MADE IN FUTURE

ADVANCE PRAISE FOR THE BOOK

'*Made in Future* is a delight to read for its panoramic, original and engaging take on the new marketing landscape. For anyone leading marketing transformation, this is one book that captures it all—data, tech, creativity—and brings it together as one conceptual whole. It's a must-read'—Pratik Thakar, head, global creative strategy and content, Coca-Cola

'*Made in Future* is the much-needed Magna Carta for the marketing discipline after two decades of alienation from and uprising against Kotleresque teachings. It invites the reader and listener to visualize marketing of the future in a breezy combination of anecdotal prose and creator-economy language. PK covers the vast interplay between media, content, data, technology and customer expectations with ease. For start-up founders looking to scale with speed, *Made in Future* provides a potent ballast for go-to-market plans. All in the start-up community must read this book, yesterday'—Jeffrey Seah, founding partner, Quest Ventures fund, Singapore

'What a thrill to be back together with Prashant through his always-thought-provoking writing! I had not realized just how much I had missed his brilliant mind, facility with words and ability to help others see the world through the fascinating lens through which he sees it. In a world that is unpredictable at best, Prashant provides deep insights into where we have been, where we are and where we are likely to go'—Matt Seiler, former global chairman and CEO, media operations, Interpublic Group

'Prashant has presented a contemporary point of view on media, customer journeys and marketing, using the prism of timeless principles. His ideas are fresh, pragmatic and yet, he has used simple examples from his successful business career. He has studied the subject, considering the areas of creativity, media, strategy, marketing and the role of marketing in society, looking at the broader sense of purpose. What is particularly refreshing is the approach, which builds on what marketers have known, and adds the perspective of what is emerging. And this is possible because of the significant experience Prashant has had building brands over the years. Practitioners will get something real and tangible, which they can apply to their craft and amplify the impact of their limited resources'—Vipul Chawla, president, Pizza Hut International

'Prashant has written an intriguing book that attempts to integrate and update the traditional perspective on branding with the changing media landscape and consumption patterns. To succeed, marketers must enable discovery, influence, experience and transaction in a seamless manner as the book elucidates'—Nirmalya Kumar, Lee Kong Chian Professor of Marketing, Singapore Management University, and distinguished fellow, INSEAD Emerging Markets Institute

'Prashant Kumar elaborates in *Made in Future* an exciting journey through the accelerated transformations that the marketing and media industry has undergone in recent decades. Also, the experiences, some bitter, others successful, that the directors of the big networks gathered in the transition to digitization. Perhaps none of us, who have been in the eye of the hurricane of this business and witnessed its evolution in different regions of the world, have been aware of the historical moments and the lessons for the future that are collected in this book. An essential book to read' —Mauricio Sabogal, former global CEO, Kinetic Worldwide, and president, world markets, IPG Mediabrands

MADE IN FUTURE

A Story of

MARKETING,
MEDIA & CONTENT
FOR OUR TIMES

PRASHANT KUMAR

BUSINESS

An imprint of Penguin Random House

PENGUIN BUSINESS

USA | Canada | UK | Ireland | Australia
New Zealand | India | South Africa | China

Penguin Business is part of the Penguin Random House group of companies
whose addresses can be found at global.penguinrandomhouse.com

Published by Penguin Random House India Pvt. Ltd
4th Floor, Capital Tower 1, MG Road,
Gurugram 122 002, Haryana, India

Penguin
Random House
India

First published in Penguin Business by Penguin Random House India 2022

10 9 8 7 6 5 4 3 2

The views and opinions expressed in this book are the author's own and the
facts are as reported by him which have been verified to the extent possible,
and the publishers are not in any way liable for the same.

ISBN 9780670096244

Typeset in Sabon by Manipal Technologies Limited, Manipal
Printed at Replika Press Pvt. Ltd, India

www.penguin.co.in

To my mother, Uma Jaiswal, for her vision,
courage and inner compass

Contents

Foreword

'The future ain't what it used to be.'

—Yogi Berra

More Life per Life

Writing a book in the times we live in has to be recognized as a singular act of courage. Technology has rendered our attention span to such transient fragments that to capture a thought in all its latent depth and coherent breadth—leave alone to gather a bookful of thinking—is in itself an everyday achievement.

The desire to squeeze in more living per life—a fundamental human obsession for millennia—now operates on three dimensions. The first is longevity—how to live more years in one life and clearly, this one is quite old. Ageing is an ageless cause.

The second is diversity—how to live a series of diverse mini-lives on an otherwise unforgiving age line. Each mini-life rises in an S curve, where people may begin a new relationship, take on a new career or job, find a new home or a new city, take on a new look and possibly even learn a new language. As soon as an S curve plateaus, another begins all over again (see diagram). And through this episodic living, one has the potential today to discover oneself in all the myriad possibilities. For eons, this used to be the exclusive preserve of the mavericks or the vagabonds, but no more.

The third is attention—how to fill in more human experience in the same moment by splitting attention across a few parallel living spheres, something that has been made a lot easier by digital devices. So, one may be discussing tonight's dinner with the family, checking WhatsApp messages on a business deal and watching a sitcom on TV, all at the same time, living more life each moment in shifting attention states. Happiness amidst this transcendental living has become an assortment of disconnected affirmations punctuated here and there by a passing satisfaction.

One may argue that such a breadth of living somewhere compromises the depth of living—the ability to think, assimilate and ruminate over the shades and nuances, the told and the untold, the extracts and the essence—of truth, love, beauty and all things worth living for.

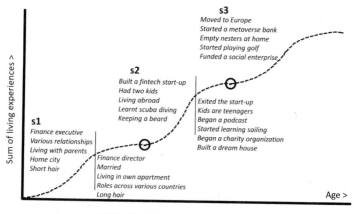

AN EXAMPLE OF LIFE AS A SERIES OF S CURVES

Yet, others may argue that such a view deeply underestimates the capacity of the human mind—at least the ones not conditioned yet—to balance higher average stimulation levels with sufficient thoughtfulness. That filling your mind with a wider spectrum of experiences and a higher state of average stimulation could serve the species' primal mandate to explore newer and varied survival pathways better. After all, when little villages became towns and towns became cities and cities got radio and then they got TV, at each stage, worriers may have voiced these very concerns.

In fact, the debate between 'filling' and 'fulfilling', between depth and breadth of experiences, is timeless and features regularly at every inflexion point of culture and technology in history. A balance, of course, is advisable, but to each generation, their own balance, really.

In addition, humankind's genetic urge for immortality has also found expression in relentless recording and sharing—possibly for eternity—thousands and thousands of photos, videos, livestreams, comments, chats, avatars, likes and dislikes, capturing moment after moment of a fast, fleeting life. Data has finally become the elixir that could render one immortal someday by capturing the information content of living and enacting some form of virtual respawn (reminds one of episodes from *Black Mirror*). Increasingly, data is the vocabulary of living.

In this rather busy backdrop with a strongly Darwinian undercurrent, one would imagine that a book is also a piece of counterculture. It's a rebellion of the slower and deeper instincts to dig more, make a deeper sense, connect things and take careful note for others to ruminate upon. Against the seemingly facile patchwork of semi-satisfying bursts of experiences that everyday living has otherwise become, reading a book can feel like an inconvenient pause of assimilation between receiving and reacting. A book becomes here a narrative ark gathering an assortment of thoughts that matter, and practices that must be recorded, hopefully for the good of others. Or at least as a pure act of catharsis.

With such thoughts in March 2020, I started writing this book. It was the time when the world had just entered the COVID-19 pandemic. It reminded the global society of the deep vulnerabilities that bind each one of us together as humans, as if we were one big 'body of humanity'—much like the Tree of Souls in the movie *Avatar*. The usual everyday routine was broken, creating more space for considered thinking. It also allowed me to begin writing what had been difficult to begin owing to my usual treadmill of corporate life.

The Time of the Possible

I joined the advertising industry in 1999, when the world was deep in the throes of the dot-com revolution. Those were heady times in Mumbai. Liberalization in India had finally hit puberty, multinational companies (MNCs) were offering unbelievable packages in campus placements and the Y2K bug had given birth to a big new software industry. Cable channels were opening Indian households to *The Bold and the Beautiful*. The Internet had brought unprecedented access to global knowledge and perspective for the first time ever. The stock market was booming and every wheeler-dealer and his third cousin in Mumbai went around sharing inside tips on which stocks to buy, helping move net worth from the naive to the discerning. Sabeer Bhatia had just made a fortune selling Hotmail to Microsoft and had proposed to actress Aishwarya Rai. It was an interesting time. It was the time of the possible.

Like many of my generation, who were attracted by things that were different and digital, I, along with a friend, Ravi Kohli, came up with an idea for a dot-com start-up—a price-comparison site called *e-bachat.com* (*bachat* is Hindi for savings). Thanks to Ravi, we managed to attract an angel investment of US$116,280 (approximately), a king's ransom for those times. The company got an office in Mumbai's posh Nariman Point, hired eighteen employees and started building the product.

We also had a fun little side hustle going on as domain squatters. Of course, we didn't see it that way then. We saw it more as monetizing our smarts in being able to anticipate how hot many of the domain names would eventually become (we also didn't use existing brands, but just followed catchy words in interesting categories). Ravi sold Baazi.com to Baazee.com, which would later become eBay India. He made US$11,628 (approximately), a pretty cool sum in those days, equivalent to three years of his salary. I managed to sell Chhutti.com (Hindi for holidays) for around US$581 to a travel agent's son from Dehradun in the Himalayas. We didn't have a lot of savings in those days, so we were super excited. That was the first money we made as entrepreneurs.

Goldman Sachs had just forecast 70 million Internet users in a few years. Rediff.com was planning a Nasdaq listing and khoj.com was still a top search engine in India. A start-up culture was taking hold in Mumbai with all its stubborn optimism and insane valuations.

My first brush with digital marketing in particular was during my first job at Leo Burnett Worldwide, a global ad agency, on the Procter & Gamble (P&G) business. P&G, as the company mythology goes, gave birth to TV advertising back in 1939 when its bath soap, Ivory, went on TV just five months after the introduction of television. It would seem that a bathing woman was the first claim to sensorial superiority of the cold audio-visual over the hot audio as Marshall McLuhan, the venerated media guru, would have called them. Chances are that before this, as some would say 'monumental happening', women hadn't realized how good they could look and feel while bathing. Bathing went from being a chore, fussing over one's bodily flaws to an exercise in agreeable narcissism and an indulgent escapade. Bathing became a lot more than bathing.

Much like obsessively fussy parents, P&G loved what it had bred. It was owned by the idea that television advertising was what really mattered. No one could ever get fired for spending their budgets on TV. A series of famed P&G memos were crafted—crisp and proud—by pedigreed P&G brand marketers aided with equal fervour by their upright agency brethren, on the hallowed certainties of TV effectiveness. Seasoned marketing directors frequently explained marketplace failures by finding ever more nuanced loopholes within loops of logic with impressive finesse. For a rookie media strategist-cum-dot-com enthusiast, this vast citadel made of memo-rocks with a moat of hallowed best practices was never easy to breach. Yet we did make some breakthroughs in secret collaborations with like-minded contrarians at P&G. In the process, I cut my teeth on digital marketing for a large corporation.

Revolution. Recoil. Reset.

Revolutions are caused by a major breakthrough in technology or ideology or both. But the unbounded optimism and the immense possibilities that such breakthroughs promise invariably result in overpromise and under-delivery. As the gap between the two widens, the bubble of sentiments bursts. A fog of uncertainty laced with confusion, disappointment and cynicism takes over for some time. This fog is the zone of reality between the breaking and the remaking. Then finally the true reset emerges from this fog. The dot-com revolution was no different in this regard. I quickly found myself in the age of overcompensation against the dot-com excesses.

As the world was slowly waking up to a new normal, in September 2003, I moved to McCann, an ad agency in Malaysia's capital, Kuala Lumpur. Malaysia was one of the Asian tigers that had managed to emerge successfully out of both the Asian economic crisis and the dot-com bubble. Growth was good, even as the country was reorienting its export and tourism economy rapidly in line with the shift of investment focus towards a World Trade Organization (WTO) ready China.

Malaysia is a small but beautiful tropical country of 32 million people (Source: World Bank), located at one of the greatest crossroads of the world for millennia—the Straits of Malacca. The country is home to a highly diverse and enterprising people who keep their ears close to global trends and technologies. Malaysia had just given birth to Air Asia, which in turn fathered online commerce in South-east Asia. Air Asia would eventually become the third largest low-cost airline in the world and the largest airline in Asia–Pacific (Source: Wikipedia). The dot-com revolution had left in its wake hundreds of digital entrepreneurs who hadn't yet had their fill of building digital businesses. It was a community that would over the next two decades incubate some of the boldest digital stories of South-east Asia such as the Nasdaq-listed Grab, Lazada (now owned by Alibaba), iProperty and iflix among several others.

Three years later, I moved to Singapore in a regional communication planning role. Singapore in 2007 sat at the crossroads of the world. Its political system was a very interesting blend of oriental patriarchy and western democracy; of liberalism and pragmatism; of oligarchy and meritocracy. And the system worked beautifully. Within a few decades the country had gone from a fishing village to one of the richest entrepôts of the world. It had one of the most effective systems of health, education and governance.

It had the potential to be the capital of Asia–Pacific in terms of location, culture, business, education and political neutrality. It was a microcosm of what Asia—if ever it were possible to conceive it as one identity—could broadly look like.

It was an exciting time for the communication-planning discipline as it had finally breached the bounds of brand planning and was being reinterpreted by ambitious media strategists in the larger marketing context. With the increasing importance of search marketing, rise of the new social platforms and with every local publisher pushing their shiny new digital incarnations, it also fell to a communication planner to place the role of digital marketing amidst the larger marketing landscape. A great shift was clearly underway and we were all trying to put our finger on the pulse of the future.

This was also the phase when the schism within the ad industry was becoming clear. Serving as a jury member for several global, regional and local awards, one found that a huge number of cases submitted were scam cases (ideas created purely for the purpose of winning awards)—and they frequently won on sheer creative power. So, the best creative gurus, instead of building real creative value for brands, focused on collecting trophies for unreal work—and pegging their payslips and egos to these. Yet there was a whole new world of marketing emerging where direct business performance was the sole currency. And in this new world, very few understood why anyone would do creative work just for the sake of creativity awards instead of actual marketplace performance of the brands. It was a world where creativity solely served business, without the pretence of some innate creative merit, which clients couldn't appreciate, thus necessitating the need to do scam work to display one's creative talent.

For the next eighteen months, I travelled extensively across Asia–Pacific, managing Coca-Cola's and Johnson &

Johnson's media investments handled by my company, and working with marketers across Microsoft, Sony, ExxonMobil, MasterCard and Cathay Pacific among others. It was an exhilarating time leading pitches, training our teams in the new discipline, getting to know strategists and digital thinkers across the region and generally seeing the world.

The future of Asia was being cast afresh in those years. China was fast discovering its marketing acumen. Chinese superstars such as Alibaba, Lenovo, Huawei, Haier and Tencent were revving up their ambitions to become global brands. Coca-Cola Japan engaged a non-Japanese media agency for the first time when we pitched for the Coke business. LG and Samsung had risen to pole positions in the Indian appliances market. In addition, Korean drama and K-pop had built a cultural momentum thrusting Korea as the new Japan. Japan and Korea had already been the most sophisticated users of mobile phones in the world. Now China leapfrogged the play to write its own story on the frontiers of tech innovation.

The new role also gave me the luxury of pondering the deeper aspects of how marketing was changing, not just in terms of the downstream tools it deployed but also the upstream reset in strategic thinking that it required. The marketers I worked with offered an extraordinary spectrum of diversity in terms of the product, the marketing job to be done and the approaches that had made them the great brands they were. Yet each one of them realized that much of what had worked so far was fast becoming obsolete. It was clear that marketing needed to be rediscovered.

Growing up as students in the 1980s and 1990s, but forged as professionals in the fires of the dot-com foundry, gave our generation a unique vantage point to appreciate both the natives and the immigrants of the digital age. The latter always sought to fit the future into the boxes of the past (or at best saw it as an extrapolation). The former saw the future as a boundless white sheet project. The need was to rethink from a white sheet but not throw the baby out with the bathwater.

With thoughts such as these on my mind in the troughs of the 2008 recession, I was assigned back to Kuala Lumpur to head the local Universal McCann office. It was a tiny office then, pitted against competitors ten times larger than us. In the very first townhall, I was faced with people's fears about retrenchment and survival of the office. It was a baptism of fire, but we resolved to fight back together.

Over the next seven years, the company doubled its revenues biennially to become the second-largest media services company in Malaysia. Two years in a row, RECMA Paris, the industry-rating body, ranked it as the number one media agency in the world out of 900 agencies on its roster. For six years out of seven, Universal McCann won agency of the year at the industry association awards. At the centre of this success was our strategic understanding of digital futures, and what it meant for marketing.

Later, I took over as the company's regional president overseeing eleven countries in Asia, trying to replicate the Malaysia success model around the region. It was a wonderful time to innovate and scale, and the profits for the region grew at an unprecedented rate over the next four years. We weren't just looking to follow the US and Europe, but innovating new services, ahead of the market. For instance, our pioneering social-media offering was launched across two dozen offices in Europe and Latin America.

In the interim, I travelled the region and the world, speaking in forums like DMEXCO in Germany, Festival of Media Global at Rome, Adtech conferences among others. I also gave a series of interviews across Bloomberg, the *Wall Street Journal* and trade magazines on how the marketing future was shaping up and how we needed to alter many of the principles that were taken for granted.

In 2015, I turned forty. Deep in my mind, a midlife crisis had been already brewing. Add to that the bug from the dot-com bubble days that still lived somewhere in my gut, I finally quit the Interpublic Group after thirteen years and started Entropia.

Made in Future

When we began, the marketing industry stood at an interesting crossroads. Global digital giants and their much-obliging buzz machine had already seeded the idea that a much more accountable marketing was possible across the world's boardrooms. This new marketing would apparently allow for every dollar spent on marketing to result in sales dollars that the finance directors could count and shareholders could get dividend from. Yet few chief marketing officers (CMOs) could give body and blood to this belief system propagated by the Silicon Valley pundits. CMOs struggled, went to Google conferences, got photographed wearing Google Glass, and then came back to find a pink slip waiting for them. It was a phase where CMOs had an average tenure that was less than twenty-four months. And they in turn churned the ad agencies with sometimes even more urgency. It was the worst of times, and—it wasn't the best of times.

For decades, the holy grail of marketing had been the question of what worked and what didn't and hence, how we could optimize the input mix to maximize returns on marketing investment. Marketers, agencies and consultancies had tried to answer this via econometric modelling and controlled experiments in some cases, and with simpler input–output analytics in most cases. The simpler methods, due to the multiplicity of soft factors involved, provided something that was more like guidance rather than rigorous answers. And the complex methods were too much of a black box and frequently mired in statistical errors for a practical marketer to follow consistently. As a result, many marketing decisions were a mix of part analysis, part precedence and a lot of gut feel. It was half science, half religion. Clearly, marketers were not exactly popular with finance, sales or technology departments.

There was a deeper shift underway amidst the more common concerns of marketing. As category after category were being disrupted by their new-age competitors, incumbents realized that they, too, needed to undergo some sort of digital transformation, if they hoped to survive. So, everyone needed a great website, an app, e-commerce set-up and indeed needed to reinvent the whole customer experience across the many types of customer journeys that may exist. Most of these areas sat somewhere between marketing and technology, and required both to collaborate closely. The complexity and chaos that all these developments created boggled many a marketing master. Some are still figuring these out.

Seeing a clear and big opportunity, consultancy majors such as Accenture and Deloitte declared their intentions to go deeper into the marketing service arena, and started a series of acquisitions to build capabilities around the world. Advised by consultancies and aided by giant digital platforms, many companies started experimenting with taking digital marketing in-house rather than depending on their advertising agency partners. In many cases it allowed digital platforms to control their share of marketing budget better, away from traditional media players, as the term 'JBP' (Joint Business Plans) came into vogue. JBP frequently started with brand business plans but, not surprisingly, more often than not ended with Google or Facebook sales plans. And through all this, the time-honoured triangle of relationship between marketer, media owner and agency was irretrievably damaged. Of course, all parties had their share of blame.

Entropia was conceived to try and plug some of these gaps and do its bit in delivering a marketing model of the future—a consulgency (consultancy meets agency) of sorts. Many of the stars in my earlier team quit to join this endeavour.

It's been five years since then. Entropia has had an explosive growth to become one of the largest and most celebrated players in the Malaysian ad industry. Brands as varied as KFC, Pepsi, Heineken, Nestlé, BAT, Danone, Grab and Lazada reposed their faith in it. In June 2021, it was acquired by Accenture Interactive to help fuel their thrust in South-east Asia.

In the process, we learnt a lot and in this book, I hope to distil some of those learnings that have been, often successfully, put to perform, and have truly earned their place in a practitioner's book.

Truth Is in the Middle

The nature of change in our times quickly obsoletes a learning, unless there is an effort to go deeper. And the faster the shift, the greater the need to go even deeper to comprehend the underlying structure of the shift. In the last two decades, the rising centrality of data and technology in people's lives has caused some fundamental changes in how people connect with brands and businesses. With the advent of the fourth industrial revolution, its core technologies such as artificial intelligence (AI), augmented and virtual reality, Internet of Things, cloud, etc., are adding yet another level to this shift.

The pervasiveness of giant global platforms, such as Google, Facebook, Apple, Amazon, Alibaba and Netflix among others, has allowed for unprecedented speed in adoption of new technologies throughout the world reflected in many having a trillion dollars plus in market capitalization. Local cultures across geographies have embraced innovative start-ups as the cherished incubators of a dynamic future. This has given way to billions in venture capital investments, most of which by design expect to fail most of the time—and that has sped up invention like never before. Together, these two phenomena have created a scenario where not just the present but even the future is changing at a rapid pace. It would seem as if every aspect of our life follows Moore's law.

On the other side, many of the promises of digitization remain unfulfilled. For instance, there once was the holy promise of digital media being the final solution to all the flaws and pains of marketing (for example, the immense wastage as pointed out by John Wanamaker in his famous quote: 'Half of my advertising is wasted, but I don't know which half'). However, twenty years after the dot-com bubble, where this claim became almost a war cry, many of those promises remain unfulfilled, just as a whole lot of new opportunities have indeed opened up.

The marketing approaches honed over a century of progress find themselves obsolete in so many ways, yet a credible new model that is holistic, scalable and brings together a certain integrity of thinking is yet to emerge. While many of the tools and contexts of the trade have changed, at the strategic level, the marketing world continues to practise principles that are at least of the boomer vintage. This conceptual gap means marketing strategy has become a schizophrenic discipline: something like trying to explain quantum mechanics in terms of Newtonian physics.

Against such a backdrop, this book is a humble effort to put in place some building blocks of this new marketing, going beyond both shallow digital evangelism and cynical traditional naysaying. The truth, after all, is in the deep and more often than not in the middle.

I sincerely hope the book is useful.

(The future cannot fit into the containers of the past. Throughout the book, I have introduced some new words, to capture the new vocabulary that needs to be there. When faced with a word like that, please refer to the Glossary of the Future at the end of the book.)

1

The New Marketplace

'Whoever said money can't buy happiness, simply didn't know where to go shopping.'

—Gertrude Stein

Happiness Traded is Happiness Enhanced

For aeons, the marketplace used to be a place where buyers and sellers met to trade goods and services in exchange for other goods and services or for money. One unmet need met another unmet need to complete each other and multiply joy in the process. In that sense, a marketplace was a destination characterized by intersecting wants.

Marketplace transactions were a win-win for both sides. Unlike plunders and wars, win-win marketplace exchanges were a force for civilization and culture, as they allowed for peaceful overlap of otherwise conflicting self-interests. Large marketplaces, the great souks and the grand bazaars—with their colours, smells, chatter and vibes—often had tremendous personality and character.

The marketplace incubated culture and helped create merchandise, rituals, icons and institutions that would bring it scale and longevity. Culture helped convert the otherwise cold, transactional marketplace into a place to trade needs and desires, dreams and meanings. And feeding each other's appetite, fair marketplace exchanges tamed humankind's raw animal spirits into what we call civilization, a role that seems to have got much less appreciation than it deserves.

High streets across the great cities—such as Fifth Avenue in New York or the Grand Bazaar in Istanbul, Ginza in Tokyo or Orchard Road in Singapore—came to symbolize the very finest of contemporary achievements of a society. With the rise of the middle class and mass-consumer economies of the developed world (and later of the cities and towns of the developing world), malls, department stores and supermarkets rose to take a central place in people's everyday lives—social, cultural and material. The marketplace became the place where one could buy happiness, if one only knew what to buy and where to shop.

With the advent of the digital age, however, the marketplace started evolving into a virtual destination rather than a physical one. As people increasingly transacted online on vast e-commerce portals for their everyday needs—big or small—the marketplace was fast becoming a set of small digital windows bringing a much bigger world of choices owing to its almost infinite shelf space. Through a tiny Amazon app in the mobile screen, one could browse through a bazaar with more than hundreds of millions of items, a scale inconceivable in the physical marketplaces. A Netflix app could allow them to choose from about thousands of titles and a Spotify could allow them to listen from a collection of tens of millions of tracks. The seller is invisible here and so is the buyer. As powerful AI algorithms are able to anticipate, queue and curate products with impressive efficiency, the windows are steadily growing narrower and less annoying even if less serendipitous (some shoppers love the last feature).

Know Your Marketplace

In fact, today, if one looks at the e-commerce marketplaces, a multiplicity of different shopping contexts has evolved, each with its own strengths and personalities. These marketplaces can be broadly mapped on two key dimensions: one ranges from the experiential to the functional and the other, from high commitment to low commitment (see diagram).

On the first axis, at one end are products or services that need a rich context and have a high experiential content. Some examples would be high-end jewellery, watches, paintings, houses, yachts, cars and luxury apparel among products; and luxury hotels, restaurants, vacations, wealth management, etc., among services. At the other end of this spectrum would be highly functional products and services such as low-cost apparel and accessories, mass-consumer electronics, loans, insurance and utility services.

On the second axis, at one end are the products and services that require a high commitment, such as insurance, wealth management, houses, loans, baby formula, etc.; at the other end are the categories where a purchase requires very low commitment per transaction and hence are driven by impulse a lot of the time—such as soft drinks, confectionary, sanitary napkins, bath liquids or low-cost apparel and accessories, etc.

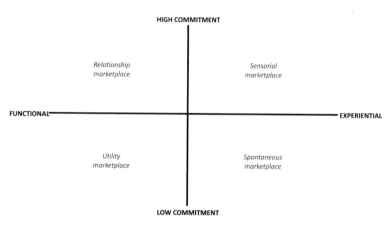

FOUR TYPES OF MARKETPLACES

The nature of the marketplace determines the attitudes and expectations of its typical customers, with implications for how marketing ought to be customized. It also reflects the nature of competitive advantage that businesses ought to cultivate for superior and sustainable growth and margins vis-à-vis the competition.

In order to develop a better understanding of how different categories compete in different types of marketplaces (even if sold on the same platform sometimes), based on the two axes of functional to experiential and high commitment to low commitment, today's marketplaces can be split into four different quadrants. They are utility marketplace, spontaneous marketplace, sensorial marketplace and the relationship marketplace (see diagram).

Let's take a closer look at these.

Now Everyone Can Buy (Utility Marketplace)

In the functional and low commitment quadrant is the 'Utility Marketplace'—a shopping context where the speed, range and cost of purchase are the dominant factors. Also, when you purchase and when you typically use are usually spread apart so that it allows for the lag it would take to deliver the product.

Most of this shopping is rapidly moving online to vast global marketplaces where millions of sellers are matched with millions of buyers each day, and the criteria for a successful transaction are often brutally focused on price, range and scale based on real-time optimization of supply and demand. Books, toys, computers, communications and consumer electronics, mass skincare and cosmetics, low-cost apparel and accessories, etc., are the typical categories transacted here, and strong brands in each of these categories must fight hard to effectively import their existing brand equity. It's an engineer's bazaar, and much as it offers unprecedented access and low-cost mass gratification, it mostly lacks multisensorial appeal and the social dimension of the good old bazaar (even if reviews and ratings do provide social validation of some sort). Window shopping can be a lonely experience in this marketplace, and margin management a brutal game (though, depending on the category, some may still love browsing).

However, this is the marketplace where e-commerce found its first reason to be—efficiency of access and cost— its true raison d'être. And this is the vast bedrock of online shopping today, a paradise for obsessive bargain hunters. This is also the marketplace that has destroyed a huge number of centuries-old offline businesses in the above categories.

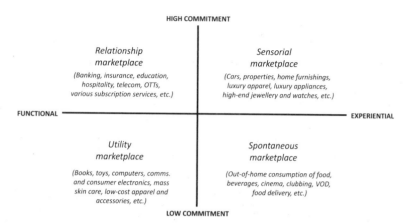

FOUR TYPES OF MARKETPLACES

Belong in the Moment (Spontaneous Marketplace)

The second type of marketplace, high on experience but low on commitment, is the 'Spontaneous Marketplace'. Here, the purchase moment and the usage moment are either one and the same or quite proximate to each other, and so the in-moment presence and experience is important. Out-of-home consumption of food, beverages, cinema, clubbing, video-on-demand, food delivery, etc., would fall into this category. A lot of such consumption is also a part of ongoing social activity and the spontaneous shared moment. Being at the right place at the right time is crucial here and can command a premium. This marketplace is mostly physical and often impulse-led and due to the relatively low outlay per transaction, the commitment required is small (even if there may be brand loyalty over time).

Return on Experience (Sensorial Marketplace)

The third type is the 'Sensorial Marketplace'—high on experience and high on commitment. This is a shopping context where the experience itself is of paramount importance to the brand choice, and the purchase has a high emotional component. These are purchases with a strong service component or where the tactile feel of the product, the trial, demonstration and physical experience are crucial. High-outlay categories such as cars, properties, home furnishings, luxury apparel, luxury appliances, high-end jewellery and watches, etc., would typically be transacted in this context. Think an Apple store, a Nike store or a Bulgari outlet. Self-image typically plays a big role in this context and can command a high premium. While the bulk of this market is physical, there is an effort to add richness to the online experience via livestreaming, influencer advocacy, social shopping and highly immersive content. The Gucci Garden inside the Roblox metaverse, or the Louis Vuitton collection for the League of Legends universe are great examples.

Best Friends Forever (Relationship Marketplace)

The fourth and last type of marketplace—functional but high on commitment—is the 'Relationship Marketplace'. This is the marketplace where the transaction involves either a service or a right to a service to be consumed later on. Banking, insurance, education, hospitality, telecom, OTTs, various subscription services, etc., would typically fall into this context. Purchases here are often mediated by a functional information and advocacy layer and require a longer term of trust and commitment. The frequency of purchases is low, even though typically the outlay is high, especially over a long period of commitment.

While the most powerful competitive factor in the utility marketplace is choice and efficiency, for the spontaneous marketplace, it is the 'momentness' (being in the moment)—

the ability to capture the zeitgeist, what will appeal the most in the time, place and mood to someone. For the sensorial marketplace, it's the quality of storytelling, whereas for the relationship marketplace, trust becomes the most powerful factor for superior growth and sustainable margins.

* * *

Bring the Bazaar to Me

It's interesting to note that one aspect of how the marketplace is evolving is not into a place or destination at all—whether physical or virtual. Like the neighbourhood peddlers and hawkers in traditional towns, who went house to house, selling their wares at the right time and right place with a lot of personal appeal, the market must now go to the buyer, and not the other way around. A product (or service) must be where the people are in their natural context, catering to their specific wants in a smooth, unobtrusive way. This has manifested itself in many ways.

WeChat, with more than a billion users in China, allows for integration of shopping into the chat windows, thus embedding itself into everyday conversations, entertainment and advocacy. As of 2019, there were over a million shops inside WeChat across hundreds of industries, with consumers opening a mini program on an average of four times a day. Alipay, China's close integration into the point of purchase, allows it to offer payment, financing and loan services, exactly where people need it—banking services embedded in an all-pervasive yet subtle manner with the help of a button. In the vast world of Ant Group that owns Alipay, the bank is increasingly a button now. WhatsApp in India is banking on its shopping button to become more and more popular and bring a more intuitive way to shop. The marketplace is getting back the chatter. Bazaar is where the buzz is.

> In the vast world of Ant Group that owns Alipay,
> the bank is increasingly a button now.

As more and more merchandise and services around the world get woven into the fabric of everyday online lives—social media, chat windows, entertainment apps, maps and ride-sharing apps, news apps, business to business (B2B) office apps, property-search sites, education sites and comparison websites of all sorts—it is highly probable that much of the online marketplace will be reduced to a button. Amazon took the button rather literally when it created the Amazon Dash, which was discontinued later. But this time, a button, informed by powerful anticipatory intelligence, will increasingly sit at the heart of all consumer commerce—personalizing what we need in a given moment from a vast repertoire of choices. At that point, the marketplace would truly live in the mind and in the moment. AI will become the curator of our lives. And moment will become the new marketplace.

> At that point, the marketplace would truly live in the mind
> and the moment. AI will become the curator of our lives,
> and moment will become the new marketplace.

Much as the nature of the marketplace is evolving, the nature of competition, the underlying sources of competitiveness and leading drivers of value-creation are also changing. To sustain and build a competitive advantage, it is important to consider what these new powers are that every business must master.

* * *

The Four Great Powers of the New Competition

A definition of the new marketplace would be incomplete without a closer look at the nature of competition, which is the life force of marketplaces. Entire categories that had evolved in a linear curve over the last hundred years are in the process of mutation. Fossil-fuel cars are to be replaced by Electric Vehicles (EVs), electric trains eventually by Elon Musk's hyperloop, jet engines by SpaceX's hypersonic travel, merchant banks by fintech players such as Stripe and Adyen, taxi service companies by apps like Uber and Ola, and hotel services by apps like Airbnb, etc. Big old incumbents are being disrupted or their margins squeezed out by competitors from completely unexpected quarters. The whole notion of keeping your eye on the five competitive forces—suppliers, buyers, substitutes, new entrants and the industry players—seems highly limiting, when the lines between categories are so thoroughly blurred.

It is important therefore to understand the new distribution of power—which in turn determines where the competitive threat may arise from and how the total available profit pool eventually gets apportioned in a particular category and the ecosystem around it.

Looking at the list of the ten largest companies by market value, six of them are companies that didn't even exist twenty-five years ago (see diagram).

Companies	In USD Billions
Apple	2,252
Microsoft	1,967
Saudi Aramco	1,897
Amazon	1,712
Alphabet	1,539
Facebook	871
Tencent	774
Tesla	710
Alibaba	658
Berkshire Hathaway	624

Source: Statista 2021

And they all rose into the place by devastating huge incumbents, sometimes spanning across several categories. Yet, it would be almost impossible to understand their success in the light of traditional competitive models.

What happened in most cases is that the powers that shaped the metastructure of competition themselves underwent a reset as the focus of customer-value creation shifted to the need for simplicity, personalization, anywhere–any time access and the centrality of customer experience in general. Fuelled by an unprecedented surge in venture capital and its appetite for bold risk, exponential change became the rallying cry of the day, best summed up in Peter Thiel's 10X rule of innovation (true innovation happens when you try to improve something by ten times rather than by 10 per cent).

It is important to realize that the new competitive landscape is controlled by four great powers that have reset how consumers view category and competition. Together they are creating a whole new ecosystem of interlocking advantages, often melting the boundaries of what was considered the industry peer group or category neighbourhood.

These four new powers are: network power, data power, UX (user experience) power and the brand power (see diagram). Although these powers are interconnected in some ways, each brings a leverage of its own and together define the emergence of the marketplace and competition a lot better today than the traditional models of competitive forces.

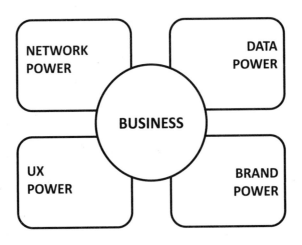

FOUR POWERS OF COMPETITIVE ARENA

For a century, businesses that invented breakthrough technology knew that the best way to conquer the market and stay put in the citadel was to become the category default or the new standard in the category itself. The famous war between the two videocassette recording standards, VHS versus Betamax, in the 1970s and 1980s had been the stuff of corporate legend. So had been the operating system war between Windows and iOS. Companies like Microsoft, IBM, Intel and Qualcomm managed to wield sustained power for decades by becoming the default in their respective categories. These standards were aggressively protected by legal armies and dominant lobbies marking their territory with patents, walled gardens and financial muscle. The economy of scale and customer habit helped fortify the margins further. For a vast global organization with hundreds of thousands of employees acclimatized to Microsoft Windows, for example, it was inconceivable to retrain them all into a whole new operating system.

However, at the turn of the century, a number of new factors started gaining strength. One of the important ones was the network effect. In the earlier era, media platforms were one-to-many. Broadcasters put out the content, and people watched the content. The most that the networks of people contributed towards this was the word of mouth that propelled the viewership of a new programme. It was an influence, but the mechanics of consumption itself was not dependent on the network of viewers. This changed at the turn of the century, bringing us to our first competitive power.

Network Power

Think about your journey with your favourite social media app. Let's go back to the time when you weren't using the app. One day you probably read about it somewhere or heard about it from friends. Then you heard again from another friend sometime later and then from another member of the family maybe. This probably intrigued you sufficiently to download the app and register. Thereafter, you added the friends and family from whom you heard about it in the first place. You sent them a message or shared a post. Further, maybe you added more people you found whom you knew or wanted to follow. Not long after, you had hundreds of connections, and now it feels almost like a virtual home. While the exact journey may not be the same for everyone, social media feeds on the power of networks. The more people join it, the more the incentive for others to join, and so there is almost a chain reaction. The mathematics of growth is no more linear but exponential as is the case with network mathematics.

What gives social-media networks (and all the businesses built atop them) immense competitive advantage is that people want to be on the social-media platform, where friends and family already are, so they can socialize with them. The more the number of friends who join the network, the more the combinations of interaction that can happen and so the more the potential number of occasions for engagement and richness of experience. So, very quickly the membership to the network starts growing exponentially. When a new competitor enters, unless the relative advantage is much higher or the differentiation is large, it is very difficult for it to pick up users, because people don't want to go where there are only a few people whom they know. The traditional linear acquisition of users from the one-to-many world of traditional media is no more relevant. Before the advent of mass media, when reputation was dependent on word of mouth, a similar process operated. Of course, the speed of propagation in that case was much slower, allowing for too much noise and distortion. To some extent when landlines first came, they benefited from the network effect as there was no point having a phone if you didn't have anyone to call.

This network power wasn't limited to social media. A whole new generation of sharing economy players emerged— in mobility, in hospitality, in real estate, in B2B trade, where the key disruptive power lay in the ability to match supply and demand with the help of algorithms. This automation delivered higher quality at lower cost based on how extensive the network of customers and suppliers they could build at speed (see diagram). Network-borne scale offered an immediate and clear machine-optimized advantage; and one could use that to create entry barriers that were difficult to scale.

Uber built their business by recruiting as many drivers as possible, so that people could get their drive as cheaply and quickly as possible, which drove up drivers' income, in turn bringing in more and more drivers, which in turn made the speed and cost of matching even better. With more riders and drivers on the network, it wasn't just the number of matches that went up exponentially, but the better cost and higher speed multiplied the advantage to yet another order.

When there are two friends in a neighbourhood, you can only find a playdate in one way, but when there are four friends in the neighbourhood, you can group together in eleven ways. But that's not all. You may be able to find someone to play with faster than usual, and with more choice, you need to spend a lot less effort persuading someone to come out.

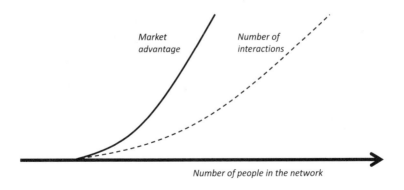

MARKET ADVANTAGE RISES EXPONENTIALLY WITH NETWORK SCALE

A string of promising crowdsourced and peer-to-peer platforms have emerged to pose serious threats to existing business models, whether in financing, job search, auctions or referrals. Social media eventually ended up disrupting the traditional media industry. Network power today continues to bring both the advantages of time and cost, changing entire industries forever. And this from players who are neither suppliers nor buyers, nor are they substitutes or new entrants in the conventional sense of the words.

Network effect and its exponential power also meant that most of these new categories became largely a 'winner-takes-all' game. As network effect became an unfordable moat, it helped build vast platforms with massive resources, which could then just acquire high potential competitors that offered a novel and promising user experience, thus eliminating any potential threat. Google's acquisition of YouTube and Facebook's acquisition of WhatsApp are two great examples of that. On the other hand, Yahoo's refusal to pay the right price for Google and Blockbuster's refusal to buy out Netflix would be examples of how incumbents that do not recognize the power of the network effect may get destroyed by it fairly quickly.

Clearly, businesses need to ponder long and hard about how to incorporate the network effect into their business. This would amount to assessing what exponentially rising value creation or cost avoidance could bring to an individual customer in a rising network of suppliers and customers, beyond the linear economy of scale (for example, a peer-to-peer customer service platform may be able to lower the average post-purchase service liabilities rapidly as customer numbers rise). Businesses needed to be reconceived to be networked-by-design across their value chain to maximize the full power of networks' exponential advantages.

UX Power

The second great power that emerged from the cauldron of the dot-com era was the power of UX (User Experience): in simple terms, how users experienced technology as a whole, making the best of function, form, perceptions and their interplay. The term UX had been coined in the early 1990s by cognitive psychologist and designer, Don Norman. As digital technology vastly expanded the breadth and complexity of human experience, a compelling need gap arose for simplicity, speed, intuitiveness, flexibility and smooth interoperability. Google with its breathtaking speed and simplicity had already set a new norm here for all dot-com survivors. They further emphasized the centrality of user experience by putting it right at the centre of their pricing model. Google Adwords offered variable pricing not just based on auction but also by factoring in Google quality scores that quantified the quality of the landing page experience as well as the relevance of the ads to the user intent as reflected in the keywords searched.

An entire generation of native digital users arose thereafter, who had little patience for design that didn't play to these expectations. The icons of design from the previous era such as Motorola, Sony and Nokia started faltering as Apple heralded a new era of UX design in mobile phones. Apple devices were so intuitive that even a small child with an iPhone in his hands could fiddle his way through to his favourite *Barney* show unassisted.

Like the watches industry that had elevated itself in the hands of sophisticated designers, refined craftsmen and brand builders to the status of jewellery, Apple decided to elevate mobile phones to the status of jewellery. (Just like jewellery, people carried a mobile phone on their person after all.) Its packaging and the store experience was perfectly in sync with this vision. Flagship Apple stores became well-known landmarks in great cities of the world, and every iPhone launch would see long, snaking queues of people waiting for hours and hours, desperate to be the first to get their hands on those coveted pieces.

All this helped Apple get more dollars per square foot in retail sales—in a ratio of 5 to 3—compared to the Tiffany stores in the US.[1] Nerd chic was the contemporary new jewellery, the new self-image with brag value. Not only that, the Apple brand and its stores heralded a whole new design vocabulary that had a unique personality of its own—brutal minimalism, contemporary chic, organic curves, refined sensuality. Apple didn't make machines like Sony or Nokia did. Apple created sleek intuitive sensorial experiences that made one feel fashionable, tech-savvy and posh all at the same time. Apple design would continue to inspire millions of designers across diverse categories the world over. It was the victory of experience over machinery. The form had assimilated the function without a compromise. Beauty had finally won over the beast.

Apple's was the new user experience, one that people were willing to pay a massive premium for, year after year, eventually adding up to more than US$200 billion in cash reserves by May 2021 and almost US$3 trillion dollars in market value by end of the same year (close to India's annual Gross Domestic Product). Apple also used the insane popularity of its iPod to start with, and the iPhones later to create a UX ecosystem that eventually expanded across its laptops, tablets, watches, iTunes and the Apple TV. Within a decade, leveraging its UX power, Apple managed to disrupt the mobile industry, the music industry and the watch industry and created a new category called tablets. Each of its products sell at a huge premium over other players, cornering a lion's share of the profit pool in the industry. People pay not just for the way the products function, they pay for how it makes them feel and for their resistance to try anything inferior to Apple. People pay for the UX.

Apple's success today is the most resounding validation that UX had now become a crucial margin driver. UX was the new competitive power that could allow a company to extend into hitherto disconnected industries simply because people loved the experience and got too hooked on to it to degrade themselves to lesser experiences. Exemplars such as these have created an opportunity for many businesses to recast themselves to put user experience at the heart of their competitive advantage.

As more and more of the customer journey across categories moves online, businesses interact with customers through a multiplicity of online touchpoints—campaigns, customer service, website, apps, online shops, social media, customer relationship management (CRM) emailers, etc. There are also multiple interaction points in the physical world between customers and brands—stores, events, sampling, offline customer service, roadshows, etc., which are increasingly digitized. The experience is no more limited to the usual audio-visual ones but has in many cases gone far beyond to include augmented reality, virtual reality, holograms and all manners of enhanced experiences. Each of these interactions are opportunities to create a powerful and seamless user experience that people love, that amplifies the brand rather than diminishes it, and that people get habituated to.

As Facebook (now Meta) partners with Ray-Ban to launch AR-enabled smart glasses, and its Oculus division launches lighter and better VR headsets, we are sitting at the cusp of a new revolutionary form factor in UX. In conjunction with Horizon VR meeting rooms and venues and other elements of its metaverse project, user experience is once again set to be transformed (more on this later). On the B2B end, Microsoft is seeking to transform the workplace around its own Mesh platform and by enhancing HoloLens, while NVIDIA has launched Omniverse to allow B2B collaborations around metaverse projects. The battle to own best-in-class UX for autonomous cars, healthtech and edutech is shaping up rapidly too.

A great UX vision can allow brands to build a powerful moat as well as give them the power to disrupt not just their own categories but also seemingly unrelated markets. UX as the new great power has finally arrived.

Data Power

For thousands of years, the merchants who travelled the great silk route, stretching across half the world from the Pacific to the Mediterranean, believed that the one who rules the silk road, rules the entire world. In the digital era, it could very well be said that the one who owns the data owns the world.

At the core of the digital revolution had been the distributed network of people and the vast granular data that the servers captured on each and every move that was made by them. Data was the fuel of these networks. Data in turn naturally became the fuel of the businesses that were erected on the Internet. Page meta data allowed Google to know which pages were referenced how many times by other websites and hence deliver the powerful search product that it built. Data also allowed Facebook to manage people's newsfeeds effectively so they only see the posts that they may be interested in the most. Data allowed Amazon to know that people who bought product A also had a greater likelihood to buy product B, resulting in its legendary recommendation engine.

Data allowed platforms to anticipate, prioritize, curate and streamline the phenomenal promises of the digital technology. If knowledge was power, to know one was to know how to manage one. Or better still, how to make money from that knowledge, by offering the person exactly what they wanted the most at the right time and right place.

A wise man once said that art imitates life. Another wise man argued that it's life that imitates art. One could similarly argue about whether science inspires life or life inspires science. But one thing is very clear that, when humans set out on the path to simulate intelligence, the first place that they looked into was the inner workings of the human mind. They peeked into how the neurons work inside our brains and how a baby's mind, starting from a white sheet possessing only a few reflexes as a sort of boot code, learns complex behaviours, pattern recognition and high levels of abstractions. So, it is no coincidence that the mathematics delving into this space was called 'neural' networks.

A neural network is a mathematical technique that aims to discover underlying patterns in a set of data in a way very similar to how human brains learn and discern. It was a technique that had, for decades, remained largely confined to textbooks and obscure laboratories, simply because there wasn't enough data to train the models for everyday application, until suddenly there was a deluge of data to model. Using AI techniques, machines can now increasingly 'see and recognize' a picture, a face, shades of emotions, voice, videos and real-life happenings. Machines can understand languages and accents, machines can feel pulses and heartbeats, machines can even see some of the things that the naked eye can't. With the help of data, machines finally have the opportunity to play human in certain contexts like never before. Data and AI are helping to create a world of pervasive, real-time and personalized intelligence, which is expected to inform and read our senses like an exobrain to elevate us to a higher level of sentience. A synchronized network of human intelligence and its artificial augmentation may just hide the breakthrough to turn us into a superspecies.

In the context of the marketplace, data allows companies the leverage to break into disparate categories, only bound together by the people whose data was collected. An Amazon with its vast data on people who bought children's books managed to disrupt the toy industry by simply extending the patterns and insights gleaned to the purchase of toys. And if, for instance, a mother was buying books and toys for a five-year-old girl, she might as well be a great prospect for buying other products for a five-year-old girl. Synergies, hitherto far-fetched, if not unimaginable, between categories became apparent.

WeChat, the famous Chinese app, started as a chat app and built a huge scale leveraging the network effect. And one delightful Chinese New Year it decided to offer a simple functionality of 'virtual *Ang Pows*' (an envelope with gift money) on its platform, so married people could pass on the ritual monies virtually to single members of their extended families as per the festival tradition. Overnight, it became a payments-industry giant in China.[2] In due course, leveraging the data it collected on its users, it started beaming content on its platform, and eventually people could buy and sell on WeChat, often egged on by all manners of influencers. Its access to user data helped it make the journey from a mere chat app to a super app, that today is almost indispensable for everyday living in China.

And in the course of this, it disrupted the content industry, built a solid position for itself in financial services and created an e-commerce giant. Grab, a ride-sharing decacorn in South-east Asia is rapidly expanding its core function into a super app like WeChat by offering payments, delivery, hotel bookings, grocery purchases and myriad household services. In India, JioMart offers through its app, grocery shopping, cloud storage, ticket booking and content streaming among other things competing for super-app status with the likes of Paytm, Google Pay and PhonePe.

Taken to yet another level, a machine-learning algorithm trained to recognize faces using data in a social network can be leveraged for security, payments, access and legal processes, opening completely new categories of application. It can prevent voter fraud, help protect against crime, and has the ability to allow smarter and smoother access everywhere. Ant Financial owes its success in financial services not just to its ready access to customers via the Alibaba platforms, but also to its access to people's purchase data that allows it to model highly credible credit scores and hence see low default on loans versus many other means of credit-risk modelling (an asset that now new Chinese regulations are trying to take control of). Stripe, the global payments platform behind the likes of Spotify and Shopify, is similarly leveraging its vast merchant data into merchant-banking products and gaining a unique edge over regular banks.

In the Tokyo Olympics, officials knew when the half-time hit based on the uptick in the flushing toilets. When you know, you can control and manage. Some experts have called data the new oil. It is clearly a potent new power for businesses to deploy.

Brand Power

Marilyn Monroe, when asked about what she wore to bed, replied: 'Chanel N° 5'.

Across the world, in category after category, in billions of purchases every day, people pay extra for brands they prefer. Very often, they pay that extra not just for the trust and functional relevance that the brand engenders, but also for how it makes them feel and what it says about them to people around. When people choose Mini Cooper, it's both a reflection and reinforcement of their non-conformist self and signals their affiliation to a certain creative culture. When people buy Nike, somewhere they buy into the passionate, aspirational mythology of a winner's journey. In the complex, fast-moving societies of today, brands offer an easy (even if lazy) matrix to pigeonhole people. We become a sum total of the brands we use or are associated with. Brands create a great impression as well as channel the most heartfelt self-expressions.

Pepsi, for generations, captured the rebellious streak of the youth, where Coca-Cola focused on keeping the world positive and together with conformist vibes. The diversity of brand personalities allows people a wide range of identities to associate with, a reference point to peg their individuality to. And it works both ways—you choose the brand you are, and you become the brands you choose.

The last of the four new powers, brand power, is also the most elusive one to conceive and control. Yet great brands have shown the power to transcend centuries, continents and great upheavals. Like a religion, a powerful brand engenders its own mythology, belief system and purpose in society.

Of all the great powers changing the destiny of businesses, brand power is the least understood one, and frequently discounted by many businesses that find themselves unable to look beyond the more countable and controllable left-brain elements of their businesses. It is also a power that's emergent from tons of often seemingly disconnected activities over a long period of time. Despite brand-measurement studies estimating top brands in the world to be worth hundreds of billions of dollars (see figure), it's frequently tricky to put one's finger on what levers must be pulled and by how much to create an expected amount of value.

	In USD Billions
Apple	323
Amazon	201
Microsoft	166
Google	165
Samsung	62
Coca-Cola	57
Toyota	52
Mercedes-Benz	49
McDonald's	43
Disney	41

Source: Interbrand 2020

WORLD'S MOST VALUABLE BRANDS 2020

The revolutionary counterculture—that of the perpetual underdogs seeking to change the world for the better—pervades the heart of Silicon Valley. It doesn't merely seek to create breakthrough innovations, it frequently lays claim to creating a radically different world. No wonder, every iconic brand in the digital era has sought to convert its journey into an inspiring story of rebellion against the status quo. In this world, every entrepreneur is a Luke Skywalker taking on the big, dark establishment of Darth Vader.

Google sought to stand for all that was wrong with the closed, manipulative, monolithic and stagnant system that Microsoft was perceived to represent by some (the supposed 'evil' in the 'don't be evil' slogan). Its brand power was counter-positioned against Microsoft. Google also aimed to put all the world's knowledge at people's fingertips and drive information productivity.

Apple, after two decades of being the radical icon of freedom and choice, had finally, with the launch of iPod, achieved mass acceptance for their vision—one where the right brain and the left brain melded together into a single piece of experience. The trade-off between the function and form had been an age-old belief in the design industry and indeed in any walk of life. Apple proved that it didn't have to be a zero-sum game.

Facebook stood for the vision of a hyper-connected human society, where the power to influence was distributed to each of the billions of its members equally. In a stroke of technological brilliance, equality of opportunity had been augmented with opportunity to influence. Facebook aspired to bring the world closer together like never before.

These brands are changing the world, each in their own way, and stand for an inspiring brand vision that goes far beyond the specific everyday tasks they help people perform. This also means that they do not see the relevance of traditional category boundaries when it comes to brand extensions. In fact, in their scheme of things, these old boundaries based on physicality, the narrow interpretation of need states and limitations of production and distribution are immaterial.

For example, Google's parent, Alphabet, isn't satisfied with remaining a search or media platform but plans to be the brains behind autonomous cars with its Waymo subsidiary. It wants to solve critical healthcare issues with its

Google Health project and provide IT cloud infrastructure and quantum computing for all businesses. It is a consumer appliance company with Google Nest, Google Home and Google Phones. And it tried to become a lifestyle company with Google Glass. All traditional norms of competition, threats and categories are blurred in the world of Google. The true constant between all these products is Google's engineering smarts, and its brand power apart from the UX, network and data power. Google and Apple probably have as much claim today on an AI- and IoT-led future of healthcare as any blue-blooded healthcare company. Already more than a hundred million Apple watches are plausibly monitoring people's vital stats every day, collating continuous monitoring data rather than the episodic data that clinics may acquire.

Facebook isn't satisfied with being just a social-media company. It would like to disrupt the content industry; it would like to create a VR-accessories and metaverse-experience industry with its Oculus portfolio, and it would love to become a financial services giant (though it is yet to find a robust model after two false starts—Libra and Diem). And most people genuinely believe that these businesses have a right to play in all these industries because of what the brands have come to stand for.

In fact, most people would love to see the Silicon Valley giants disrupt newer and newer industries. For instance, it wouldn't be an exaggeration to say that a company like Apple already has a captive market if it wanted to launch an 'Apple car' someday or an Apple VR headset (both supposedly in the pipeline). Similarly, a 'Facebook bank' or a 'WhatsApp mall' or 'Google schools' and 'Tesla yachts and trains' are all categories that the respective brands have already earned the 'permission' to enter from customers. And the secret is their extraordinary brand power.

Brand power is not a creation of the digital era in itself, however. The iconic brands of the Valley represent a conception of brand that rises far above the narrow function, physique, need state and category lines, thus multiplying its potential leverage and power. Never has marketing been so free of production, distribution and sales straightjackets. Never has a brand been so free of the product.

The Interplay of the Four Powers

The four powers are connected in some ways. Data is the fuel of the networks facilitating connection, prioritization and conversation. Data also keeps the UX honest and smart. Network power is best experienced via a good UX. And the best UX is often infused with network power mirroring the naturally social state of living. The greatest new-age brands of today are often perceived as inseparable from the network, UX and data power that helped them become great. Yet, each is a power in its own right, creating unique advantages and bringing a multiplier effect when deployed together.

To understand a marketplace today is to understand the dynamics of how the four new powers apply to a given category. It requires an incisive understanding of what kind of data creates leverage; the type of brands in the market can be easily extended into the category in question; the network effects that are relevant to the category need state (and value chain); and the role a powerful UX can have in carving a unique position within the category. Entire categories can be reconceived on the basis of these four powers, and new opportunities and threats uncovered.

* * *

The Open-House Advantage

Much as the marketplace and the nature of competitive powers in the marketplace have evolved, the concept of competitive advantage has also progressed in the digital economy. In this section, we will discuss what a cutting-edge competitive moat looks like, taking Amazon as an example. We will also note how it leverages the four competitive powers we outlined earlier.

At the turn of the century, Silicon Valley threw up some revolutionary new rules of engagement. For one, companies increasingly realized that they were competing less with each other, more with the future. As technology evolved categories faster and faster, a lot of the traditional norms of protecting one's competitive advantage were a lot less important than seizing the next wave of innovation. Open-source revolution was a gift of the dot-com era—and a product of Silicon Valley's counterculture—as armies of software developers came together in an altruistic spirit to build open platforms and ecosystems such as Linux, that were free and available to anyone, thus lowering the divide and inequality that access to technology itself could build.

> Companies increasingly realized that they were competing less with each other, more with the future.

As companies understood the power of ecosystems in keeping competition at bay (learning from the spectacular success of Microsoft), the race to own the ecosystem by gaining rapid scale resulted in companies like Google offering their Android operating system (OS) free. The idea was that if you owned the ecosystem, you had a captive base of people who couldn't do without you, and hence there would always be other ways to make money. At the least you ward off the competitor.

Company after company opened their codes to allow millions and millions of developers at large to code on their base.

Facebook gained their first advantage over the likes of Orkut, Friendster and Myspace by allowing developers and companies to build their own apps and embed it into their open platform (think 'pokes' and Farmville). This ensured that people on the Facebook network had tons of fun things to do together with their friends. Both Apple and Google allowed and encouraged people to create apps for their app stores. In this new world, competitive advantage was crowdsourced. This approach to rapid ecosystem development by co-opting downstream players also meant that the chance of a major threat appearing downstream was reduced (how the power equation here is dramatically skewed in favour of the ecosystem owner is aptly reflected in the lawsuit between Apple and Epic games, the makers of Fortnite). A generation of developers voted for the platforms by coding for it, and the most popular few would win it all. The new advantage was advantage by democracy.

It was a very opposite approach to the closed system approach that Microsoft (and players like Walmart) had followed in an earlier era. For almost twenty years, Microsoft became one of the most envied but also reviled players in Silicon Valley with its closed system, tight controls and a repeated tendency to suffocate innovators by copying their innovations and giving it away free as a part of their office suite. Google chose 'Don't be evil' as its slogan and promised to herald a new world. Of course, the erstwhile rebels, now big establishments themselves, have since created their own walled gardens. All great revolutions begin in dreamy idealism and end in cold, calibrated pragmatism.

Notwithstanding this, there is little doubt that most popular platforms today are a lot more open architecture, less as a matter of principle, more as a sound business practice. The app stores are a source of rapidly growing, high-margin revenues for both Apple and Google. Today Tesla and almost the entire automobile industry—BMW, Mercedes, Chevrolet and Honda—all have one thing in common: their cars all run the open-source Linux as their underlying operating system. This would have been unthinkable not very long ago.

All these new rules of the game have forced a reappraisal of what competitive advantage means. And as the leading players of the era seek to navigate their way through unpredictable technological cycles and a complex competitive landscape, Amazon has heralded a whole new way of building competitive advantage.

Amazon was built on Bezos's single-minded focus on building scale as rapidly as possible. Online retail had near infinite shelf space and the incremental cost of offering new stock keeping units (SKUs) was literally zero. Even in traditional retail, with a much smaller fraction of SKUs on offer, a company like Walmart had built an economy of scale that had proved impossible to challenge. Retail had been a brutal scale game, where almost every cost item fell as one built size. This allowed one to offer lower prices, which in turn drove scale further. In this business, scale was everything, the rest was all optimization. Bezos latched on to this simple idea, captured the first mover advantage and started his journey selling books, a category where, by and large, you didn't have to touch and feel before buying. It was also a category where returns were rare and cost of delivery not too high. For fourteen years after its Initial Public Offering (IPO), Amazon never made any money, but it built the kind of scale that would finally turn Bezos into the richest man on earth (and his now divorced wife the richest woman), and Amazon into a trillion-dollar-plus company.

But unlike Walmart, Amazon didn't build a closed system of interlocking advantages that would keep the competitors miles away. Amazon open house model was an open architecture model (see diagram). The platform allowed literally any legitimate seller to sell. Amazon's algorithms deployed AI-based recommendation engines to make purchases as efficient as possible, while maximizing average basket value, but its AI reco engine capabilities were available to anyone on its AWS cloud. Amazon's vast miles of servers were available to anyone who wanted to use them and this made AWS the unquestionable leader in digital infrastructure. Amazon warehouses and logistics were available for anyone to use, including its competitors. Amazon pricing system was open and allowed sellers to reference and benchmark. Amazon's marketing system allowed anyone to sell ad space as well as place their ads.

> Unlike Walmart, Amazon didn't build a closed system of interlocking advantages that would keep the competitors miles away.

In theory, any competitor of Amazon could be using its servers, its warehouse and logistics and its pricing guidance to compete against it. And even though within Amazon the various components of the businesses fit in snugly, in itself each component is not seen as a competitive advantage to be denied to competitors, but as an opportunity to monetize better, collect data and benchmarks and use the open architecture model to build dominance at every point in the value chain, which deters any organized major alternative to build. If you have to take on Amazon from a white sheet in markets where it plays and dominates, you have very little choice but to play the Amazon game.

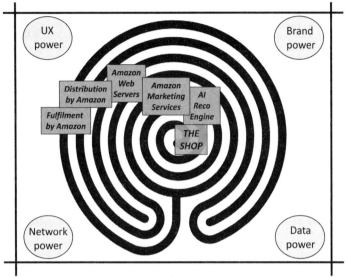

AMAZON 'OPEN HOUSE' COMPETITIVE MODEL

Whether in terms of the product and pricing choice its platform offers or the speed and efficiency of its logistics and warehouses, the more users it gets, the more value is created for each user, thus leveraging on network power. Amazon realized the power of UX quite early, inventing the one-click purchase button that makes purchases brutally simple; Amazon Dash physical buttons could be stuck to your washing machines to order detergents with a mere push of a button; as well as correlative recommendations that suggested to the customer to buy a particular book because people with similar interests bought that book too. It leverages the power of data across each and every aspect of the business, deploying powerful machine learning. Amazon's brand power has helped it build a credible presence in categories as diverse as over the top (OTT) streaming services, cloud services, voice assistant, consumer appliances, media and payments.

'Keep your friends close. Keep your enemies closer.'

—Sun Tzu, *The Art of War*

Through all this, the Amazon open house model has turned each stage of its value chain into a platform and opened it to build scale and competitiveness, thus building layers of crowdsourced advantage. The four powers of the new marketplace aptly inform the architecture of advantage it has built.

In the great Indian epic, the Mahabharata, Drona, the commander of the Kaurava army deployed a sophisticated battle formation called Chakravyuh (the wheel formation). Chakravyuh had seven layers of battalions merging each other in a maze, with alternate layers constantly moving clockwise and anti-clockwise respectively, in a highly disorienting manoeuvre to exhaust the enemy. A great warrior could always open a gap in front but the highly synchronized movement quickly allowed the gap to fill. Even if a wide open gap was made, the layers were intertwined in a maze so that the enemy would keep going in circles and get killed before reaching the prize at the centre.

Chakravyuh was considered impregnable by all but a rare few because it was designed to co-opt the competitors in a formation that was designed to squeeze out the competitors' energy, by creating an illusion of progress, yet offering a battle that would never end. As the outer layers closed in on the attacking forces, there was no choice of withdrawal. In fact, the farther the competitor engaged with the maze, the stronger the maze became, sapping the enemy's stamina and morale.

Amazon's competitive advantage is multilayered, transcending across the value chain, is open architecture in so many ways, yet is designed to benefit from the cost advantage and intelligence edge that access to the resultant scale, network effect and all-knowing data can bring. Amazon's open house model is reminiscent of the impregnable Chakravyuh that thrives on co-opting the competition.

As new competitive powers arose in the new architecture of the marketplace, it is not just the competitive moats that evolved, but also the competitive tempo. The customer became an active cheerleader and partner in the innovation process, rather than a passive purchaser. Let's consider for a moment, how that changed the speed and cadence with which companies moved in the marketplace.

* * *

The New Competitive Tempo

Air Asia is one of the world's largest low-cost airlines. It has historically sold most of its tickets via its booking website. At any point of time, it knows exactly how many people are browsing its website, how many went beyond a certain step in the booking engine and how many actually booked for what price and what date. It also knows how often this person travels, what they paid for the same ticket the previous time, and so on. It has a fairly reliable estimate of how many site visits it can expect to get each day and each hour at different times of the year. This gives it a truly granular picture of demand data across all its routes for a given date. Since its total inventory doesn't change every day, it has the ability to institute a highly dynamic real-time pricing mechanism that ensures its filled seats remain within a high utilization zone, while maximizing average price. This gives Air Asia an incredible ability to model its revenues and profits against any new product innovation—very, very quickly.

Similarly, Netflix can know very quickly which titles are flying and which ones are a dud, as it's capturing real-time response data to new innovations it introduces. Facebook knows through its Oculus VR headsets just how many people are using what new features and where exactly they are getting stuck in its Horizon meeting rooms. Four trends, somewhat interrelated, have made it a lot cheaper for companies to launch quickly and learn-n-improve rather than wait until the product achieves perfection to introduce it. Let's spend some time over the four key trends that are setting the new competitive tempo.

The Automation of Demand and Supply Chains: The last two decades have seen increasing digitization of both the supply chain and the demand chain. Demand generation is often activated and calibrated via a performance-marketing machine fuelled by powerful targeting data, that can be optimized and dialled up and down. Supply chains have become increasingly real time in their responsiveness to demand. With the rise of Industry X technologies that has allowed factories to use sensors, data and digitization to simulate optimizations, there is a whole new degree of responsiveness that's being created. Where the automated demand and the supply chains meet, there is the possibility of a margin utopia, as real-time inventory management and optimum-price mechanisms meet an adaptive, demand-generation engine. This requires a unified and responsive data architecture that runs across. Therefore, data is increasingly becoming a powerful factor in margin maximization in many categories. Data begets margins by leveraging asymmetry of information on the supply side, by delivering tailored value on the demand side, and by creating efficiencies in general, etc.

Where the automated demand and supply chain meet,
there is the possibility of a margin utopia.

The Cult of the New: We live in a global culture where new is celebrated sometimes for being merely new and not always practical or useful in a traditional sense (think Google Glass or the blockchain-based rights to the virtual real estate inside the Decentraland). The smallest of feature innovations—not yet real products—can overnight become unicorns. In this culture, where there are rare categories that are not threatened by wholesale disruption, innovation is the new fetish. As a result, categories are evolving fast, product life cycles are becoming shorter and shorter, and the pace of change itself is accelerating. Survival of the fittest has a more specific expression as survival of the most innovative, as ability to innovate becomes the leading indicator of adaptiveness. The electric truck company, Rivian, had a valuation of about US$2.3 billion (approximately) at its IPO without even a product in the market.

Faster Feedback Loops: As people live more and more mediated lives rather than situated lives, they react to brands online in subtle yet highly credible ways—in social media conversations, on blogs, in chats, in discussion groups and just by clicking something or watching a video to the end. Each of these reactions add up to a data trail that provides a precious feedback loop that can be almost instantaneous. The same applies to popular culture and rising trends. No more do businesses need to wait for their market research company to come back after several months to tell them what's working and what's not. This allows for higher agility and faster course correction for brands. Agility is the antidote to fragility.

'Everyone has a plan until they get punched in the mouth.'

—Mike Tyson

Fail Fast. Learn Fast: For decades, a new product launch would take years or at least months to perfect and plan its roll-out before it would see the light of day. Those were times when getting it right was more important than getting it out first. In a world worshipping at the altar of Silicon Valley, the whole approach has been replaced with a 'fail fast' paradigm, where the idea is to get the betas out rapidly and let the people judge, but use the speedy feedback loop to evolve fast. It matters less how lasting the product is, because the basic premise is that nothing lasts forever and must continuously morph to fit the next window of opportunity. Speed to market is becoming the basic criteria of survival for businesses.

In this process, by surrendering the right of marketers to decide what's good for their customers to the customers themselves, for once, businesses are moving from a traditional top-down approach to a bottom-up approach. The market rises and reveals itself on its own and customers end up creating the suitable choice, shorn of intermediary executives second-guessing on their behalf. What the so-called decision makers have to focus on is to throw different possibilities into the mix in the shape of betas and add-ons, and listen in very closely. It's the vision of a true democracy of choice built around the survival of the salient. And this culture is championed eagerly by hordes of early adaptors and alpha users, for whom trying new things—even if work in progress—has tremendous badge value. Beta is considered as cool. Beta has a reputational currency.

> It's the vision of a true democracy of choice
> built around survival of the salient.

In such a context, naturally, the marketplaces across different categories are evolving rapidly. A global marketplace of constantly colliding new ideas, new technologies, new ways of looking at data, evolving needs and specific niches, and differing visions of the future are forging a new era. In this era, there is a relentless pressure on organizations, business models and brands. The marketplace today is a highly dynamic, shape-shifting organism—with huge profits for those able to anticipate, lead and capture the most lucrative windows of margin—but with increasing pains and eventual destruction for those forever trying to second-guess. Both entry and exit barriers have gone down and the flow of capital—and increasingly, skills—is both more brutal and daring. Dealing with uncertainties and finding the sweet spot between a martyr and a game changer is the single biggest test of management wisdom in these times. To that end, every leader is wearing or ought to wear a venture-capital hat today.

SUMMARY:

A. We discussed the four types of marketplaces—utility, spontaneous, sensorial and relationship. This was based on the two dimensions of functional versus experiential and high commitment versus low commitment. We also discussed what mattered the most in each of the four marketplaces.

B. Then, we discussed briefly how the marketplaces, especially utility and relationship marketplaces, are getting condensed to ever-present, all-knowing AI-enabled buttons in digital spaces where people live their lives.

C. Thereafter, we discussed the four great powers that are changing the metastructure of competitive threats today— UX power, network power, data power and brand power.

D. Then, we considered the new architecture of competitive advantage informed by these powers and exemplified by the Amazon multi-layered moat.

E. Last but not least, we discussed the new competitive tempo—the speed and cadence—built around the fail-fast culture, the cult of the new, faster feedback loops, automation of demand and supply chains; and what it will take to succeed in this new tempo.

Having understood the nature of the new marketplaces and competition, let's move to how a business can choose its prospects more carefully; where the decades-old paradigms of segmentation stand in the new milieu, and how businesses can create advantage by answering the question of 'who is the prospect' better.

2

The New Prospect

'If you don't know where you are going, you might wind up someplace else.'

—Yogi Berra

From Anybody to Somebody

About ninety years ago, Henry Ford, who had just rolled out the Model T, quipped that you could have any colour you wanted, as long as it was black. Model T was for everyone, and it was black, take it or leave it. However, somewhere in the mid-twentieth century, wise marketers discovered that in order for a brand to be successful, it couldn't be all things to all people. Just as it is for a normal person, so, too, for a brand, it's important to be known for something, and depending on what that is, it would appeal to one segment of people more than the other. About half a century after Ford's famous quote, the concept of segmentation was discovered, followed within a decade by the concept of brand positioning (we will discuss this in another chapter).

The two concepts have been carved into the cornerstone of marketing for half a century. But today they lie challenged at the altar of technology and data.

The truth is, different people may buy a product for different reasons, and they may choose or not choose one brand over another for reasons that may be very personal to each (see diagram). So, while some people may prefer a Mercedes-Benz over a BMW because it looks more elegant, another set may prefer the brand because they perceive it to be more reliable; for a third set, it may remind them of childhood memories of rich people; and for yet another, it may stand for people who are generous and kind, for example, and so on. Most of the time, the reason people choose one brand over another has less to do with what the brand offers and more to do with their own unique context, needs, wants and influences in life. And just as there may be a huge number of drivers of preference for a brand, when aggregated over a population, there may be a huge number of barriers to a brand.

In the era of mass marketing, the dominant wisdom was to look at the marketplace, analyse who is good at what, then find a gap in the market where you could have an advantage among a large enough segment of people and then focus there to build your shares. However, this way of thinking was based on a simplified view of the market suited for the times. For instance, when marketers mapped the competitors, they basically focused on certain associated perceptions generally shared by people—sort of a lowest common denominator.

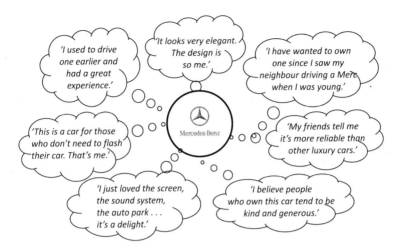

EVERYONE HAS THEIR OWN REASON TO BUY A CAR

This airbrushed the greater truth that each individual was unique and even in a market with a limited number of choices, there were scores of constituents with varying specific needs and perceptions within the larger picture, many of which mattered a lot more than the lowest common denominator.

Mass Segmentation a Compulsion, Not a Choice

'A group experience takes place on a lower level of consciousness than the experience of an individual.'

—C.G. Jung, *The Archetypes and the Collective Unconscious*

The reason why marketers continued to see things from the majoritarian perspective, however, and why it worked great for a hundred years, is because of two key reasons. First, the economy of scale that made products and services affordable to the masses required maximum standardization in turn leading automatically to a focused point of advantage.

And the second, because the most powerful touchpoint for reaching out to people for a mass consumer product was mass media, where a single brand message would be viewed by tens of millions. A brand looked for the lowest common denominator and hoped that its inability to better meet individual consumer needs would be more than made up for by the affordable access that economy of scale brought to both, the supply and the demand sides. Also, the scale that mass-media targeting brought meant that, despite a large number of exposures being wasted and merely annoying people who were never going to buy the product, the cost per prospect was still reasonable. Marketing for the most part didn't have a choice but to be mass, due to the limitations of mass media and economies of mass pricing.

To Each Their Own

In fact, even in the mass era, brands that involved in-person selling always tended to be many things at once, with their mass image projection often quite broad in order to allow for in-person customization. In categories such as life insurance, wealth management, properties and B2B selling, brands would always seek to cater to individual wants that could be highly diverse. A smaller role for mass media allowed one to avoid inefficient generalizations.

One of the great promises of the dot-com revolution was to minimize wastage in marketing. Evangelists, dot-com entrepreneurs and their groupie mediapersons interminably repeated John Wanamaker's famous quote about advertising wastage promising to fix the wasteful part. This promise still is the single largest driver behind the rise of the great media giants of our times—Google and Facebook. Also, because of the lean-forward nature of consumption in the new media and dropping attention spans of the new generations, quality user experience required one to be a lot more relevant and hence, less annoying. This made the spray-and-pray approach of mass-segment targeting even less tenable. Players like Google punished businesses with higher prices by lowering their Google-quality scores for being irrelevant.

The dot-com promise is premised on the fact that digital media allows for individual traceability and records the data for each and every activity of the surfer. It means that a brand can talk to an individual one on one. Also, since by looking at this data, there is a lot a brand can know about the person, a brand can mostly reach out to those who are real prospects— who it believes have a fair chance of buying it. In addition, with the information it has on the prospect, it can customize its message to improve its chances of converting the prospect into a customer.

In that sense, the real big opportunity that digital brought is not just in terms of minimizing media wastage (which is less relevant if you are truly a mass brand—say Coca-Cola, since you anyway want a huge number of people to see your message), but in being able to micro-target with highly relevant messaging. So, if someone is googling 'Beat Saber' (an extremely popular VR game), you know there is a good chance he or she (or they) may be a prospect for a VR goggle ad. Or, if someone has been watching videos about 'pregnancy rashes', you know she might be an apt target for a premium formula milk for would-be mothers that uniquely helps with allergies. In fact, if her location is an affluent locality, that improves the odds that she can even afford it. This hyper-relevant micro-messaging is the real holy grail of digital media. This is the conceptual justification for almost half a trillion dollars in digital spends each year and growing by leaps and bounds. Yet, it's also an area that is deeply underleveraged and in fact, often forgotten in the marketing ecosystem today soon after the hype and hyperbole of the digital sales pitches are over.

Advertising, the Opium of the Masses

The concept of near-zero wastage is revolutionary in so many ways. A few years ago, the famous rapper, P. Diddy, when invited to talk at the Cannes Advertising Festival, started with: 'Everybody hates advertising. I do.' It may be an exaggeration but there is some truth there. One thing is sure, the traditional interruption-based advertising—sort of a tax people paid to subsidize their programming—increasingly tested the patience of the attention-scarce generations. It was a huge waste of time and attention, as people on an average spent more than a thousand hours each year watching, reading and listening to ads for stuff that was not relevant to them at all—their minds overwhelmed by too many messages that would never be useful for them or that carried little genuine meaning for them. Digital media via its hyper-relevant messaging offered a panacea for this grand ill of mass marketing.

Karl Marx spoke about religion being the opium of the masses. In the age of television and all its mind-numbing imageries, consumption and advertising became the opium of the masses. Advertising stuffed and blunted people's minds with frequently irrelevant products and messaging prising it away from plausibly more fulfilling pursuits.

The new media platforms intensified their focus on user experience built around relevance. So, as mentioned earlier, the Google search engine would price their ads based on an auction model, but also incentivize ads that were more relevant and would least annoy people. In fact, they would put relevance right at the heart of their pricing, not charging for ads that were not clicked. Facebook and YouTube followed up on this commitment by similarly incentivizing ads that seemed to get more likes and interactions with much higher organic (free) views. Relevance became the new discount and offered higher cost leverage to those who cared more about offering good value in exchange for people's attention. It was a powerful attack on what had been seen as an acceptable collateral damage of mass marketing. However, this was not the first time a marketing approach had challenged its wastefulness. That honour goes to direct marketing.

From Direct to Digital

Fifty years ago, as direct marketing rose as the new weapon in a marketer's arsenal, it claimed to offer higher levels of customization, deeper levels of engagement and reduction of waste, somewhat on similar lines. However, for most mass-marketed products the cost per contact for direct marketing remained exponentially higher than mass media. The only way the higher impact it offered could justify itself was for products that were high involvement with long purchase cycles and consideration periods, and involved higher value per transaction. Sometimes this higher value could be justified on smaller outlay products with expectations of higher lifetime value on account of loyalty as soon as someone was converted. However, a common feature of direct marketing initiatives was its ability to be highly targeted towards a much smaller but higher potential segment, not unlike digital marketing today.

Direct marketing, which at one point of time had ambitions to replace much of mass advertising, in due course settled down to a useful, but considerably limited weapon. However, it had already cued a model of where the big new disruption for mass marketing might come from in the eventual future.

The only barrier really was the cost per contact relative to mass media. It also validated how an aggregation of smaller discrete segments with customized messaging could provide higher returns on marketing investment. This is why direct marketing is the spiritual father of digital marketing.

> Direct marketing is the spiritual father
> of digital marketing.

* * *

So, What Should a Marketer Do?

Digital microsegments took on from there, building on the momentum that low cost per contact of digital media brought. Today, it is quite clear in most categories that a best-in-class marketing plan ought to work with a targeting spectrum, rather than one mass target audience (see diagram). A brand needs to have a mass layer with a mass segment focus (typically 8–30 per cent of prospect base) to convey its overarching image and a message based on the lowest common denominator within this segment conveyed mainly through mass media and messaging.

This further needs to be complemented with a personalization layer, where it works with a large number of microsegments, each of them often less than 2 per cent of the prospect base—where the whole idea is to gain disproportionate impact by a high degree of messaging relevance. Sometimes, a third and intermediate layer of mini-segments, typically in the range of 3–7 per cent of prospects may be added with customized messaging, especially for highly commoditized and contested categories. (These percentages may differ based on brand maturity and category life cycle.)

In the context of customer relationship management (CRM), where a business has access to the individual data of its customers and the cost per contact is low, with the right automation, it is not uncommon to act upon each individual as a 'segment of one'. This targeting spectrum would still have the original mass segment as its epicentre but taps higher and higher relevance and efficiency as it moves from the mass layer towards the segment of one.

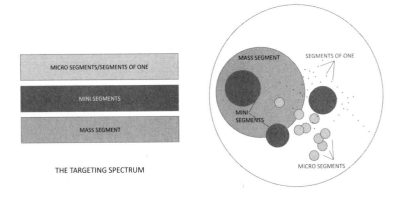

THE TARGETING SPECTRUM

From a Target Segment to the Targeting Spectrum

A 'targeting spectrum' approach versus a one-size-fits-all mass 'target segment' approach doesn't just promise to bring higher efficiency of targeting, but also helps manage the marketing risk better. No longer does a marketing budget need to be completely risked on one blockbuster mass campaign idea, hoping that the gamble pays off. It allows marketers to work with a portfolio of messages, with the ones getting better returns attracting higher allocations in the media-optimization process. For once, marketing campaigns can be less of a gamble.

Imagine a new car being launched. The car is more spacious than its peer group (important for families), it's also more macho in its look (many men love that) and the fuel consumption is clearly low. The big debate in marketing rooms often is about what benefit to dial up. Each of the benefits may appeal to somewhat different even if overlapping segments of people. In the traditional segmentation approach, it will result in one big, unwieldy uber-segment—which is roughly the superset of the three beneficiary groups—as the target segment, say all adults, 25–49, in a broad income group. And then the messaging will need to find a primary focus on, say space. So you end up talking about a 'big car for big hearts' (for example) and target a very wide segment.

Compare it to a targeting spectrum approach, where for mass awareness we may deploy the above overarching message of a 'big car for big hearts' to the mass segment but, at the mini-segment level, we may decide to activate each of the three mini-segments. We could target, say the 'Spaceloving Simon'—families with more than two kids or with grown-up kids plus multigenerational families. We could separately target 'Manboy Max'—grown up men, 30–44, who define themselves by their macho possessions. We could also target the price-conscious 'Smartpick Sally'—someone more value-conscious, younger and relatively less affluent typically who takes pride in well-thought-through choices with a long horizon in mind. Each of these mini-segments can be targeted with specific marketing programmes designed to convert them and activated through media choices today.

To complement the mass and mini layer, a micro-layer could be conceived either through digital media or by leveraging the CRM data or both. Better space in cars could be very important for weekend picnickers, outdoor sports lovers, family caregivers, tall individuals, those with a permanent leg handicap, families with pets, painters who have to carry big canvases in their cars, and so on. None of these may be big segments in themselves, or even mini-segments (depending on the country), but a spacious car is a godsend for each of them, and aggregated, can be quite a chunk. In the age of mass media, it was not cost-effective to talk to each of them specifically, so you just hoped they would know about the car, and also get that it's great for them. Now, with micro-targeting and micro-messaging, it's possible to talk to each with a separate custom message tapping their specific need gaps.

This three-tiered view of targeting also offers a natural balance between reach, relevance and returns, allowing a brand to continuously test its relative appeal to different constituents. As investments get allocated to higher conversion segments increasingly, it allows brands to naturally expand their constituencies and test different growth hypotheses against the reality.

Come to think about it, hyper-relevant marketing may not be all that new. In fact, it has a vintage as old as civilization itself. Personalization is old, it's the personalization at scale that is new—aided by automation and granular traceability—and hence lower cost of sale on digital platforms.

Original Marketing was All Personal

In an interesting déjà vu, before the advent of mass marketing, most products and services were customized at a personal level. In the village economies that dominated human civilization for thousands of years, the artisans knew everyone in the village. They knew the customer, his or her family, personality and what might be truly needed (no need for a focus group). And the artisan would handcraft to cater to that. It was highly personal. And since so many people were involved in producing such personalized products and services, it resulted in deeply interdependent, sustainable and largely self-sufficient microsystems. Personalization was not a value-addition allowing for higher margins, but a reciprocal communal understanding. (This was the crux of the Gandhian economy expected to be a complete, sustainable and responsible-by-design economic system.)

As towns and cities grew, and the first wave of scale manufacturing started, aided by merchants, artisans and their highly organized guilds, high quality artisans used personalization to drive up their margins by catering to merchants, noblemen and royalty, while leaving the bulk produce for the hoi polloi. This was also how many of the French luxury brands today originated.

Cut to modern times and once again, personalized product and pricing is set to be the future of commerce. Apart from several digital products, sectors such as hotels and airlines have already begun to experiment with how personalization, not just in communication, but also in product and pricing can help command better margins apart from helping gain loyalty from customers. Category after category has chosen to go for personalized pricing based on specific needs, available inventory and expected demand. Telecom companies have launched packages where one could personalize their communication needs to customize the pricing. Highly flexible subscription bundles are becoming commonplace in categories with fewer choices.

Also, virtual interactions have opened new avenues of personalized selling at scale. In areas such as wealth management, the principle of 'money begets money' was premised on the thought that wealthy people have unique access to higher return opportunities due to the high cost of access and mediation. However, as technology helps provide access and customized advice at a much lower marginal cost, wealth management is set to undergo its own robo-adviser revolution. No wonder some have gone so far as to say that Personalization could be a whole new P of marketing (apart from the 4 Ps of Product, Price, Place and Promotion). Personal is the new premium, and if deployed well, brands have an unprecedented opportunity to command it.

Personal is the new premium.

As we will see, slicing and dicing crowds of people is not the only way to drive higher relevance. Depending upon the product and how it is different, it's also possible to focus on other dimensions, for example, specific moments.

Moment is the Message

'Life is not perfect. Moments can be.'

—Anonymous

Let's consider Laurent Kelly, a thirty-four-year-old mother of two. At her breakfast table, she is an archetypal mother not much unlike her boomer mom; an hour later at her workplace she is a millennial executive; and on a Friday night out with her girlfriends, she doesn't mind shooting and uploading a funky TikTok video, like her young Gen Z cousins. How she reacts to brand messaging is influenced by the moment she is in at a given point in time. To club the many personas she takes on in her day-to-day life into a specific segment may be highly wasteful for a brand, depending on the category.

The untethering of the messaging from a monolithic segment brings a new level of dynamism to the targeting spectrum by opening new ways of looking at how to define focus. And one way is to look at the targeting spectrum as a collection of moments rather than differently sized segments.

Hence, a targeting spectrum could also be populated by a collection of moments the brand wants to focus on and own.

As people try to squeeze in more life per life—postponing maturity, innovating new lifestyles and defying the traditional norms of age-appropriate mindsets and behaviours—it could be argued that people live more and more in moments rather than in broad, generic, static, pigeonholing segments.

People live more and more in moments,
rather than in broad, generic, static, pigeonholing segments.

In the old world of mass media, whether you were a coffee brand for morning consumption or a condom brand for say evening consumption, you had to advertise on prime-time television, because that was when people watched TV. However, now that the screen travels in our pocket around the clock, brands have an opportunity to plug into very specific moments like never before.

Beyond moments, another targeting dimension that offers interesting opportunities for designing a brand focus around is the social communities or affinity groups. As more and more people become creatures of their social network, just as individuals make the network, the network makes the individual too. We are defined by where we belong at the intersection of community, content and influences—in a reality shaped by social media imagery, we become what we share. And a brand can seek to belong in there too. If you are selling very powerful sunscreens, it makes sense to focus on, for example, the top five outdoor sports that may account for 90 per cent of the usage occasions for the product, and each of those sports can be targeted as a community—in social media or otherwise, with marketing programmes that will ride the network.

Thus, targeting spectrum is a dynamic approach that it can incorporate different perspectives on which a basic unit of targeting can offer the highest elasticity of demand in a category—be it a multiplicity of segments, moments or communities, etc.

Last but not least, in every population, there are people who are conformists, who seek the comfort of the crowd and make the safer choice. And then there are those who are curious and novelty seekers. Brands have a strong interest in the latter ones, as for a new product innovation, they can bank upon such people to try it out first. The diffusion curve is about mapping people on a spectrum in the light of their tendency to try out new things. The percentage of people who are early triers in a given category makes a lot of difference to how quickly a good product can be successful (or get rejected). So, a discussion on targeting won't be complete without touching upon this aspect.

* * *

The Diffusion Curve and the Rise of Newism

When an innovation is launched, the group that's the first lot to try are the innovators—curious category users (on an average, they tend to be younger, more savvy, but also from an above average income group relatively) or alpha users of the category, who have a stronger need consciousness compared to the rest of the population and are willing to try new things more readily than usual. Once the innovators share the feedback around, they are followed by the early adopters, people who are curious but need the validation of the innovators before they would buy a new product. They are followed by the early majority, who in turn are followed by the late majority and laggards (see diagram).

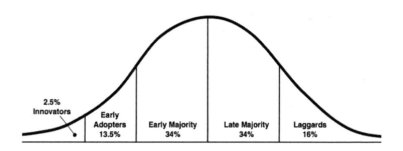

THE DIFFUSION OF INNOVATIONS CURVE BY EVERETT M. ROGERS

One of the residual trends that the dot-com revolution left in its wake is a large-scale recognition by societies around the world that innovative ventures sit at the heart of productivity growth in an economy. As discussed before, innovation by definition would entail rapid experimentation and hence a high failure rate, so the emphasis went to celebrating the fail-fast culture as the crucible of bold transformative innovations. As the fail-fast culture took hold, companies started taking pride in launching their beta products, and people at large began to love participating in co-creating the product to help achieve better reliability and relevance.

It didn't matter if the product was designed to last, what mattered was that it pushed the frontier of what was possible. Fuelled by hundreds of billions of new stock market value, the hustle and jostle of the unicorns, rapid global scalability built into most platforms and the global media hype, a 'cult of the new' arose with tens of millions of followers in every part of the world. Celebrating the new for the sake of being new became the basic ritual of this 'Newism' and that forever changed the traditional diffusion curve of innovations, accelerating it but also bringing new motivations into play (see diagram).

Today, for new tech innovation, in the beginning come the 'Techsetters'. These are frontier scouts made of nerds, hipsters and the bargain-baggers (the last one being the opportunists who are looking for those early deep bargains, knowing that venture capital's first priority is to rapidly scale the network effect, with less regard to the actual cost of sale). The 'Newists' pick up right after providing it the street creds that would thereafter attract the digital 'Natives'. These are the millennials and the Gen Z who find natural resonance with credible innovations that bring them currency in their day-to-day life. This has the effect of making the innovation mainstream. The network and ecosystem impact compel the digital 'Immigrants' (older generations who love digital) to get onboard. And finally, there is a long, slow trickle of digital 'Pilgrims' who may join the train, if it stops at the station long enough.

The perfect symmetry that the diffusion bell curve was, due to the network effect as well as the cult around Newism, is now skewed towards the front rising steeply with the rear part dropping off into a long, slow tail.

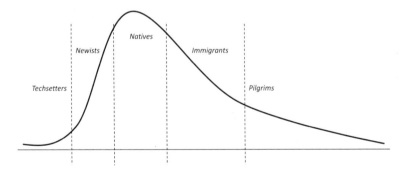

THE HYPOTHETICAL SHAPE OF THE NEW DIFFUSION CURVE

While we have discussed a more sophisticated new
targeting spectrum—made of segments, moments or
communities—it's important not to forget that the biggest
barrier to realizing this had been the cost. So a closure on
the subject requires one to ponder over the economics of
personalization in marketing. Here we will discuss the
demand side in particular; however, the principles can be
extrapolated to the supply side as well.

* * *

The Sweet Spot of Margin Maxima

As more and more data is available, media targeting can
move from buying an opaque audience set to buying a target
segment who are potential buyers of the product. This can
be further fine-tuned to focus on category relevance seeking
those who are already in-market for the category. However,
the power of the data takes another dimension when we can
reach these in-market people in the moments that are most
relevant to the product (see diagram).

Of course, as the level of selectivity increases, the cost of
each contact increases exponentially too, due to declining
inventory volume and higher data cost. Having said that,
with far higher conversions, the conversion per media
dollar grows in an S curve. Depending upon how mass-
focused the product is and how differentiated its category,
the sweet spot of optimal margins per media dollar may
lie somewhere between category relevance and moment
relevance for most products.

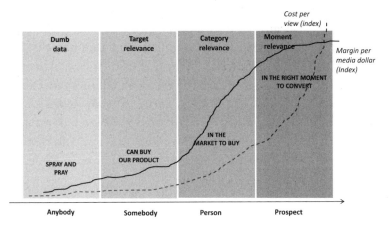

Dumb data	Target relevance	Category relevance	Moment relevance

Cost per view (index)

Margin per media dollar (Index)

IN THE RIGHT MOMENT TO CONVERT

IN THE MARKET TO BUY

CAN BUY OUR PRODUCT

SPRAY AND PRAY

Anybody   Somebody   Person   Prospect

HOW COST AND MARGIN TYPICALLY MOVE AS DATA GETS MORE SPECIFIC

Let's take an example of a premium formula milk with anti-allergy properties for pregnant women. Let's assume the sale of one unit allows for US$10 in profits before paying for media (see diagram).

Now the brand can target women in general, where the media cost per view may be inexpensive (say, 1 cent) but the conversion from view to sale is 0.1 per cent, which means the cost per sale comes to US$10 and net profit is zero. However, let's say if we target mothers, the cost per view goes up to 3 cents, but the conversion is now 0.5 per cent, which brings the cost per sale to US$6 and net profit to US$4.

Let's get more focused and target pregnant women. The cost per thousand may go up steeply to 15 cents, but the conversion is now 5 per cent. The cost per sale hence is US$3 and net profit goes up to a high US$7.

We can go even further and decide to target pregnant women with rashes—it's definitely not easy to find enough of them—so the average cost per view really shoots up to 50 cents this time. Now conversion must shoot up as well;

however, it's possible that the conversion may only go up to 10 per cent, because of affordability constraints. This means that the cost per sale instead of going down, goes up to US$5 and our net profit falls to US$5 from US$7.

Finding that sweet spot is the crux of many a marketing-optimization scenario depending on the priorities. A single-minded focus on share growth may need a different approach from margin growth, for example. Also, the cost of creative development and automation must be added to the media cost in real life.

Category: Premium Milk Formula				
Differentiator: Anti-allergy properties for pregnant women				
Margin per unit: $10–media cost per sale				
All monies in USD				
Media Target	Cost per view	Sale per view	Media cost per sale	Margin per unit
Women, 18+	1c	0.1%	$10	**0**
Moms	3c	0.5%	$6	**$4**
Pregnant women	15c	5%	$3	**$7**
Pregnant women with rashes	50c	10%	$5	**$5**

FINDING THE SWEET SPOT: AN EXAMPLE

This opens new opportunities for media companies, who can charge a premium for inventory that's highly specific. They can also charge a significant premium for the same inventory if they know that a piece of inventory holds a high value for a brand specifically. In a world where people are living via media half the time, generic inventory is almost limitless.

Smart useful data that can qualify the inventory to fit a brand's specific need is, however, limited.

Data can turn dust into specks of gold. And this explains the gold rush of third-party data companies that prevailed for several years. This also explains why most global digital platforms are walled gardens protecting their data rigorously and inventing new ways and means to be able to plug into the marketer's customer database. A lot of the media buying is now highly automated via opaque auction mechanisms, with asymmetric information—where a platform's ability to make higher margins is frequently dependent on how much they know about what a business needs and how they can pit its needs against those of its competitors, thus squeezing out more and more profits. It's a margin paradise, reflected in the valuation multiples which global platforms enjoy.

SUMMARY:

A. We looked at the origin of segmentation as an approach. Then we discussed why and how targeting needs to evolve from a monolithic mass segment to a multilayered targeting spectrum—with a mass layer, a layer of mini-segments and at the base, an always-on pool of microsegments or segments of one.

B. Then we briefly looked into how targeting spectrum could also be composed of moments or communities built around different affinities.

C. We also looked at how the diffusion curve—which set expectations traditionally about what kind of people to expect when you launch a new product—is changing. And we considered the rise of Newism—great for rapid innovation, but which also carries a higher risk for incumbents.

D. Finally, we looked at the cost versus margin dimension of targeting narrower and narrower segments and how to find the sweet spot.

* * *

Having analysed the marketplace and the competition, and a more sophisticated picture of who and where to focus, let's delve into the 'what' question—what should a product or brand stand for? This is the crux of the next chapter.

3

The New Positioning

'It takes all the running you can do, to keep in the same place. If you want to get somewhere else, you must run at least twice as fast as that!'

—Red Queen, *Through the Looking Glass,*
Lewis Carroll

Positioning refers to the place a brand occupies in the mind of its target audience. Defining the right positioning for a brand is one of the trickier tasks in marketing. To create a generic mapping to reflect how people see the brand vis-à-vis its competitors is relatively easy; however, the task of positioning the brand as an insightful decision device is more complicated than that. Also, it is not enough to know where the brand is positioned today, but also where it needs to get and where it has the best 'right to play'.

Categories are rarely stagnant. In fact, like the Red Queen said in the book *Through the Looking Glass*, a brand must keep running in order to even stay in the same place, because the category is always evolving. Rigveda, the ancient text of the Hindus, asks readers to keep moving— with exhortations of *'Charaiveti, Charaiveti'*[1]—espousing the central place of motion in life. However, identifying the most relevant dimensions on which the category is moving— from the various established as well as new functional and emotional attributes—is an important factor in defining the desired positioning of a brand. This ensures that the brand is primed to ride the more important trends in consumer lives, providing it that tailwind for growth.

Let's discuss some important considerations we must ponder in order to be able to arrive at the right positioning for a brand.

Different Marketplace, Different Rules

Which of the four marketplaces—utility, spontaneous, sensorial or relationship—a brand plays in, is yet another important consideration. A brand positioning required to win in the sensorial marketplace needs to have a deeply emotional dimension steeped in the brand mythology, and that is different from what is required in the relationship marketplace, where trust is what matters the most. Also, the larger strategy to leverage the great competitive powers of network, data and UX ought to be in sync with the way the brand is positioned and vice versa. Positioning also serves as an important overarching umbrella that the different levels of messaging on the targeting spectrum must abide by in order to avoid conflict of identity.

Find Your Place in the Marketplace

It goes without saying that a market leader must always occupy the most mainstream positioning in the market and evolve in line with it, so that it always has the largest catchment area of all its competitors. A challenger taking on the market leader should, instead of trying to defeat the leader on its current turf, seek to take the lead on the future trajectory of the category, thus making it more mainstream, hopefully, in due course.

Disruptive challengers, on the other hand, may often have the insight to be able to open unrealized constituencies and a future path, which may help step change the mainstream in the category, leaving the leader to keep trying to play catch up. The difference between challengers and disruptors is that disruptors have little to lose, they have not been co-opted by the incumbent category gameplay, are trying to leapfrog the category rather than seek incremental gains, and hence tend to play a riskier strategy, hopefully with pay-offs that are worth it. Niche players should strive to find specialist positioning where they, instead of trying to play the game of the larger players, seek to own a smaller (yet big enough to provide ample growth) catchment area. It should be an area that can be dominated and also, hopefully, is one that offers faster growth rates, lower risks and sufficient margins.

The Right to Play

As David Ogilvy, the famous adman, observed, great marketing can only make a bad product fail faster. An apt example of this is the Tata Nano car. The great global buzz and interest that Nano received for its 'shockingly cheap' perceived positioning even before the launch only hastened its death, as a few cars blew up due to faulty wiring, validating people's secret suspicion that the cheapest car may have compromised in critical areas. A more low-key introduction, mainly focused on the value-end rather than solely on the cost-end, may have allowed time and space for calibrating up the quality issues to a more robust platform. Ultimately, there was no second chance for Nano.

It is important that the product—and the value bundle it represents across price, place and promotion—is always the starting point for a positioning exercise. A good understanding of the relative strengths and weaknesses of the brand—real and perceptual—is important to ensure that the brand has a good chance to own a desired positioning in due term. These reasons to believe (RTBs), fact-based arguments to support why consumers should trust the positioning, are crucial and keeps marketing honest, effective and sustainable. Without at least some measure of RTBs, it's like a wise man said: 'You can't fool all the people all the time.'

It is quite clear that a positioning exercise requires both right-brain and left-brain understanding of the deeper fabric of the customer minds and the evolving category landscape. In fact, for a small player in the category, defining a positioning in generic terms that other bigger players might be using already, leads to playing a game where the rules are set by someone else—a game that they can seldom win.

Let's discuss the choices that a positioning decision typically entails and some of the important things to keep in mind while navigating them.

The Tug of War

Overall, a positioning decision is often a tug of war involving three major trade-offs. The first is revenue against profitability. A brand can go for more volume by pitching itself at a lower price point, or it can play a predominantly margin game by focusing on the upper end of the price point. Secondly, a brand can focus on today's need gaps—better-improved solutions to the known problems or opportunities that already have a large constituency, thus playing it safe and incremental. Or it can go for the emerging need gaps, where the scale of opportunity is still an open question and the brand is a market maker. Lastly, it can primarily emphasize the functional advantage where it may have a clear edge and the confidence to make people switch in a logical process, or it can try to gain an emotional advantage, either due to a lack of clear functional differentiation or as a choice because it sees greater upsides in dialling up the heart.

An optimal positioning decision at the intersection of the three axes above, involves both science and art (see diagram). Let's understand this better with an example.

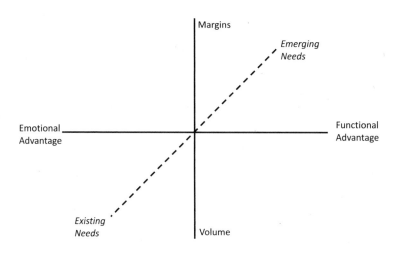

A TYPICAL POSITIONING TUG OF WAR

An iPhone chooses to own the most premium positioning in the mobile phone category, catering to the mass affluent customers who attach their self-image with best-in-class aesthetic standards and user experience. It can go for a more mass positioning, but it is likely that the extra volumes it will get may not be worth the profitability it may sacrifice. It may also mean quality compromises and image dilution, creating a risk for its exclusive image as well as the self-image it evokes among its buyers. The brand is also scrupulously particular about delivering a perfect emotional experience across the complete customer journey, de-emphasizing the functional advantages which are a lot easier to replicate (and which a lot of its competitors obsessively emphasize, as fighting the battle of image with Apple is a whole lot tougher).

Also, much as every new version of iPhone incorporates some new features, it has been forgoing the temptation to try to launch a VR or AR device extension, which may be an emerging need, as it probably deems the world (and itself) not yet ready to bring a game changer in that sphere. Samsung, on the other hand, has experimented with VR gears, tries to project its functional strengths aggressively and sells at lower prices for lower average margins, but high volumes.

Positioning the Portfolio

The issue of positioning takes on added sophistication for more complex brand portfolios, adding new ways to manage the above three trade-offs. 'Line extensions' serve as forward scouts for the brand, exploring the emerging need gaps for the portfolio, as the mother brand is often preoccupied with today's need gaps. Sometimes, the line extension may be an image leader bringing emotional advantage for the portfolio due to a sharper, edgier image unsullied by the ravages of time and girth. 'Brand extensions' on the other hand, are deployed to carry the same brand into other products, sometimes new innovations, within the larger category need-space. Thus, they leverage the core brand equity to further drive revenues and profits. A 'flanker brand' with an independent but highly differentiated positioning of its own, forays into territories that are deemed too far from the main brand.

So, a BMW deploys its line extensions—BMW 3 series, BMW 5 series, BMW 7 series and BMW X6, etc.—to cover different price points and need segments. Mini Cooper plays the role of a flanker brand for the portfolio, allowing it to win over the highly individualistic, urban, creative hipster constituency. BMW Motorrad would serve as a brand extension into motorcycles, leveraging the larger equity of the brand as muscular performance machines among the macho, urban sophisticates who love their bikes—that mirror their own smooth power.

All these devices allow a powerful brand to be able to extend its positioning into newer domains on the positioning map in order to widen its catchment area as a portfolio, manage risks better, leverage mutual synergies and continue exploring and evolving. They turn brands into dynamic living organisms.

Having sensitized one to these important considerations, let's come back to a simple process made of four questions, the answers to which can help throw up the brand positioning at their overlap.

The four questions are, what do customers need, what does the future bring, what can the brand offer and what are competitors doing (see diagram).

FOUR QUESTIONS OF POSITIONING

The first question relates to expressed or latent needs of the customers; the second one relates to how technology can evolve the category; the third question is about the right to play and reasons to believe; and the last one ensures that brand positioning's prime role as an enabler of customer preference over other choices in the market is not forgotten. That positioning doesn't become a narcissistic pursuit in the echo chambers that large successful incumbents can sometimes become.

It's important at this point to delve into how 'positioning' for a brand needs to evolve in light of the new trends that seek to make traditional assumptions obsolete, and also open new opportunity spaces that ambitious brands can latch on to.

* * *

Culture and Consequences

The megatrends that can create new positioning opportunities typically emerge from three important shifts: cultural, technological and economic. In turn, they affect people's expectations in terms of their preference for one brand over the other.

These expectations can be explicit or implicit. When explicit, they may be articulated by people or reflected in how some consumers interact with the category already. When implicit, people may not be able to articulate what they want or show clear patterns of choice, simply because it's difficult to conceive what doesn't exist yet (Bitcoin, the pioneering cryptocurrency is a very good example of a product tapping implicit expectations, so is the iPhone). It is one reason why traditional market research can sometimes be limiting. You can't drive by looking back all the time or expect consumers to envision what can be.

To be able to read the signals in the wind—both explicit and implicit—one would need structured (e.g., market research, internal sales, etc.) and unstructured data (social-media trends, search volumes, consumer interactions, etc.) on the three shifts to be analysed, assimilated and meditated upon by teams that can bring together both analytics and creativity in a conceptual whole. Here are a few important ways the cultural shifts are taking place in the consumer mindspace that affect many categories.

Ingenuity is the New Smart

As mentioned before, we live in times when people worship technological innovation sometimes to the extent that they buy something new, merely because it's new rather than useful. In such a backdrop of Newism, brands are expected to keep their customers continuously stimulated and inspired with relentless innovations (even if the innovation may be temporary—think Google Glass). A perception of ingenuity has become the hallmark of a smart brand. It also marks out a brand as adaptive and agile, which is seen as the new criteria of strength, rather than the traditional pillars of size, seasoning or solidity. Some of these attributes have become a common influence on positioning maps. When it comes to brands, ingenuity is the new smart today and agile, the new strong.

The leading Silicon Valley giants such as Alphabet, Amazon, Microsoft, Tesla and Apple are great examples. They enjoy extremely high valuation multiples because they have built an image of relentless ingenuity (even if many launches may be failures, for example, Google Glass or Facebook Libra) and hence have been able to sustain confidence among stakeholders in their ability to stay relevant year after year. In comparison, the traditional car makers, who were massive in scale and solid on the books, just couldn't sustain the same level of disruptive ingenuity, and hence, are worth a lot less.

Technology is not Just Utility but an Expression

Digital presence with high quality user experience, speed and efficiency further contribute to this perception of brain and brawn. As people live more and more tech-mediated lives today, technology has taken a pole position in the contemporary lifestyle, culture and self-image. Brands that are perceived to be in sync with the latest technology—whether through great UX or via new technology-led experiences or via products embedded with exciting new tech—are seen as 'getting it'. It allows such brands to tap into people's latent desires and self-image. Brands need to recognize that technology is the new contemporary. Technology can't substitute the human experience or culture, but increasingly, culture and technology are getting intertwined in a deeply symbiotic relationship. Technology is not just a cold, incidental facilitator of human expression and experience; using inspiring, novel technology is a defining cultural expression in its own right. This is how Ariana Grande drew 78 million players to her virtual concert inside Fortnite Metaverse beating Lil Nas X's Roblox performance, which had 33 million viewers.

This shape of technology is nothing like the mechanistic view of technology—championed by the likes of HP, Motorola, Dell and Microsoft—that dominated the previous century.

Transparency Begets Trust

Social media rules of engagement necessitate that brands behave more like normal humans in order to be relatable and to embody trust. A certain degree of authenticity and transparency is key to earning the street creds in this social village. People on social media have a fundamental aversion to the big, opaque patriarchal chest-beating. Just as between a modern parent and the child, people expect businesses to treat them like adults and communicate to them openly. Trust is borne of transparency.

Good examples are companies like Tesla. Despite Elon Musk's unconventional behaviour, quite unlike what corporate-communications departments of large listed corporations would advise, it is his accessible image, authenticity and transparency that allow him to thrive. People trust him despite his throwing all the rule books out of the window.

Empathy Begets Loyalty

A certain degree of empathy on the part of the brands is the price of entry towards the organic network of shared consciousness in social media. This empathy needs to be overt and not just limited to product design. Ability to embody and project that human-like 'connectedness' makes brands more real in social media. All in all, at its very core, social media is a village; and the peer-to-peer fabric of relationships—not just functional but also emotional—is the dominant norm of behaviour here. Listening, being responsive, treating people as people rather than legal entities, showing you are on the same side as your customer, sympathy for the underdogs, etc., are the qualities that brands must engender on top of their functional reliability to build loyalty.

> A certain degree of empathy on the part of the brands is the price of entry towards the organic network of shared consciousness in social media.

The Crisis in the Middle

Apart from the above cultural and technological shifts, an important economic shift that's shaping the fortunes of several categories globally—although the picture may vary country to country—is the increasing polarization of markets in many categories.

On one end are the emotionally led prestige brands, which you buy in high-experience contexts, where you pay a premium for self-image and other higher order needs (e.g., luxury handbags, expensive resorts, posh cars). On the other end are the products that leverage the global supply chain and economy of scale to deliver the minimum acceptable quality in the cheapest and fastest way possible (much of what is sold in supermarkets and the generic online marketplaces could qualify for that). In many categories, the middle seems to be shrinking under pressure from both ends and creating a crisis of positioning choices there, as people in the middle are either trading up or trading down. In categories, where using multiple brands in parallel is a norm, it may sometimes be the same consumer displaying both behaviours, aligning high-end brands with a specific set of occasions and the low-end brands for the rest.

There are two key reasons behind this. One reason is the nature of demographic shifts. There has been a marked hollowing out of the middle classes in developed countries such as the US in the last few decades. Parallel to that, hundreds of millions of erstwhile poor in countries such as India, China, South-east Asia and Latin America have entered the global consumer economy at the lower end. Also, the increasing concentration of wealth across both developed and emerging economies riding the wave of globalization and technology has exploded the upper end of the pyramid. Exclusive excludes a lot less than it used to.

The second important reason is that, in this experience-obsessed world, people are a lot more exposed to high-end brands, and open to buying them, even if for very specific occasions. In addition, the clutter of brands in the middle trying to play both up and down the pyramid and the information overload in general means customers seek the simplicity and clear gratification that sharper, top-of-the-shelf brand positioning provides. Brands, it's obvious, need to be clear about where they play. People naturally block out anything fuzzy. You cannot both be and not be.

Computers, consumer appliances, apparel, accessories, household care, personal care, hospitality, luxury retail, etc., are some of the most directly affected categories by this squeeze in the middle. The pyramid is becoming an hourglass. Brand aspiration used to be a climb on a ladder. In many categories, it is becoming a leap now.

> Brand aspiration used to be a climb on a ladder.
> In many categories, it's becoming a leap now.

Looking at the premium and the risk buffer that an excellent brand positioning can provide, a fundamental step to creating accelerated growth for a brand is to start from a clear, robust positioning exercise based on an insightful picture of cultural, technological and economic trends that are relevant to the category. It should be based on an original (yet credible) and unexpected view of how the category is laid out and how a breakthrough could be made. Consumer mindspace is seldom too simplistic and obvious when it comes to placing one brand against another. Therein lies the opportunity for a unique perspective that opens hitherto unseen doors. A perspective that is original, clear, believable and one that can bring the full force of conviction from the entire company towards actualizing it in the consumer's mind.

Growth in its core essence, after all, is born out of a point of view. An original one.

* * *

Developing the Brand Identity

Once we have a clear picture of where the brand is and where it needs to be positioned, the positioning and its informing analysis can be extended into a brand identity framework, that provides a more complete picture of the brand we intend to take to our customers (see diagram).

Brand identity encapsulates looking at the brand in six important dimensions, three each for what the brand is internally and what the brand is to the world. Let's delve deeper into this. We will be using Tesla as an example.

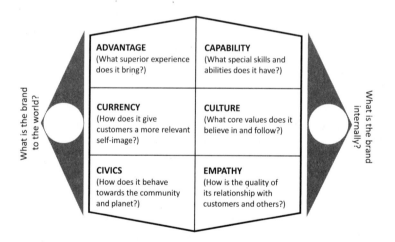

Capability alludes to the differentiated skills and competencies that the business has internally, that begets trust and respect towards the brand's dynamism, reliability and long-term competitive advantage. Capability as a dimension of the brand identity dials the more authentic, tangible, sustainable, trust-building aspect of a company, that then can be seamlessly leveraged into new products and markets. This is the aspect that allowed Elon Musk to attract capital and customers for Space X, even though spaceships may not be in exactly the same category as cars. For Tesla, the capability box would include their transformative leadership in battery technology and production; their expertise in cutting-edge, autonomous technology; and their top notch design skills, that allowed Tesla to become an aesthetically appealing lifestyle choice (see diagram).

Advantage summarizes the functional and emotional advantages that the brand provides its customers in relation to the product. For Tesla, they would be best-in-class engineering, support infra and services and excellent aesthetics. Clearly, capabilities directly impact the advantage that a brand brings.

The third dimension in the brand identity framework is *culture*, which refers to what core values does the company believe in and follow in all it does. For Tesla, the key elements of this dimension would be courage, tenacity, agility, irreverence and being planet-aware. These clearly are the values that helped Tesla (despite naysayers) recast the entire industry of a hundred plus years vintage. This leads us to *currency*, which reflects how the brand gives its customers a self-image that is relevant to the times.

The importance of currency underlines the fact that self-image is a far more dynamic construct in the social media age today than it ever was. There is a premium on social currency rooted in a higher degree of shareworthiness, contemporaneity and topicality. People seek beacons rather than bedrocks. There is a natural preference for brands that help them be 'in circulation'. Buzz is the new bazaar. Tesla makes a customer feel they are a non-conformist leader, whose eco-awareness puts them on a higher moral plane. There is also a contemporary silicon valley break-and-remake swag the brand comes attached with. And, of course, it assigns a certain premium status.

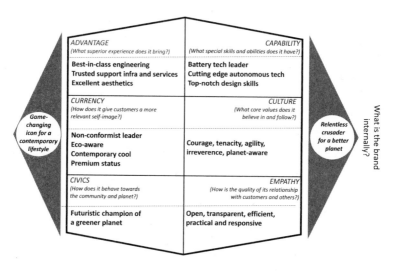

BRAND IDENTITY: TESLA

The fifth dimension that is getting increasing importance is *empathy*. Empathy engenders the social persona of the brand, what kind of relationship and chemistry it builds with its customers and other stakeholders. Tesla's relationships are open, transparent, efficient, practical and responsive.

The empathy of a brand naturally leads to *civics*— how the brand behaves as a larger citizen of the world— its communities and the planet in general. Tesla is a deeply respected global citizen owing to its bring a practical pioneering leader that became one of the most powerful catalysts towards a greener planet.

SUMMARY:

A. We discussed brand positioning decisions and the three important trade-offs—revenue versus margins; today's need gaps versus the emerging ones; and emphasizing functional versus emotional advantage—that must be made in the process.
B. We also discussed some of the important cultural, technological and economic shifts that are affecting many categories globally.
C. We briefly summed up with how breakthrough growth often requires an original view of your positioning vis-à-vis the competitors'.
D. Towards the end, we discussed how to put body and flesh on the positioning to build a brand identity framework.

We established a picture of how an optimal brand positioning can be arrived at and how we expand it into a brand identity framework. Now let's think about how we will use this to lead our target prospect from where she is to where we want her to be—in other words, what a typical customer journey looks like in this time and age and how businesses can make the best of that journey—in the next chapter.

4

The New Customer Journey

'Sometimes it's the journey that teaches you a lot about your destination.'

—Drake (Rapper)

For thousands of years, great journeys gave birth to great stories. Whether it's the Greek story of Odysseus, the king of Ithaca, and his journey home after the Trojan war; or the story of Rama and his travels from the north to the south of India and the resultant battle with Ravana; or the story of the monkey king in China inspired by the story of Xuan Jang's travel west to India; or Marco Polo's stories about the legendary Kublai Khan and his Xanadu. As in life, so in these stories, the journey is as important as the destination itself. And often there is a greater moral point that only the right journey can lead to the right destination. As Mahatma Gandhi said, 'Only the right means can lead to the right end.'

As for these epics of history, so for the brands of today, the journey we want the customer to have and how we hand-hold them on this journey ought to be the epicentre of all marketing. An incomplete customer journey, even if it somehow sells the product, may not result in post-purchase gratification and lasting loyalty. It's not enough to sell the product, it's also important for customers to imbibe the full story for a sustainable relationship. Let's delve into the best way to do that.

The Journey of Gratification

As soon as the target prospects are identified as discussed in chapter 2, it falls upon marketing to hand-hold the prospects on a journey from where they are—'Never heard about the brand', for example—to a point where the business needs them to be 'Used it, liked it and would love to recommend it'. It's a journey that can, at the end of it, generate meaningful value for both sides—satisfaction for the prospect and profit for the business.

For about a hundred years since its discovery in 1898 by an American businessman, marketers have used the AIDA model to map what's sometimes called the ladder of effects. AIDA is an acronym for Awareness, Interest, Desire and Action. The assumption was that if you took, for example, a raw prospect and introduced a new brand to him, marketers had these four tasks before the prospect converted to a buyer. He had to be aware of the brand, had to be interested enough to get more information on the brand, had to feel a desire towards it and finally, there had to be a way to make him or her act on the purchase.

Of course, the reality was that the process was never as sequentially linear. People could transcend multiple steps in one single interaction with the brand, especially for impulse purchase categories—for example, feeling both interested and desirous to purchase a concert ticket, say, upon a teen listening to the latest album of Taylor Swift. Or they could feel the desire first and get more information later—for instance, if a friend asked to them to taste a piece of chocolate, they may try it, love it and only later know what the brand name was and what it was made of. A sales action could be elicited by a compelling price discount, where a category need existed, even if one had no 'desire' for the brand itself and so on.

However, the AIDA model still provided an excellent conceptual model of how brand messaging was processed. (Somewhat unfairly, the sequential linearity of AIDA became a favourite flogging horse of digital evangelists. It never had been intended to be strictly linear, any more or any less than a customer journey in the digital age.)

Today, the advent of several new digital media choices that created new roles in people's lives and hence in the typical customer journey, has changed several aspects of the customer journey. The new model, for simplicity's sake, can be broadly summed up in four non-linear nodes in a loop—Discovery, Influence, Experience and Transaction (DIET).

From Curiosity to Discovery

Discovery entails awareness of a brand but is a lot more than that. People usually hear about a brand or category somewhere and are intrigued, thus creating what ad tracking would call aided brand awareness (if one can recall when prompted). Thereafter, people bring their curiosity about the brand to search engines in order to know more about it, either from the brand's own website or on third-party sites. This high-context awareness has become an important gateway for brands today and forms a critical moment of truth (see diagram).

Another important difference is that while the awareness in the AIDA model assumed a certain passive push-based awareness creation in the new world, an intriguing hook can, in certain cases, be both necessary and sufficient. Necessary because attention spans are getting shorter and shorter and only an intrigue can bridge the gap between shallow brand awareness and further information-seeking; and sufficient because people can always proactively search online if they want to know more to continue their journey.

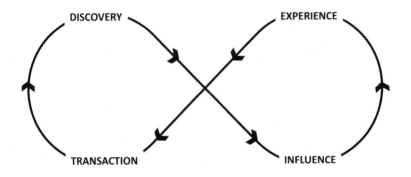

A TYPICAL CUSTOMER JOURNEY AS A NON-LINEAR DIET LOOP

The higher the involvement and information-rich the category is, the more important the process of discovery becomes. Awareness, in large measure, is a lean-forward activity now triggered by curiosity.

> Awareness, in large measure, is a lean-forward activity
> now triggered by curiosity.

Let's take for example, a Gen Z girl called Selena. Selena may see a cool new headphones brand on a billboard and feel intrigued. Her natural next instinct would be to google it and click on the URL there to go to the website. On the website, she will find out all about the specs, the colours and possibly the price. It's not cheap and she is still not sure. But she is loaded with a decent amount of information about the headphones now (see diagram).

Seeking a Credible Validation

The next important change in the funnel is the influence. Due to the pervasiveness of social media content—both peer-to-peer and influencer content—people often see, seek and share opinions and advice online. They visit discussion groups, read reviews and ratings, check out blogs and comparison sites, read about what experts or other opinion leaders may have to say about the brand, or just ask their friends and family via their WhatsApp group. They seek from these sources all that a brand campaign may not tell you about the reality of the product experience and its specific relevance to them. The cues exchanged, even if subtle, can be quite powerful. For new brands or small brands, having the comfort of knowing that someone in your circle of trust has bought it and is happy with it, becomes an all-important criterion for trust. Referrals, too, have become a lot easier as the social network hosts an expanded circle of trust.

Depending on the category and the brand, the nature of influences that a brand can leverage varies; however, it is quite clear that influence has become an important step in a brand's adoption. This is unlike the traditional media era, when mass media had managed to establish a direct dialogue with the people, shrinking the space for peer-to-peer social influences. Social media didn't just pass on the power back to the friends and family in the situated world, it greatly expanded one's circle of influence via the mediated world.

So Selena may now, after loading herself with information about the headphones, decide to go to a blog where an influencer has reviewed the product with tons of likes and positive comments from people who bought it and love it. She may mention it in a WhatsApp chat to her best friend who may tell her that she has heard about it too and that it seems quite cool. Two days later, she sees a posting by a cool boy from her college wearing it and notices how the photo has elicited tons of likes, some people even commenting on how awesome the sound is. She mentions it to her dad, who is not quite sure yet if that's what her birthday gift should be.

However, for brands and categories where typical preference is driven more on emotional considerations, an immersive experience or a trial or demo is particularly important. And this is where the third node in the loop—that of experience—becomes particularly useful.

Feeling the 'Feeling'

As clutter levels get higher, attention spans shorter and mental filters and ad-blocking tech sharper and sharper, the time-tested way to elicit desire by manufacturing photoshopped reality is often not enough. In order to differentiate, brands are tapping deeper participative experiences, either physical or those aided by new-age technologies. The business of creating 'desire' is no more limited to sleek video editing, generic on-ground events and print visuals. It can also be evoked via highly intuitive and sophisticated UX, branded utility, a sensor-infused shopper experience, or a cool IoT-enabled personalized device.

Experience design today has risen to become a complete discipline in itself, helping brands create seamless, alluring, technology-led interventions throughout the customer journey. The emotional desire for brands today comes not just from traditional experiences but also those that are adaptive, participative and much more immersive.

So let's go back to Selena, the headphones prospect. She is now well-informed about the product, she has the endorsement of her peer group around it on the key parameters that matter to her, but she is still wondering if she should rather go for a Google home speaker for her room on her birthday.

Three days later, however, Selena sees an awesome music video of one of her favourite celebrities wearing the device. She loves the song, the setting and how great the headphones looks with her hairstyle, which is not very different from her own. She clicks on the video and enters a webapp where she can customize the headphones' skin to her own unique liking for a custom order. Selena's mind is made up now.

Closing the Sale

The last but very important node in the loop is the transaction. The big difference in the digital era is that the transaction is not limited to the physical space. Not only has e-commerce become a large part of transactions taking place in many categories, but also the traditional line between media and the shop has finally blurred. In the old world, brands advertised on television and on the weekend, when you went to the shop, if you still remembered what you saw and liked, you might have switched. Today, the shop and the media are often just a click apart.

This has fundamental implications for the two hitherto disparate disciplines of marketing and selling, one that focused on creating pull via media by owning the mindspace of the consumers, and the other focused on creating push into stores by driving last-minute incentives and visibility. As media and shop are now just an impulsive second away or a moment of conviction apart, there are enough grounds for them to merge into one common discipline in many categories (or at least have deeper interoperability).

Let's call this hybrid discipline 'marselling' (marketing and selling)—built around one unified view of the customer and his end-to-end journey—to describe all the push and pull measures taken by a business — right from the discovery stage all the way into the transaction and thereafter. The segment, the moment and the mood—and all the other relevant data that we may have on the customer side can be used to not just inform the pull message of marketing but can also be seamlessly synchronized with the right product, pack size, the price and the sales pitch to maximize impact. If the customer came via a particular keyword query on Google, it's possible to make a custom sales pitch via the relevant text ad to hook the customer in and then place just the right SKU on the landing page to reflect the search key word.

> Let's call this hybrid discipline 'marselling'
> built around one unified view
> of the customer and his journey.

Also, pricing in many categories has become highly elastic due to its ability to talk to inventory, thus creating high-synergy opportunities between demand management and supply management. Large e-commerce platforms may offer real-time benchmarking of relative price in the category, allowing for highly responsive margin management. Optimizing the 'share of shelf'—what percentage of shelf (or screen in this case) is occupied by the brand and its variants; and 'shelf visibility'—how visible the brand is in the store (its rank in the search results for example)—can be optimized in real time online.

It is also possible to work backwards the most optimum path to the last mile by interpolating the data trail—basically looking at data to see what worked and what didn't work and hence what kind of browsing behaviours provide the best conversion pathways. All these possibilities offer great opportunities in marrying marketing and selling into one seamless discipline. The age of Marselling is upon us. Unfortunately, few age-old organizations are designed for this, and tend to stay slaves of their organization charts.

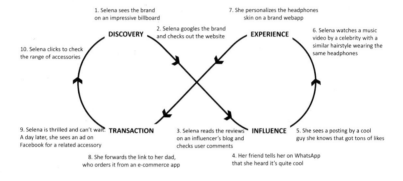

SELENA'S DIET JOURNEY TO BUY A HEADPHONE

Selena is ready to order now and with her birthday looming, forwards the purchase link to her dad, who immediately confirms the order only too happy that his beloved daughter has probably found something that she will genuinely enjoy for a long time. In another era, this would have worked a lot differently.

Targeting the DIET Loop

The DIET loop mirrors the targeting spectrum in an interesting manner. The mass segment layer in the targeting spectrum is best activated in the initial stages of the loop—especially for creating intrigue. The microsegments work most effectively for the latter part of the discovery phase—information provided via search for instance can be customized via the right ads as well as the right landing pages against the search keyword intent. Microsegments are also very relevant for the transaction phase to maximize last-mile conversion. However, to plan the influence and experience, one should generally use mini segments to provide the best balance between relevance and cost.

Taking the Selena example, let's assume the mass segment for the headphones is M/F, 15–34, from mass affluent households. We may further choose the four mini segments conceived around affinity groups—music lovers, gamers, video callers and fashionistas. We may further build microsegments around different gifting moments, designs of skin choices available and the personalities they engender, price-sensitivity, linguistic groups and their varied combinations.

The Myriad Fulfilment Pathways

The DIET loop represents a summation of some of the greatest trends that has defined the new digital era. However, it is possible to double-click on the transaction and the fulfilment that follows after to look at the complexity of customer fulfilment pathways that businesses must contend with today. As lifestyles have become more and more differentiated, there are multiple choices that people have in terms of not just where the brand communication happens, or how the influences work, but also how they can buy the product, have the product delivered, ways they can pay for it, the ways they can consume it and the ways they can avail of customer service.

So, a fast-food dinner, for example, can be ordered at the store, or via phone, own website, food aggregator sites, mobile app, etc. It can be paid for with cash, credit card, mobile wallet, loyalty card, etc. It can be physically accessed via drive-through, dine-in or delivery boys. And one can eat at the store, office, home or in an outdoor picnic spot (there indeed are delivery start-ups specializing in delivering to unstructured outdoor spaces such as a park or a hiking trail). Every realistic combination of these steps (and there can be scores of them) is a unique customer journey that has to be catered to by a seamless brand experience informed by powerful underlying data, something we will talk in more detail in later chapters. A masterful design of such pathways is both an art and a science.

Last but not least, the DIET loop must be customized based on the brand, its maturity, its place in the product life cycle and the key bottlenecks it is expected to encounter in a typical journey of choice. In the new marketing world with tremendous chaos and complexity, the DIET loop captures some of the key shifts in how people make choices today. It also makes a clear point that whatever we do in the marketing space must ultimately make a difference in making the customer journey smoother and more effective. This test of how it makes the journey better keeps marketing focused and the marketing investments honest.

SUMMARY:

A. We discussed the AIDA model and the transition to the DIET loop across the four nodes of Discovery, Influence, Experience and Transaction.
B. We discussed how the targeting spectrum can be married to the DIET journey in a general situation, focusing on the mass segment for building intrigue, mini segments for the influence and experience stages, but activating the microsegments for the rest of the discovery as well as the transaction stage.
C. We also discussed how the DIET journey can be double-clicked on to reflect the complexity of access points, payment and sales channels, and the need to maintain

optimal experience across all the varied permutations and combinations possible.

Having discussed the marketplace and the competition (where do we play?); the target audience (who do we convert?); the larger positioning question (what do we want to be known for?); and their journey (what's the journey to conversion?), it's time to delve deeper into the intricacies of brand building (the 'how' question). We will focus on the two nodes in the DIET loop, that of influence and experience. In the next chapter, let's ponder over how influence has evolved in the last two decades.

5

The New Influence

One day, in ancient Athens, a man came running to Socrates to tell him something.

SOCRATES: What business do you have?
MAN: Kyrios, I have something important to tell you. Something that I only just came to know about.
SOCRATES: Are you sure it is true?
MAN: Not quite sure, but I heard it from someone.
SOCRATES: Are you sure it is kind?
MAN: Er . . . well, not a pleasant thing to hear, really.
SOCRATES: Are you sure it's useful? It'll help if I know that?
MAN: Well, I doubt so, Kyrios.
SOCRATES: Well then, I really don't need to hear it.

In this chapter, we will start with the notion of truth in our society and how it has been conceived, influenced and propagated over millennia. And how it has been central to the evolution of society in general and brands and market-making in particular. (It would seem the man wanted to tell Socrates about a rumour that his [Socrates's] wife was having an affair.)

The word 'brand' originated from the ancient practice of branding livestock with the owner's mark using a hot iron, so there was no doubt who the animals belonged to. This practice was also carried over to the branding of slaves, as they were considered part of 'stock'. While the word itself may have taken its contemporary meaning in more recent times, the notion of brand is as old as god himself.

God, Truth and Branding

Great emperors of yore who ruled over vast empires, with scarce means of communication, needed to maintain their authority—fear, order and goodwill—by erecting pillars and obelisks across the farthest stretches of their empire. These carried the emperor's name and his words, as a symbol of his power—temporal and moral. (That makes outdoor media the original mass medium—with a shelf-life that could stretch across millennia).

For thousands of years, information moved via such imperial installations, fireside chats, gossip in village stalls and town squares; messengers reading out the royal edicts; merchants exchanging tales in highway inns; soldiers by campfires; performances by itinerants—bards and minstrels, for example; and priests and saints teaching their flocks. Brand reputation originated in these whispers, chats, songs and ballads that travelled from one village to the next, radiating along highways. They were often mediated by wise men—like in the Socrates anecdote—with a keen eye for the true versus the untrue, useful versus the useless, and the kind versus the unkind.

Brand reputation originated in these whispers, chats,
songs and ballads that travelled from one village to the next,
radiating along highways.

As people were the most important purveyors of information, and often there were very few means to validate it, the credibility of the purveyor was all important. In small communities, individuals were known over a long time by those around them, and hence such credibility was earned over a lifetime by those with discerning eyes and good judgement. A brand was created by decentralized advocacies fuelled by a network of hard-earned reputations.

However, this communication machine was highly inefficient in many ways. As information flowed from person to person over a chain involving a large number of people, even with the best of intentions, the original information invariably got distorted and lost—much like a Chinese whispers game. Also, the speed at which the information travelled was painfully slow, sometimes taking months and years to reach the farthest villages, changed beyond recognition by the time it arrived. Truth for the masses became a function of the spectrum of the biases and prejudices that it travelled through, each assigning its own colours to it. Truth was statistical and through narratives and counter-narratives, the good old wise men of the villages were left to distil 'facts' for a local community. In essence, this meant that each village had its own truth.

This opened perilous gaps for anyone trying to maintain control; for instance, an emperor who needed people far and wide to believe in him. It allowed rebels on the outskirts to gatekeep and manipulate information. The emperor could isolate the populations under their influence until they could gather a critical mass of soldiers and accumulate sufficient wealth to fund their larger forays. Years before an emperor fell, it was his brand that was destroyed. (No wonder, good kings didn't just rely on an extensive spy network, but also often went around the kingdom disguised as ordinary traders or pilgrims, doing mystery shopping for their brand.)

Also, pace and distortion were not the only problems with this branding machine. It was also very difficult to scale in a dependable way. In this model, beyond a point, the reach was dependent on a receiver's natural urge to propel the message forward. The power to communicate was highly diffused without any systematic incentive system fuelling it and so the machine worked as good or badly for an empire as it did for a popular rebel or a renowned scholar, a penniless sage or a great new invention. One could seed the message, even deploy a few carriers, but beyond that there was little control as to how far it would travel.

Over time, age-old reputations of great leaders got laboriously inked into parchments, and etched into temple walls and pyramids. Over long periods of time, their brands and stories would be polished, embellished and perfected into myths and legends giving them a godlike reputation. Entire religions would be built around them, some of these religions becoming the most powerful and lasting organizations in human civilization. Great branding fossilized people into gods.

Forging of the 'Mass Truth'

With the invention of the printing press about six centuries ago, the age of mass media began. Now those with resources in their hands could take a message, create millions of copies with zero information-loss or distortion and get it into the hands of people far and wide.

As the first newspapers were born out of this revolution, they built a new information system. Newspapers built dedicated collection and distribution machines that could collate news and spread printed information at a very rapid speed to the farthest outposts, only limited by the fastest modes of transport available. As newspapers achieved wide circulation, they offered a vehicle that could be used by businesses to get their message across either by doing something newsworthy or by paying the newspapers for it. People paid to read newspapers and businesses paid to have their information carried as ads. This created a strong incentive system which in turn brought both control and scalability for mass producers over their brands.

Within a few centuries, newspapers changed many aspects of how reputation was now forged. It shifted power from the vast networks of people into the hands of those who owned and managed these powerful machines or had the resources to pay for advertising there. Since this empire of the written word required learned people to run it, it transferred more power into the hands of the intellectuals—the editors, the thinkers, the artful writers and the resourceful journalists— at any point in time a very small niche of the population. Dominant media and the interests they represented became arbitrators of truth. Winston Churchill, when asked about his role in history famously said, 'History will be kind to us. Because we will write it.' No wonder the world is fully aware of Churchill's heroic defence of Great Britain against Hitler (and his truly impressive wit), but very few know about the millions who died in the Bengal Famine of 1943 due to his policies).

Truth became highly mediated and institutionalized rather than crowdsourced as it had been for eons. Media became the fourth estate, creating a bridge between the masses and those with wealth, intellect and power—thus becoming an important pillar of democracy. A small bunch of editors were now the wise old men of entire nations.

A small bunch of editors were now the wise old men
of entire nations.

When it came to brand reputation, newspapers also allowed businesses with quality and ambition to convey messages about their product with consistency and attractiveness. This gave them the ability to better control perceptions of their brands and allowed them to charge their customers higher for the trust and satisfaction they could bring to them. This helped raise profits and cumulate capital, which in turn fuelled economies of scale, thus feeding mass production. Radio followed newspapers, and TV followed the radio.

Mass media and mass production made each other bigger and better, and mass marketing was born of their marriage. As a reputation machine, it offered unmatched speed, scale, control and power, and heralded the modern era of branding.

The Decline of the Wise

Mass media eventually helped build some of the greatest brands of the last hundred years. The value of the biggest global brands exceeded the GDPs of many countries. Amazon's brand value in 2020 was assessed by Interbrand to be US$323 billion which was ahead of the GDP of countries like Greece, Finland, Qatar, Ethiopia and New Zealand (World Bank estimates).

They also exercised immense soft power, moulding the popular culture, endorsing specific values, rituals and lifestyles, and creating powerful dreams and icons very systematically. As the twentieth century progressed, brands became the main sponsors of mass media, thus creating a counterweight to editorial power. Profit-obsessed proprietors put increasing commercial pressure on the editors. And in the blind pursuit of ratings and profits, what had been a rather hard line between the commercial and the editorial started blurring. Under a new breed of increasingly pliable editors, television as a medium began to cater to its baser instincts.

As a medium, TV with its fast-moving images was designed for cognitive suspension, emotional abduction and relentless addiction of minds. Reality TV took this to the next level starting in the late 1990s.

The rise of 24/7 news TV eventually became a deadly assault on the wise editor, as 'sensational' took over the 'wise' and their considered, nuanced wisdom. News anchors competed with reality television for ratings and revenues, and ended up being hired for oversimplified melodrama. News editors increasingly started peddling the sensational and the superficial, polarizing opinions and dialling down the moderating wisdom. Editorial versions of shrill demagoguery arose, obscuring the vast difference between the two-penny theatre and the editorial in many cases. The line between the business and the editorial had already faded before. Even before social media gained prominence, the ground for the fall of mass media from its 200-year-old perch had already been prepared.

With loosening editorial controls, media became one with the mob. Media was changing the crowds and crowds were changing it back. Viewers sought truth, yet expected their favourite channel to confirm their version of it, thus sending the news content spiralling down the rabbit hole of people's prejudices. Truth is often in the middle and the middle is boring. Truth is also often nuanced, and television as a medium was never designed for nuances. It was a medium that was made to fill people's senses with rapidly moving stimuli that didn't allow viewers time and space to think, but to feel and experience. Media began to appease narrow, emotional narratives, rather than be open, hand-hold and lead people's minds towards objectivity. Media became the circus mirror that showed people their distorted reflections—ugly, banal and juvenile.

An apt example of this is a leading Indian news anchor and his highly popular 'newsdrama' on the channel, which often beats reality shows on viewership. He himself plays the angry hero here, channelling ordinary people's deep-seated biases, impatience and contempt. In the pigeonholes of the TV screen, some are paid to be allies and some others, cast as villains. The broad narrative is by and large decided in advance, cutting through the grey haze of a vast complex democracy to cast issues as black and white. 'Villains' often get muted live—in order to assist the hero and to maintain the 'integrity' of the outcome. For the viewers, the feeling of disillusioned powerlessness against a complex faceless system is replaced by an addictive dopamine release in the face of this instant justice. In Bollywood films, often a hero will deliver a long cathartic dialogue before delivering the coup de grâce. He may not dispense real justice, but his vitriolic verbal violence sure is cathartic to many.

Not surprisingly, with the loss of credibility of mass media, the credibility of mass-media branding fell as well. People realized that one may end up spending a significant percentage of one's life watching television, for instance, on ads alone. In a single hour it could mean watching dozens of ads, out of which not more than a few may be relevant to the individual.

While many ads went straight for the hard sales pitch, many others conjured up a fake world of plastic beauty and unrealistic perfections, delivered in a manner that wasn't just inauthentic but also frequently insulted the intelligence of people. When advertising didn't annoy, it didn't evoke much trust either.

The Return of the Crowds

It is against this backdrop that social media exploded, building a reach that has now crossed more than half the planet. It offered a platform where people could curate their lives, just as they wanted, or at least just as they wanted others to see it. It put a megaphone in the hands of each and everyone, which, with the right message, could be used to reach up to four billion people in no time. A fifteen-year-old Greta Thunberg became an overnight global phenomenon owing to this power and access. The speed and scalability that was hitherto only available to the guardians of mass media was now available to everyone.

The way news travelled on social media was very different as one-to-many communication now became many-to-many communication. In the old days, editors set the agenda for the day by deciding what news deserved the front page and the largest coverage. Now, news mostly got shared forward by friends and family around us, based on what they thought was important enough to share, thus bringing a dramatically higher level of relevance for individuals. Laced by likes, dislikes and comments, it offered further context to the news, a picture of the dominant sentiment around it—often by people you knew well—and even allowed for users' own participation, commenting, mashing and sharing forward. One didn't just inherit the dominant sentiment that accompanied the news in its reactions and comments, but also felt compelled to conform due to the personal proximity of the network and eventually committed themselves to a partisan stance by commenting or forwarding.

The mechanism was incredibly powerful. However, it also meant that truth, as one perceived in social media, was curated by the crowds of people in one's network. The pressure to conform, especially against the backdrop of emotional biases along with the reactiveness the efficiency of the medium brought, soon overwhelmed the credibility of the information itself. Facts became incidental if the biases were already deep-rooted. If you liked something, you believed it to be true, giving the benefit of doubt to your prejudices. Emotional clarity obviated the need for truth.

> If you liked something,
> you believed it to be true.

So, for example, if you were a white, unemployed man in a town in Nebraska, each time a buddy posts a WhatsApp story of a new factory coming up in Mexico, your suspicion towards your Hispanic neighbour keeps increasing. As the buddy's sentiment is gradually mirrored by some others, in a leap of hate, you start attributing your personal failures to his presence in town. And you are inexorably drawn farther and farther down the right-wing spectrum, deeper and deeper into the fog of biases, as the most innocuous of observations and incidents start feeding your own sense of disempowerment. Life is simpler if we have an external enemy and social media makes it easy.

People in general started showing a preference for crowdsourced truth over institutionalized versions of truth. It recreated certain elements of the communication dynamics of the age before mass media, albeit this time, the scale and speed were very different.

The Rise of Mediated Living

Today, ordinary people on social media have thousands of 'friends' and 'followers', thus building a relationship fabric that has impressive breadth, even if it may compromise on the depth of interactions. To be able to participate in the lives of so many people, with a click here and a like there, a comment here and a share there, is magical. The erstwhile six degrees of separation has become the six clicks of separation.

People wake up first thing in the morning and go to social media to get their little dollops of dopamine and spend the rest of the day in an addictive daze induced by these micro-stimulations. In the 1970s, Pope John Paul II once famously said about TV: 'If you are not on TV, you don't exist.' In the social village of today, where content is the currency and sharing is the essential ritual—if you do not share, you do not exist.

> In the social village of today, where content is the currency
> and sharing is the essential ritual—if you do not share,
> you do not exist.

As people spend hours and hours each day living almost parallel lives on social media, the mediated living has started to shape its own reality versus the actual physical situated living. It's a case of persistent perception creating its own reality. If an exciting new filter makes a teenage boy look like his favourite idol, and if that is the visual that 90 per cent of his network see 90 per cent of the time, and say, 70 per cent of the network may ever see, then this raises important questions about the innate assumption of superiority of the physical reality over the virtual. This growing eminence of the mediated over the situated is set to take another leap with the mainstreaming of the metaverse eventually.

All these changes led to a very different notion of truth, as people perceived it via social media. Let's look closer into some of the usual distortions that we all experience.

Social Media and Truth-Bending

The limitations of the social-media algorithm and the lack of editorial mediation have given birth to systematic new cultural distortions. On social media, private lives of people often look better than they are in reality. However, the public life—how a nation or society is faring in general—feels a lot worse than what the real world is like. The secret to this is the simple fact that people rarely put up bad or boring aspects of their personal life on social media. And when they do, often very few tend to click on such posts and hence very few people get to see it, as social-media algorithms prioritize posts that get more reactions on the assumption that more people would like to see them. Similarly, as traditional mass media had already proved, good news doesn't sell as much—and hence, it once again gets de-prioritized by algorithms due to fewer reactions. This ensures that the public news often feels grim and hopeless.

On social media, private lives of people often look better than they are in reality. However, the public life—how a nation or society is faring—feels a lot worse than what the real world is like.

The other important phenomenon is that people can't discern between outlier news and perspectives versus the mainstream ones. So, an extreme opinion by an insignificant person could never be heard by people at large in the old system, as there were editors to filter these out (or consign it to page 23 in a measly few column-centimetres). But now an extreme opinion—even a stray remark—immediately provokes reactions, and that means more and more people end up seeing it, effectively putting it on the hypothetical frontpage. As the reactions propel it to mass reach, people may perceive it as mainstream opinion. Whereas the mainstream opinion, which can frequently be relatively boring often gets very little reaction and hence no one gets to see it, effectively relegating it to the position of an outlier opinion.

The classic Overton window—basically the range of ideas on a given issue that mainstream society might be willing to accept, beyond the range considered too niche or extreme—is expanding rapidly, as social media can turn outlying ideas into mainstream opinions due to the algorithm's profiteering bias towards extremes.

Given that many people are anonymous on social media, and there are few checks, this mechanism also allows for fake news to be posted, which can cause major damage to the fabric of truth. Thus, the vocal extremities continue to overwhelm the silent majority, who are being slowly and steadily nudged into one or the other extremity. As the Cambridge Analytica case showed, social media is a medium perfectly designed for the extremes, the centrifugal force of its prejudices creating one of the most powerful brainwash machines ever invented by mankind.

Social media is a machine perfectly designed for the extremes, the centrifugal force of its prejudices creating one of the most powerful brainwash machines ever invented.

A dictator now does not need to cancel the newspaper licence of a recalcitrant editor (or abduct him). He just needs to build content factories that can churn relentless hate that cater to the prejudices of the ordinary people, and social media algorithms are capable of and keen to do the rest of the job of turning them into rabid mobs. It's the stuff that Hitler's propaganda chief, Goebbels's dreams must have been made of.

Quite naturally, the manipulative power of social media first attracted the attention of extreme radicals. Al Qaeda, ISIS and Lashkar-e-Toiba were some of the first organizations that became expert users of social media for recruitment, fund-raising, instructions and the propaganda spectacle. The spectacular blowing up of the second tower of the World Trade Center with an airplane full of passengers on live television was only surpassed by hundreds of millions around the world watching the series of ISIS beheadings on social media and its livestreamed terrorism (later, it inspired incidents like the New Zealand mosque shooter).

However, the second wave of social media leverage brought in a generation of idealists and social progressives. In the US, Obama sought to use social media to sell hope and goodness and Arab Spring used it to try replacing the despots with democracy, for instance.

However, the last few years have seen the third wave of social media leverage where, in country after country, the system is now falling into the hands of the xenophobic ultranationalist conservatives, who have found in the medium a perfect ally for their divisive agendas premised on stoking insecurities.

Beyond the political impact of social media's crowdsourced truth, another dimension is its impact on the quality of human relationships. In the world of the social, the scale and efficiency of human relationships have multiplied manifold, sometimes at the cost of depth. Much like immersive AV entertainment, there is just enough unbroken attention span for one to react in the moment to relationship stimuli—rather than to ingest, assimilate and ruminate over it and let it grow on oneself. Spontaneity, instantaneity, instinct and diversity have replaced consideration, resilience, depth and constancy. It's the age of the ephemeral love, made-to-order dreams and transient joys.

A thing of beauty is a joy of the mere moment in the overstimulated synapses of the beholder. Promising human encounters can sometimes be kangaroo-courted on the relentless 'fail fast' paradigm of the social age.

Having considered both the power of the new shifts as well as the distortions it can bring, let's delve into how it affected marketing in general and brands in particular.

* * *

Brands are Networks

Brands used to live in the minds of people as a set of perceptions. Now in the social age, they live in the link between mind and mind. Brands have become networks. They are networks of people with shared need states, affinities and experiences. Brands grow market shares when people invite other people to join in via subtle but powerful cues, influences and advocacies. And they decline when people start influencing others in their network to abandon the fare. Riding a media platform built on network effects, as mentioned before, growth today has become a function of the network effects too. Networks breed profits and influence is the midwife.

> Brands are networks of people with shared need states,
> affinities and experiences.

The paucity of trust in advertising gave social media a big advantage when it came to validation. People usually trusted the experts for technical knowledge and, depending on the category, the type of experts would differ. People loved to hear from their favourite celebrities about what they use and what they would recommend. While traditionally, brands had deployed experts and celebrities in their advertising, the selection of the same was always based on who the most popular or most suited to a vast number of people was. Now all these experts and celebrities are on social media. And brands can deploy not one but several of them, targeting different affinity groups. In fact, millions of so-called key opinion leaders have arisen, people who are not a celebrity or an expert in the traditional sense but have big enough followings on account of their attractiveness, some degree of expertise or ability to engage. These social-media angels, much closer to their network than a mega celebrity—who may have a wide but shallow appeal—can now be deployed at will to serve brand messages in a way that is a lot more authentic, relevant and adds a more genuine slice-of-life appeal.

People universally trust their friends and family a lot more on their views about what product or brand would be most suited to their needs and is more trustworthy. At the least, they would look to people who were more or less like them. If it was something more technical, they would again trust someone in their extended circle on the truth behind conflicting or confusing brand claims. Now the entire circle of trust and its larger extension is on social media, merely a click away. And when they love a brand, they often speak. In fact, if they have a bad brand experience, they speak several times louder. Either way, its power can't be denied.

Let's do a deep dive into the types of influencers that exist around us and how they are different (see diagram).

* * *

The Pyramid of Influence

Usually, at the bottom of the influence pyramid are the vast majority of ordinary 'masses', who may have strong credibility on account of their specific understanding of what's good for their very close friends or family with

respect to a given category, but this set's influence is
extremely limited in width.

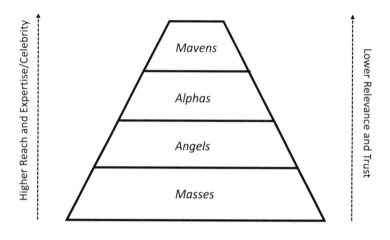

THE PYRAMID OF INFLUENCE

At the next level are what could be called 'angels', who are
typically individuals who can be visualized as that someone
in your extended friend or family circle, who you may turn
to for advice on a certain category, because his or her level
of knowledge or exposure to the category is better than
those close to you. For many categories that are either high
involvement, high outlay or information intensive, this
layer of influencers becomes extremely critical, as they are
expected to understand the functional and emotional needs
of the individuals they advise, sharing a lot of context with
them. Their credibility is derived more from their expertise
in knowing a customer's specific needs than expertise in the
category itself or the scale of their network.

Above this level are the 'alphas'—who have many more
followers than an average person, and are somewhat aware
of their status as an influencer or opinion leader by virtue

of being an expert or a minor celebrity, either due to their functional expertise or due to their emotional connection with a larger number of people. Alphas may sometimes be paid key opinion leaders (KOLs) who are willing to advocate a brand for money. What they may lack in understanding a specific person's need, they make up for by offering larger reach as well as higher expertise or celebrity status.

Right at the top of the pyramid, of course, are the 'mavens' who command a very high reach. They are either major celebrities or famous experts typically.

As we go up the pyramid, understanding of the individual needs goes down and the category or 'lifestyle' expertise (in the case of celebrities) goes up. For example, for a new gadget brand, an angel may be the neighbourhood boy to whom one might go for advice on all things tech, whereas a maven may be a top film actress who has a vast following but is still too distant from our personalized needs and identification. At an overall level, there is also a trade-off between credibility and reach per influencer, as we go up the pyramid. A good influencer strategy would bring together the mavens, the alphas and the angels in a powerful mix—as authority, catalysts and connectors—to activate the bottom mass of the pyramid.

There Is Influencer and Then There Is Influencer

It is important to realize that not all influencers are the same on a given level. When considered for a brand, it's useful to look at six key parameters that can help improve the effectiveness of influencer leverage (see diagram).

Catchment scale is the first criteria, which refers to the size of the influencer's follower base, basically indicating what kind of relative reach could be expected. Multiplatform proactivity shows how many diverse platforms the influencer is active on and how proactively the influencer typically promotes, thus cueing the unduplicated coverage and extra mileage an activity may bring. Brand proximity is an indication of how close the influencer persona is to the brand personality—if the influencer can represent the brand and be true to it. Affinity correlation is a measure of how close the influencer's interests overlap with where the brand and the category operate. For example, an influential nutritionist may share her affinity group with a healthy sauce brand, rather than a cricket-bat brand.

1. Catchment
Scale

2. Multiplatform
Proactivity

3. Brand Proximity

4. Affinity
Correlation

5. Engagement
Rate

6. Social Credibility

SIX PARAMETERS OF INFLUENCER SELECTION

Engagement rate indicates how interactive the base of followers is with the influencer (it's not uncommon to have a large 'bought' component in many commercial influencers' follower base). And finally, social credibility captures how much credibility the influencer holds among her followers—which may depend on how sincere and authentic the content usually is, how many brands she promotes and how much authority she may carry in relation to the brand message, etc.

The first two parameters, catchment scale and multiplatform proactivity, capture the quantity of influence; the second two, brand proximity and affinity correlation, its relevance to and impact on the brand; and the last two, engagement rate and social credibility capture the quality of influence.

While individuals are the basic unit of social networks and influencers its key nodes, usually individuals and influencers are also parts of many communities. The ease of creating and maintaining online communities means that social platforms may typically have hundreds of communities around a category with members sometimes running into millions. Such communities can be broadly categorized from a marketing point of view into paid, owned and earned communities.

* * *

Brands at the Centre of Communities

Owned communities are typically the brand's own social-media profiles or YouTube channels or owned blogs. These are communities where they have higher control, even though they usually have to pay the social platforms to have any decent reach within even their own brand communities. Social platforms also often allow deeper one-on-one interaction either for customer service or sales with individuals in the owned communities. These communities usually consist of the most loyal and socially active among a brand's customers and serve as the innermost circle in the brand's network.

Paid communities may be communities built around paid influencers or networks of people and small influencers who get incentivized to spread a brand message or they may be blogs and discussion groups who post messages for money. Many of these communities start seeding outside the global social platforms, for example on an online news portal, though eventually, much of their reach may come from social media. They may also sometimes be attached to a media channel with communities built around an affinity or a content brand. Paid communities bring together a degree of control but also help build a certain reach level. Brands that are looking to drive frequency, to take customers away from competitors or to create a new market, gain very little by just focusing on owned communities and must leverage the paid and earned ones.

Earned communities can be either communities built around influencers who may spread the brand message simply because they find it share-worthy or they may be organic communities built around different passions or affinity groups where once again the brand message gets spread from people to people due to its sheer share-worthiness. For example, a genuine music lover may love a Coke Studio clip received via a WhatsApp group, and may share it on a Facebook music community without getting paid for it. The mileage received for Coca-Cola is truly an earned benefit free of cost. Earned communities are highly credible and involve minimal or no media cost. A breakthrough into earned communities can be made either on the creative power or a high degree of relevance of the message to the communities.

An influence strategy designed around the specific needs and perspectives of different communities around a given category holds a lot of latent potential; however, this approach means brands need to think differently from the conventional view of their social position—and start seeing their brand as a network of networks.

Brands need to think differently from the conventional view of their social position—and start seeing their brand as a network of networks.

* * *

Brands as Memes

Today, this network of influences and communities has become a powerful arbitrator of a brand's destiny. Even though a large part of these networks continues to be tough for brands to penetrate as the bulk of social media is dark social (e.g., WhatsApp chats, private conversations on Facebook, Snapchat, etc.), to which brands have very limited access. Also, a vast majority of influencers do not work for paid influences. And despite content professionals aggressively trying to tame social media with professionally generated content (PGC), most of the content consumed continues to be the extremely fragmented user generated content (UGC).

It has not been easy for most brands to penetrate private social spaces such as Facebook Messenger and WhatsApp. Social media at its heart is a medium of memes, and this was displayed most prominently by Donald Trump. His was a meme government, policies were declared via memes, he believed his legitimacy derived from the virality of memes; journalists and stock traders hung on to every meme of his, and a presidential meme could literally change the world under him.

The formats deployed range from the more serious short stories and articles to jokes, caricatures, GIFs, greetings, photo mash-ups and video mash-ups among others. Brands proud of their pristine design sense struggle to adjust to these formats. Given the extremely high credibility that these private spaces enjoy in people's lives, for effective reputation building, it is important to formulate a creative strategy that is native to these spaces and gets sufficient flexibility within the larger brand framework.

To make the best of the social-media narratives, brands need to master the art of harnessing influencers, communities and dark social memes. They also need to understand carefully the range of specific roles that social media can play in their business. Let's spend some time pondering that.

* * *

Return on Conversations

The advent of social media had a profound impact across the various components of the marketing value-chain. These roles and opportunities can be broadly classified under eight points of intervention—insights, customer service, campaigns, content, CRM, commerce, internal communications and crisis (see diagram). Let's have a brief look at each of these.

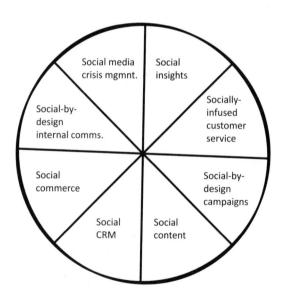

EIGHT KEY ROLES SOCIAL MEDIA CAN PLAY

1. Social Insights

To start with, social-media conversations offer a fly-on-the-wall view of how the category and the brand is perceived by people in real time. It is now possible for brands to monitor street-by-street and moment-by-moment (through a whole host of social-listening tools that crawl the world of non-private social chatter), how the conversations are shaping in their categories and where the exact sentiments lie for them in a specific context. This can offer powerful insights into product, packaging, price, consumer promotions, communication and customer service. The geographical mapping of sentiments for a brand can be a useful surrogate of staff or franchisee performance in a specific catchment area for many categories. More structured surveys can also be run on the base of loyal customers.

Brands can also look at who is saying good things about them and who is not, which of those speaking are highly connected, and how the network of influences in relation to the brand and the category functions. This offers brands an opportunity to talk to their social graphs, carefully nurturing them into their advocates and promoters.

2. Socially-Infused Customer Service

For any brand with considerable size, there will always be some disgruntled customers (as no brand is perfect), their numbers and intensity accentuated by the reactive and not-well-considered world of social media. A brand that does not have a good social-media presence has a major opportunity loss because people will still converse and complain about it without the brand being able to intervene, shape or solve the issue. As soon as a brand has social-media presence, it is automatically sought out for customer service-related queries, as more and more people prefer to tag or chat via social media rather than call the customer hotline, and a social-media presence, if managed well, can prove to be a good safety valve.

While on one hand, brands must sincerely try to be as responsive in redressing their issues as per what is fair and feasible, the truth is, there will still be complaints. It is not always possible to try to erase the red line entirely; however, as mentioned earlier, brands can draw a big green line in front of it to overwhelm and drown out the red line. And that is why it is critical that brands have a proactive, always-on engagement with people in social media with a sufficient volume of positivity and advocacy around them.

In fact, in many categories, brands are being assisted by their more informed, experienced, loyal and connected customers in answering customer-service queries posted on social media. Peer-to-peer customer service, as mentioned before, continues to be an area with excellent potential especially in categories with high information content, some degree of complexity or need for demonstration. (YouTube is full of 'how to' hacks about products, paid and user-generated. In fact, it is not uncommon to even see tons of improvised brand hacks, not unlike 'fan fiction' in literature.)

3. Social-by-Design Campaigns

As social networks breed new cultural memes and zeitgeist every other day, it has opened a unique opportunity for brands to ride these topical trends, thus displaying responsiveness, originality and candour. While on the one hand, integrated campaigns can be extended into social media allowing for viral amplification, campaigns can also be conceived to be centred around social-media participations. In fact, if conceived well, entire campaigns can be crowdsourced in terms of ideation and propagation (though push-based media support would be needed for most in order to gather reach).

New formats are being introduced by social-media platforms on a continuous basis to allow creative minds with more tools to play with. Also, different social-media formats are designed to play different roles in the customer journey, thus offering a diversity of choices. For example, the Instagram carousel allows brands to display a range of product variants or benefits it offers, while Facebook augmented reality ads allow users to use their smartphone cameras to superimpose 3D assets in the real world around them, thus allowing for engaging participation.

4. Social Content

The most common way to use social media for brands has been to do social-media posting with text, photos and videos, and to pay Facebook to drive up its reach to a wider audience. Given that at its core, social media was not conceived for advertising, but for propagation of content in the larger sense, social-media platforms also offer opportunities to engage the prospects with non-advertising formats that can go deeper in building trust and bringing alive the experience. Livestreaming, Instagram TV (IGTV), articles, interviews, surveys—there are so many ways brands can customize their form factor to suit the jobs to be done. In fact, every brand needs a well-thought-through content calendar in social media (including advertising content, but not limited by it).

5. Social CRM

The ability to integrate a brand's CRM (customer relationship management) database into social-media platforms allows an opportunity to further drive referrals, advocacy, upsell and cross-sell opportunities. It can also play a very effective role in managing down the churn and drive frequency and loyalty in a category. For example, if the BMW CRM database knows that someone bought a 3-Series five years ago, it has an opportunity to target a 5-Series ad via Facebook, as long as the CRM database is integrated with the Facebook platform.

6. Social Commerce

Integration of chat—via bots or humans—allows not just for one-on-one customer service but also offers opportunity to upsell and cross-sell. Of course, social commerce on platforms like WeChat have taken it to another level via a vast number of social shops, many of them run by influencers—thus integrating networks, conversations, influences and content in a complete loop of commerce. High-context virtual selling—whether in the B2B space or in consumer categories such as insurance, skincare, cosmetics, wealth management or counselling—is another promising area that can move a lot of information and perspective-rich customer engagement online.

7. Social-by-Design Internal Communications

As the power of professional editors has gone down, top-down management of reputation has become that much more difficult. Amidst this, an important need is to manage how employees, vendors and other stakeholders (beyond consumers) of a business communicate in social media about the company. Each of the individuals associated here sits at the heart of his or her own network. And a corporation sits at the centre of that internal network of networks.

A whole host of tools such as Yammer, Slack, Facebook Workplace, etc., are on offer today that are dedicated to managing internal social networks within organizations, boosting collaboration, workflow, knowledge-sharing and team-bonding. Carefully conceived internal communications programmes designed to elicit natural interest and ride the peer-to-peer synergy and validation can work wonders in a company. Unfortunately, while many corporations are trying to leverage internal social networks, the defining spirit remains adoption-by-fiat than by popular bottom-up choice. This is a missed opportunity as an internal network designed to engage genuine employee enthusiasm can help corporations weave authentic human connections at the core of their culture.

A network view of organizations is more fluid, transparent, collegial, innovative and knowledgeable and hence can be much more effective than a traditional view of organizations.

8. Crisis in the Social Age

Last but not least, no business or brand is fully protected from a social-media propelled reputation crisis. A crisis can quickly take a global dimension hammering brand trust, consumer sales and stock prices, costing billions in no time. Companies like Shell, Nestlé and Malaysia Airlines have learnt this the hard way. In such a scenario, social media can also serve as a powerful customer-communication platform in times of crisis. An always-on, proactive reputation building as a transparent, sincere, responsive, empathetic and engaging social citizen is often the best buffer when such crises hit. In a crisis bred by a network of people, people alone can be the best allies and antidotes.

In a crisis bred by a network of people,
people alone can be the best allies and antidotes.

For brands that do it right, their social-media advocates become their first line of defence, sharing and arguing the brand's perspective and neutralizing the negativity.

Let's for a moment consider the persona, tone and manner that brands need to wear in order to earn street creds in the social space.

* * *

Brand as a Social Animal

Wanting to be as good a part of the new, social-media living as that of the physical one, in the beginning, brands started their social-media pages to offer single-click access to anyone anywhere in the world.

But this also meant that many things could not simply be brushed under the carpet. Customer complaints, if not served well, would spill on to social media. Sometimes even before people called the customer hotline, they would complain on social media first. Brands that for a hundred years had managed to curate a carefully orchestrated image of near perfection, suddenly were vulnerable to angry customers like never before. In the early years of social media, marketing and customer-service departments struggled to manage this effectively—and many continue to struggle even today.

For long, traditional corporate communications or PR (public relations) were often found wanting in this respect. Social media as a space, with the power it vested into the hands of the small, was made to distrust and challenge the big. Big corporations with their big-brother attitude and corporate replies, vetted by elaborate legal departments, would frequently find themselves ravaged by angry mocking crowds of thumb-downs and abusive comments. The crowd could be wise, the crowd could be nasty. The customer could

be the levitating god, and could be the obsessive troll. It was
all out of control.

The crowd could be wise, the crowd could be nasty.
The customer could be the levitating god, or the obsessive troll.
It was all out of control.

This necessitated a new way of crafting the social persona.
A Facebook or an Instagram or a Twitter, just like any
other media platform, has its own sub-culture and rules of
engagement. First and foremost, businesses needed to get
down from their big-boy perches and be humble. Social
media by definition was a social space, so the tone and
manner needed to be conversational and friendly, instead of
formal and stiff. It also was a space, which in the manner of
a small community or a village, demanded a higher degree
of authenticity. Brands had to realize that they couldn't
pretend to be perfect all the time. Just as no real individual
was expected to be perfect, brands would be allowed some
slack too, as long as they were transparent, authentic, sincere
and well-meaning. People could forget and forgive mistakes
but not bad form. And it is thus that transparency became the
new trust.

As discussed before, social-savvy brands also realize
today that they need to bring a certain amount of empathy
to their social presence in order to be accepted as a normal,
sentient entity. They need to have a voice on issues that
matter to people, as they can't stay hidden behind the
veneer of their narrow role-plays and be singularly devoted
to the business of profit maximization. Social media
allows them an almost human-like presence beyond the
1930s commercials of TV and a stray customer-service
interaction. They need to be more whole. And it is okay to
be a somewhat imperfect whole.

Having delved into the social persona for businesses, let's zoom out a bit and discuss how brands can take a high-level view of social, and how it impacts not just marketing, but the larger business reputation as well.

* * *

Run the Game or Be the Game

There is a popular grandma fable of the cat and the pigeon. When a pigeon sees a cat, it closes its eyes. The pigeon thinks that just because it can't see the cat, the cat is no more there. But then the cat is there. And it's not going away. In fact, it's preparing to pounce on it. And by the time, the pigeon realizes this, it will be rather late.

The first reaction among big businesses towards social media was to ignore it, not unlike grandma's pigeon. Social media was overlooked as a strange place where young people do their 'things'. Then it was seen as a place where many people did share things, but what did it have to do with business and branding? Not much later, it was seen as a place where you could also put up advertising and press releases, maybe. However, it all changed quickly.

In recent years, as big businesses realize that their destiny is closely affected by social media's take on issues that sit at the intersection of their business and the government or important other stakeholders in the civil society, managing advocacy around the corporate brand has become as critical as managing perceptions with lay people. This is true especially for industries that entail huge upfront capital investments and are highly regulated, which means that small policy shifts can impact their long-term profitability and risks significantly.

A 400-year-old tale of the Moghul emperor Akbar and his favourite courtier Birbal might be relevant here. Akbar and Birbal had an ongoing battle of wits, and Birbal always managed to delight the emperor with his. One fine morning, Akbar took a large piece of paper and with a pen he drew a line on it. Then he challenged the courtiers to make the line smaller without erasing it. It seemed to be an impossible problem. It was beyond everyone. Then Akbar looked at Birbal and asked mockingly if the cleverest man in the empire had been outwitted at long last. Birbal laughed softly, walked to the table, took the pen, and drew a longer line next to the original line. The line was shorter now. Without erasing it.

Companies realize that they are sometimes only one comment away from a fully blown global crisis—which may end up costing billions. And hence there is a need for them to be proactively managing their reputation. It is impossible to be in perfect control of a brand's image in social media, so a red line of negative chatter can always emerge at a very short notice.

While it might be difficult for a brand to be able to erase the red line altogether, it may help—as for Birbal, so for brands—to draw a big fat green line next to it (see diagram). Towards that, brands must proactively and continuously drive positive narratives around itself, especially in areas of vulnerability, so that when in distress, while the resolution is in process, the negativity can be overwhelmed by the positive with the aid of carefully cultivated advocates and influencers. Brands must be the ones setting the agenda for conversations around them relentlessly as, when people do not have anything to talk about a brand, in this communication vacuum they are more prone to pick up or exaggerate negative stories.

Birbal line

Akbar line

HOW BIRBAL MADE THE AKBAR LINE SMALLER

As a brand you can either run the game or be the game. Let's therefore spend some time discussing a simple five-step process to run this game.

1. Map the top reputation opportunities and risks for the brand.
2. Look within to identify the key narratives that can drive each of the opportunities and the risks.
3. Frame the story angles with which to propel favourable narratives and counter the unfavourable ones. Define what success looks like.
4. Populate the story angles with a stream of specific stories and advocacies, and craft the content in suitable formats.
5. Distribute it to the relevant audience via paid media channels as well as owned and earned (or viral) ones.

First and foremost, a brand needs to map out a clear picture of the key long-term and short-term reputation priorities in line with the business strategy and the perceptual risks. It is important here to prioritize, depending upon what the brand and business is most sensitive to and what the low-hanging fruits are in terms of feasibility to address.

Behind every reputation there is an interplay of myriad narratives. Understanding the metastructure of these narratives allows one the insight to be able to modify it.

Some narratives conflict with a corporation's own narrative, some support it, but many are tangential in that they may be adding to or taking away from what a company wants to project, but in an indirect manner or without explicit intentions behind it. The narratives may originate in and be fanned by competitors, vested interests of all kinds and a multitude of stakeholders in the larger ecosystem. A careful analysis of these may help us determine our short-term and long-term focus in terms of what narratives to strengthen and what to distract from. A narrative arc can be conceived to lay out how we would want the thinking to evolve to suit the corporation's interests.

A clear picture of the strategic narratives allows one to then frame the right stories with the right angles to help entrench the preferred narrative and counter the conflicting ones. It also allows a brand to systematically recruit and nurture the right influencers and advocates in the right roles to add further credibility to the story.

Let's understand this further with a brief example. In the context of Indian politics, let's take what has been a troublesome brand situation—that of Rahul Gandhi. Let's start with the first step.

Put simply, the top three reputation opportunities could be (1) to convey to the people of India that he is fit to be a prime minister, (2) to convince potential allies that he has the will and the plan to lead them to power, and (3) to inspire his party workers and leaders to believe, come together and bring their best to win the general elections.

Top reputation risks could be summed up as (1) the image of Rahul Gandhi as someone who is patently unfit to lead the country, (2) the perception of Congress as old, tired, divided and rife with corruption with nothing new to offer for this age, and (3) the equivalence of secularism with being anti-Hindu.

In the second step, let's look within the first risk identified—that of Rahul Gandhi as someone unfit to lead. We dig deeper into the narrative metastructure and try to list some key sub-narratives that make up this risk. Of course, the narratives are perceptions and may just have little to do with reality. (Reality creates perceptions, just as perceptions create their own reality.)

Some of them could be (1) Rahul Gandhi is almost a foreigner, who is completely out of touch with the real people of the real country, (2) Rahul Gandhi is a half-hearted princeling, is not particularly smart, lacks a strong character, and often has no idea what he is talking about, and (3) Rahul Gandhi has zero leadership skills to be able to really connect with his party workers, give confidence to the allies and backers, and to be able to win, leave alone lead the nation to greatness.

In the third step, let's focus on the first sub-narrative. This sub-narrative has been masterfully grafted on to elements playing to commonly held systematic stereotypes, such as his Italian mother, his foreigner-like looks and his silver-spoon upbringing. Further, it has been very carefully magnified and given flesh and body by the thousands of memes manufactured by his detractors in myriad creative ways. Every iota of his history, every minute of his public appearance has been scanned, every speech has been deconstructed to isolate, pivot and mash-up content—sometimes overlaid by made-up stuff—that can feed this narrative to a billion people's social feeds across public and private spaces relentlessly. So, a solution to the problem would require well-thought-through counter-perspectives based on a set of angles that can credibly overwhelm the sub-narrative. These may again need to dial up another set of biases, symbolisms and stereotypes for mass effectiveness.

In the fourth step, the story angles need to be developed into streams of continuous stories and well-crafted content.

In the fifth step, the content must be seeded and fanned across the population with an intensity and frequency sufficient to overwhelm the entrenched memories as well as create a sharp and compelling counter-narrative. Of course, part of the strategy could be to play offence by repositioning the competitors but that again would follow a similar process of reputation reset as a complement to the organic effort.

When it comes to propagation of course, as discussed, the role of traditional news is shrinking and of crowd-curated news is increasing. However, between the two extremes is a space that's been occupied by a new generation of news purveyors, who play a very important role between yesterday and tomorrow. Let's call them 'native' news to denote the fact that, by and large, they are a product of the social age and are pure play without any offline avatars. Let's spend some time discussing these.

* * *

The Long, Long Tail of Native News

As soon as the stories are in place, they need to be distributed. Corporations have historically used professional content from large established publications and channels towards this. However, their power has gone down significantly. Digital PR has come into prominence with the rise of pure play 'native' news portals that plausibly offer a lot more currency among the netizens. While opinion on their credibility may vary—because on the one side they offer an alternative to mainstream news content that represents a certain institutionalized version of truth (even more relevant in countries where media is controlled), and on the other side they may lack—especially the smaller ones in the long tail—the rigour and depth that traditional news systems have. Of course, coming from a native digital background, they tend to offer higher share-worthiness and hyper-specialization.

Today, there is a vast number of long-tail news portals, blogs, discussion groups, YouTube channels, reviews and ratings sites that are native to the digital age and often command decent credibility. Brands need to be systematically able to stitch the right advocacies and influences from such third-party players. Given that the field has to some extent been levelled when it comes to influencing opinions between the big traditional players versus the native news portals, it's possible that using the power of virality, a David with the right story can overpower the Goliath of today.

One limitation of native news portals is the high degree of fragmentation in the interminably long tail; and as the business models are not yet robust and sustainable for many, their openness to feature paid news can be a lot larger. In fact, content-discovery networks, such as Outbrain, offer at-scale, paid-media style, controlled placement of branded content that looks like editorial pieces across a multitude of these online portals (they also include, to be fair, some major mainstream news portals). Also, a new breed of highly automated PR release distribution players exist to help brands tap the long tail of online news covering thousands of native news portals globally.

In fact, to complement this trend, 'brand journalism' has emerged as a discipline to help find and curate the newsworthy stories hidden inside organizations to help ride the elusive share train. These stories, of course, can be carefully selected to drive specific narratives that are relevant to the reputation needs.

The discipline at the centre of this, historically speaking, is public relations (PR). Let's spend some time on that to complete the picture.

* * *

The Triad of Relations

To stay in sync with the times, PR as a discipline needs to also evolve into newer dimensions if they have to stay relevant with the times. The acronym PR ought to be expanded to include Private Relations and Personalized Relations (see diagram). 'Private' relations may refer to the need for brand news to be able to enter the more intimate but less controllable spaces—with permission, of course—private social forums such as Facebook Messenger, WhatsApp, Snapchat, etc. However, by and large, the success of mainstream brands in infiltrating these spaces has been quite limited due to their inability to convert brand news into genuinely share-worthy memes.

Personalized relations may refer to the micro-targeted versions of a piece of brand news propagated via customized brand newsletters or multiple versions of social posts, each catering to specific affinity groups to drive maximum impact.

A good PR strategy must mix and match the three to convey the right narratives with scale and credibility. Some of the most successful general elections of our times around the world have leveraged this triad of reputations very effectively.

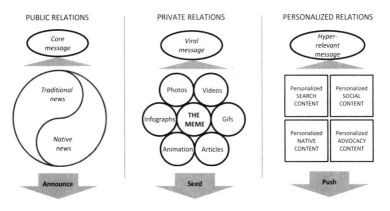

THE TRIAD OF RELATIONS

So, in the 2016 US presidential elections, while the likes of Fox News and the alt media constituents helped Trump maximize the PR opportunity, thousands upon thousands of memes were given birth—some of the biggest by Trump himself—and seeded and made viral by the most passionate of his supporters into intimate WhatsApp groups of families, friends, colleagues and neighbourhoods, leveraging private relations. Last but not least, hundreds of thousands of right-wing stories—fake or not—were micro-targeted via social-media advertising into people's everyday newsfeeds to tap their most personal interests, beliefs, insecurities and value systems using highly sophisticated analytics.

SUMMARY:

A. We discussed the nature of truth-making across the ages, starting from the era when each village had its own truth, to the age of mass truth and finally to today's crowdsourced truth.

B. We discussed how these changes mean that brands are themselves networks. We looked at the influence pyramid and the relative power versus reach of different levels—angels, alphas and mavens—and what role they could play for brands. We also understood the six key parameters of influencer selection—catchment scale, multi-platform proactivity, brand proximity, affinity correlation, engagement rate and social credibility.

C. We took a peek into how brands sit at the cusp of various paid, owned and earned social-media communities. We discussed the role that memes have in brand-building today.

D. Thereafter we investigated the eight points of intervention that social networks can have for businesses—starting with social-media insights, social-by-design campaigns, social content, peer-to-peer customer service, social CRM, social commerce, internal communications via employee networks and crisis management in the social age.

E. Then we discussed briefly the persona, tone and manner that brands need to reflect in the social-media space and how that's different from how corporations usually see themselves.

F. Finally, we looked into how brands and businesses can control their reputation by unravelling the structure of the narratives around them. We discussed a five-step process to be able to manage that better.

Having discussed the world of influence in sufficient detail, let's look closer in the next chapter at the nature of brand experiences and how businesses could make the best of that. This will allow us to understand deeply the two most critical steps in a customer's journey.

6

The New Brand Experience

'The broader one's understanding of the human experience, the better design we will have.'

—Steve Jobs

Brand experience is the heart of the customer journey. This is the stage when brands hope to appeal to the deepest desires, the subconscious needs and the trickiest psychological barriers of people. Of all the disciplines of marketing, brand experience is one of the most elusive. Sitting at the interface of people and business, it holds the most challenging brief of all in any business—how to understand people and what they need, be able to cater to it in a way that's different and superior to others, and then be able to convert that into a unique but salient set of associations in their mind and their heart. Understanding people in all their diversity and fluidity to be able to zero in on a specific utility bundle, even at the best of times, is half plumbing, half poetry.

Typical business managers attuned to quantifying their technology, resources, risks and revenues often struggle to fathom its inner workings. It can at once feel intuitively

simple and accessible to anyone (everyone, including the
CEO's wife, has an opinion), yet it refuses to be nailed down
in its predictability. For example, it is not uncommon to
find business managers who have very strong opinions on
marketing decisions, but when actually put on the decision-
making hot seat turn out to be abject failures.

It is important, therefore, to take a look at how to capture
key aspects of a brand, and how a brand experience in these
times can be approached the best. One of the most common
tools deployed in the space is the brand house (see diagram).
Let's look a little deeper into this.

Building a Brand House

A brand house is a small tool to capture the key building
blocks of a brand. A simple brand house can be constructed
with a set of brand values as the foundational plinth (see
diagram). The key functional and emotional advantages that
the brand has versus the competitors become its pillars. And
the overall brand positioning which must derive from these
advantages becomes the roof that rests upon the pillars. Brand
vision sits here at the top as the higher order summation of
what a brand wants to be in the long run.

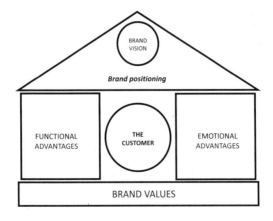

A SIMPLE BRAND HOUSE

Let us consider a brand house for Nike. Nike caters to every athlete in the world, and those who are inspired by them. Nike's brand values include inspiration, innovation and authenticity, among others. Nike offers the emotional advantage of wearing a winner's attitude and that of trust by virtue of being a brand most trusted by athletes of the world. To buy Nike is to emotionally commit at some level to push your boundaries with courage and tenacity. Functionally, Nike seeks to offer the world's best and most innovative performance technology in footwear at an affordable price. Nike's vision is to bring inspiration and innovation to every athlete in the world. And one way to sum up its brand positioning could be, 'Inspiring one to be their absolute best.'

Depending upon the complexity of the brand portfolio and the stage in strategic thinking—from the simplest campaign strategy at one end to the rebranding strategy at the other— more sophisticated versions can be deployed. However, the simple brand house mentioned above must be retained as the kernel, one way or the other. Its simplicity also allows it to be applied across varied aspects of business such as internal culture, customer experience and operations.

Operationalizing a brand house requires one to incorporate the entire brand ecosystem—the internal and external manifestation of the brand derives from the brand house (see diagram).

A brand ecosystem model has the brand vision at its core, enveloped by the brand values as its internalized essence and brand positioning as its externalized expression. In order for the organizations to live up to embrace the brand, the values need to be operationalized as organizational culture. The culture is enabled by four internal dimensions, namely structure, processes, platforms and currency. For instance, if a brand seeks to be open and transparent to its customers, the company's internal structures and processes require transparency, a culture of mutual trust and openness too. A brand can't be for the outside what it is not inside, and this integrity is critical for scalability and consistency.

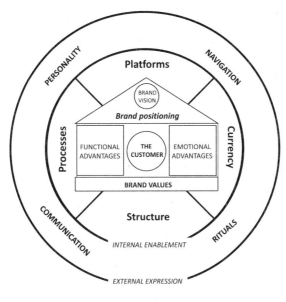

A BRAND ECOSYSTEM

Similarly, if a brand wants to be dynamic and agile in responding to its customers, it must have the right internal technology platforms that allow for a high level of responsiveness and flexibility. With the deeper integration of technology and customer data into business processes—and how UX and AI are bringing new value to customers—the role of brand-aware platforms has taken on a whole new meaning. Last but not least, the right currency for the internal reward system needs to be aligned with its brand in order to drive an incentive to co-own the brand across the wider organization. Marketing can champion brand building, but everyone across the organization must live the brand in a personified state as well as a shared culture.

In terms of external expression of its brand positioning, the brand manifests itself most importantly as customer experience (CX). The overall customer experience can be broken into four components: Personality (what kind of personality is reflected in the way we deal with our customers), Rituals (what kind of unique activities and gestures are attached with the brand), Navigation (what kind of journeys we offer the customers) and Communication (what kind of image we put out there in different communication vehicles).

People's instinct to assign human personalities to everything they connect to is as old as human civilization itself—be it inanimate rocks and toys, animals and birds, or abstract concepts such as God and Satan. A brand needs to have a well-defined personality that is reflected in all it does. The personality must manifest itself in how people representing it behave with customers across all its touchpoints and can be marked with some distinctive and defining rituals as a signature, not just run-of-the-mill processes and clichés that are category standard.

The brand must also be seamlessly embraced in how it designs its navigation across all its online and offline interactions. A brand with speed and efficiency at its core can't have a slow landing page. A brand that stands for the future can't have a dated website navigation or an app full of bugs. Last but not least, the brand must express itself through every piece of communication that the business has with the customers.

A brand vision that pervades the full spectrum from the internal culture to external customer experience in one integral whole is extremely well-placed to succeed in the marketplace. It also has the requisite DNA for scalability and consistency.

Having discussed the basics of how we can define a simple brand house and customer experience as part of a holistic brand ecosystem around it, let's look at how the experiences that build brands have evolved over centuries, and what tools it has at its disposal in the contemporary age.

* * *

Four Generations of Brand Building

As technology evolved, and people's relationship with media, image, stories and technology changed in response, new types of experiences emerged that could inform the brand-building process (see diagram). Let us delve deeper into this.

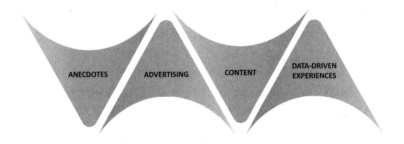

FOUR GENERATIONS OF BRAND-BUILDING

1. Brands Made of Anecdotes

As discussed in the previous chapter, for thousands of years, brands were built on the power of word-of-mouth. Durability and function were central to innovation, and the secrets of the craft were protected generation after generation by keeping it within the family or through a system of apprenticeship that valued lifelong loyalty and secrecy. Be it the best warhorses or the strongest swords or the most alluring rubies or the finest muslins or the noblest kings, brands were forged with stories and anecdotes. These anecdotes worked like little time capsules which, over generations, turned brands into legends. They had another very practical use. For instance, long before the bloodthirsty Mongol hordes arrived, the stories of their brutality arrived, allowing them easy walkovers over surrendered towns and fortresses.

This, of course, also necessitated that unconventional armies with transcontinental ambitions needed to create exemplary anecdotes of brutality or technical effectiveness to minimize resistance and win the psy-warfare. In an age where nation states as a sharp, unifying ideology had not emerged and typical armies were full of peasants and irregulars, brand anecdotes were a particularly effective weapon.

However, as we will see, while efforts to retain some form of anecdotal storytelling remained, the way the story was told became very different, in both form and vehicle.

2. Brands Made of Advertising

As mass media took hold in the early twentieth century, the second generation of brand building emerged and this was predominantly via mass-media advertising (and sometimes public relations). It allowed for a high level of control over brand messaging and an unprecedented scalability. Brands became the new icons of culture—often taking over from human leaders, who, unlike brands, could be criticized at will (and, in fact, news media loved to pick holes in, in order to keep leaders grounded). People used brands as important cultural references, defined themselves by the brands they loved, took inspiration from brands and were willing to pay a huge premium for it. This clearly was the golden age of brands, helping build a lot of the great brands we know today, such as Coca-Cola, Toyota and Microsoft.

Advertising did try to take inspiration from storytelling but, in truth, the limited and standardized format rarely allowed for much of the narrative arc. The story of a brand, if at all, was more emergent and cobbled together from tons of fragmented advertising experiences people had over a long time.

The advent of social media brought about third-generation brand building, putting social content and influences at the heart of the branding process, reducing dependency on advertising and PR. In certain ways it resembled the storytelling era of branding given the highly distributed influence; however, in speed and scalability, it was a whole different beast. A lot of new-age brands, such as GoPro, Airbnb, Spotify, Tesla, Netflix and Uber, were, by and large, entirely built on social media, whereas older brands like Dove, Nike, Sephora and JetBlue have deployed the third-generation brand building around social media to powerful effect. Brands like Air Asia, even if in a brick and mortar (or bum-on-the-seats) industry, have been native to the social era of brand building, using it to great effect for their business. Let's delve deeper into the third-generation brand building that has been primarily built around social media, though continued to deploy advertising, PR and physical experiences in different roles.

3. Brands Made of Content

As the credibility of traditional advertising went down at the turn of the new century,[1] smart brands discovered a way to leverage the new forms of content and the new norms of trust and currency. In the pre-digital era, brands, by and large, were communicated via advertising. Today, it is clear that brands must be made of content, not just ads. Each brand needs to define its content architecture, where different types of content can be deployed in their right roles to address the relevant bottlenecks that may exist in the consumer journey.

A look at the lives of people and the sources and characteristics of the content they consume in their day-to-day life shows that, broadly, there are five pipes of content that run between people and brands. The five pipes can be largely defined as peer-to-peer, influencer, editorial, experiential and advertising. These pipes vary significantly on two major criteria—credibility and control (see diagram).

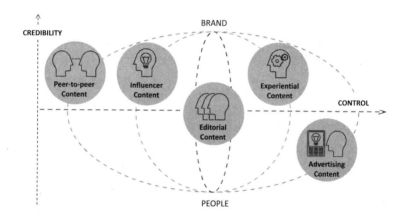

How much credibility a pipe has in the minds of people affects how much trust people may assign to the brand messages that come via that pipe. The pipes also vary widely in how much control brands can realistically exercise in how the brand messages flow through them, how they change shape, how much reach can they attain and how controllable that reach is.

People as the Most Important Medium

The first pipe, the *peer-to-peer content* pipe can be quite credible but offers a low level of control and can be scaled up only by aggregating a huge number of peer-to-peer shares.

This pipe pervades not only the general social-media platforms, blogs and discussion groups but also the most intimate spaces of social interaction such as private chats. It opens many latent opportunities for brands. At its best, memes can build brands and brands can be memes.

For instance, a lay customer may impact a brand in different ways depending on where he or she is in the customer life cycle. An 'excited prospect' can be a proto-customer, who can't wait for a new product or brand to launch (think all those lining up outside the Apple stores for new launches). Or it can be a 'first experiencer' who has experienced the product for the first time and, for instance, is surprised with how his or her initial barriers to the brand were so misplaced. It can also be an 'alpha advocate'—an evolved or specialist customer who uses the brand in moments, occasions and for purposes that help drive frequency or share of basket in the category. Or it can be a 'loyal propagator'—a current customer, who loves to talk publicly and openly recommend the brand to those in his or her circle of influence. Each of these types of customers and their advocacies, if deployed rightly, can play unique roles in helping address the varied bottlenecks that may exist for a brand.

From Social to Sales

The second pipe running between the brand and the people is the *influencer content* pipe. Now while the advertising and editorial pipe had existed even before the digital era, this pipe, by and large, emerged strong as a direct result of social media, just like the first one—the peer-to-peer pipe. Historically brands often deployed in their advertising either technical experts—a doctor or an engineer or a scientist, for example— or lifestyle icons, such as renowned celebrities, for an image rub-off. However, the format was still advertising which got placed via highly controlled media buying and the messaging was framed in a rigid commercial form. The influencer pipe in the digital world is a whole new organism in comparison, with its own unique formats, propagation mechanism and impact parameters. It's a global industry today in its own right, worth billions.

For every brand, if you look at the universe of people who are familiar with the brand, there will be those who are its positive advocates, the promoters, and there are those who are its negative advocates, the detractors, and then there are those who have neither a positive nor a negative opinion about the brand, the neutrals. For many brands, while the majority of people who are familiar with it tend to be neutral, it is the gap between the number of people who are its promoters versus the number who are its detractors that makes the biggest difference to a brand's fortune and may, in fact, be the leading indicator of the shape of the brand's future. There are several research instruments available to help quantify the net promoters or net detractors for a brand. Normal consumer behaviour in most categories also shows that while a consumer who is happy with a brand may tell a few people about his positive experience (if at all), an angry customer, however, has a lot more propensity to complain openly on social media given the access that it has facilitated. And this is a reality that brands often struggle to handle.

A campaign designed to be shared on social media (also sometimes called 'social by design') may typically involve influencers in different roles depending upon the stage of involvement. At first, a typical campaign meme may need to be seeded into some affinity groups where it is expected to have the most appeal by a few major influencers. This would give it the best chance of triggering the initial momentum of sharing. However, as soon as the reach within these affinity groups exceeds a certain point, the content must break out of these groups to cover a much larger catchment area. Parallel to this, paid-media support may be needed to provide sufficient tailwind in most cases.

At this point, a brand may deploy a slew of catalysts to fan the fire into a multitude of disparate groups. This is also a point where such catalysts may mash up the content or introduce new versions and formats to give it further and repeated sharing possibilities. They may also invite people to create or mash up and share their own version, thus potentially turning it into a mass participatory campaign. This participation also adds extra shelf-life to the memes and helps drive the depth of engagement with the campaign.

The campaign may have yet another leg where a climax may be designed in a big coming-together of the story to heighten the brand experience to yet another level, thus re-enacting a complete story arc. It is easy to imagine here that the bulk of the campaign moves via a snowball effect, which can't be closely controlled by a campaign architect. It's also important to realize that, as the campaign snowballs, the brand itself has less and less control over the shape the message takes as people take control and the process of self-selection begins leading to survival of the salient. The only aspect that marketers can hope to control here is the paid media support that is usually needed.

In countries like China, paid influencers have gone far beyond producing and propagating branded content to actually selling the product, running little online shops and getting paid by the number of sales made. This can be incredibly powerful for high context and high overlay products. Since social media assigns everyone a higher power to influence than the physical world, it is possible to imagine a future where ordinary people will be referring and advocating products they like in a natural and seamless manner. This may further be bought with a simple click by people who like what someone likes, and a sales commission is assigned to that someone. This would put everyone behind a selling counter. Everyone will be a shopkeeper in the future, potentially.

Programming the Brand News

The third one—*editorial content* pipe—refers to the PR activity, where brands use their newsworthy content to belong to the historically high-credibility space of editorial coverage itself. A brand launch covered by news reporters, a positive feature on the business and a brand covered by a business journalist, or a socially aware initiative covered by the city beat, would all form crucial components of it. PR historically was a complement to advertising and was considered much more precious than advertising based on impact per column centimetre of space in newsprint (some used a normative multiple of three—so for the same size of coverage between a PR story and an ad, a PR story would be deemed worth three times as much in value or impact).

Another dimension of the editorial pipe is branded content, which applies to professionally generated content beyond the news genre that is fully or partially produced in collaboration with brands. These typically may allow brands to infiltrate the script or the sets in a way that helps the brand convey a message either about a function, occasion, demonstration or image. Depending upon the quality of the content, and how smooth and natural the integration is, it can be quite powerful, even if expensive when done on a large scale.

Do It to Love It

The fourth pipe is the *experiential content* pipe. This pipe helps elevate 'storytelling' to 'storydoing'—beyond creating, mashing and sharing communication. It could be a physical experience or a virtual experience involving multiple senses and allowing for deeper participation. It could be an experience centred on functionality—like sampling, demonstration, trial, roadshows, etc., or it could be purely an emotional brand experience such as sponsored sporting (e.g. Red Bull space jump) or musical events or educational seminars.

The high-tech participatory formats in the experiential pipe are still in their early years. When people 'do' something rather than read, listen or watch, and that 'do' is something they have never done before or if it makes them feel great about their self-image, it gets etched deep into their minds. As millennials and Gen Z around the world prioritize collecting experiences over gathering possessions, this content pipe is set to be more and more impactful.

When it comes to conceiving and designing best-in-class activation experiences, it is important for marketers to apply some key criteria. The relevance of the experience to the target audience is of utmost importance. The activation idea must be conceived with the specific bottlenecks the brand is trying to address, in order to hand-hold customers on a sales-minded journey. The experience must be designed to be participative and to be able to trigger virality. It also needs to enhance the brand equity and amplify the integrated campaign (if it's a part of one). In general, the emotional impact of an activation (commitment, advocacy, referrals, etc.) needs to go beyond the functional interaction in order to allow for the usual high cost of contact to be worth it.

Pay for Play

Given the level of control that the last pipe—*advertising*—offers, not just on message but also on how scalable one wants it to be in terms of reach, frequency and recency, still allows it to attract a lot of marketing communication investment.

However, the credibility of this pipe has become low. To start with, this is one pipe where the line between the commercial message and editorial is relatively clear, so people know that advertising content is, well, just advertising. Added to this, the overwhelming level of clutter, frequent lack of relevance and the make-believe framing of messages which has become the default tone and manner, juxtaposed with shortening attention spans of people and their increasingly efficient mental filters, have meant that advertising investments make a big trade-off between credibility and control.

It is critical here to note that even though the credibility of claims made by brands via advertising—because of the way the message is often framed (and due to conflicting and confusing claims by different players in a cluttered market)— is relatively low, consumers still expect to hear from a brand, about what its own stand on its superiority is. That is why brand websites in many categories have become an essential reference in the customer journey. It's an important constant in the battle of divergent brand narratives that consumers must collate their one truth from.

The five content pipes expanded the repertoire of weapons a brand had in its arsenal and the leading brands of the last decade have led the battle to win share of mind by deploying each of the five in the right roles in their customer journey. However, once again, technological progress was brewing yet another set of brand-building opportunities, which we would group under fourth generation brand building.

4. Brands Made of Data-Driven Experiences

As algorithms married to vast granular data pervaded our daily stimulation, regime and self-image (some called it 'algodithm'), it gave birth to a host of new attitudes, behaviours and experiences. This had a direct impact on how brand experiences were conceived too. UX took a central place in this new lifescape, along with the still blue ocean areas of micro-utilities, artificial intelligence, the Internet of Things, extended reality and a culture of co-opting the newists in the beta versions of products. Let's delve briefly into each of these.

The first weapon in this arsenal that took on a whole new level of importance in marketing in the digital era was UX—the user experience. User experience is often confused with its subset User Interface (UI). UI focuses on designing the aesthetic experience of a product centred on people. UX goes deeper and ensures that the user journey is structured in a way so as to solve the various customer pain points in the most efficient and effective way.

If you look at the greatest brands in the world today, especially those which were minted in the post-dot-com era—Google, Facebook, Apple, etc.—one remarkable aspect that differentiates them from the great brands of the previous era, such as Coca-Cola, Toyota or Microsoft, is how little they have invested in advertising as a weapon towards brand building. If we think about where a lot of the perceptions we hold about these brands and businesses come from, we realize that they are brands built around user experience. And, while in the larger picture, UX is one of the big four powers in helping disrupt today's marketplace, in the context of brand building it also has a very specific and decisive role.

Back in the dot-com era, Google first broke through the clutter of other search engines on the power of their page rank algorithm but also the ruthless simplicity and speed of its interface. Even before people absorbed the intricacies of why its algorithm gave superior results, they were truly delighted by how great the interface was. It did what it was supposed to do much better than anyone else via an experience that was as user-friendly as it could be. After using Google a few times, it was not difficult to 'feel' the brand difference from the experience it offered.

Facebook followed the same trail. Facebook was not the first social network; it wasn't even the second. In fact, it was rather late to the scene, yet it grew up to become the unchallenged giant in the space, because of its user experience. Like Google it brought brutal simplicity, speed and intuitiveness—but it also brought a fun, open, collegial and cool contemporary experience. The brand had a personality that arose out of the user experience. You didn't have to see its advertising or read a lot of literature on it to know what the brand stood for, what value it brought, what image it evoked. And the same could be said of Apple and its user experience that was suitably mirrored in its packaging, stores and its website.

Today, irrespective of the category—and whether there is a physical product involved or not—more and more of the customer journey is moving online. People interact with brands in so many ways today beyond the product itself. It can be with the company's website, online customer service, digital sales interactions, the online shop, the apps, the emailers, in-store interactions and so on. People have certain levels of expectations that the Silicon Valley UX icons have built into people's minds and now they expect every brand to fulfil them irrespective of which category they are a part of. Too many businesses are failing to deliver the quality of user experience that people expect. And this has serious implications for how those brands are perceived.

As we discussed earlier, in many categories, people come to know of a new brand and the first port of call is to go to its website or download its app or visit its social page to find out more. Based on what people experience there, there are serious judgements that get made on how dynamic, efficient, agile and innovative the company is. Little things matter there—how fast the page downloads, how relevant the information is, how intuitive the navigation is, how efficiently information can be served to help someone and so on. As mentioned before, in an era where big is not necessarily seen as strong, as it might as well be a ripe, fat target for disruption—agile is the new strong. And user experience is a precious opportunity to mirror that agility. Of course, it may not be sufficient, but it's a necessary window for managing brand perception in most categories.

In services, where the product is often in the form of information and experience, this is a fundamental fulcrum for great brand building, as UX has become a potent way to present information and convert customers. But also, in categories that entail high involvement with significant digital intervention in the customer journey this becomes the deal-breaker. UX is the new brand for these categories.

With the advent of AI, the importance of UX in the eventual customer decisions is only going to increase. Just as the future of living is highly assisted by smart, all-pervasive AI technologies that will anticipate people's needs and curate personalized solutions for the more repetitive, logical or predictable tasks, the future of all commerce is personal and anticipatory too. Already businesses like Netflix, Spotify and Amazon deploy a significant level of AI to anticipate what we may want. Based on anticipatory data, many businesses are creating personalized products or services that are offered to people via personalized media targeting and messaging and as soon as the sale is made, a personalized brand experience is offered across the subsequent customer service, upsell and cross-sell. AI is raising the power of UX further to make it even more powerful as a force for brand building.

For millennials and Gen Z, high-tech experiences are not just very engaging, but also lifestyle statements. Brands clearly have an opportunity to bring these experiences to such consumers, either to enhance their innovative and tech-savvy image or build engagement or to offer more functional value. In fact, the seduction of new experiences has allowed Silicon Valley brands to deploy 'betas'— unpolished proto-products—to be launched, tested and tried by people. To go public in an unfinished form is no more clumsy, embarrassing and unprofessional, but about transparency, thought leadership and pride. It's an act of brand building. Some of the most iconic brands of today regularly deploy this content pipe to enhance their brand— for example—Google cardboard VR goggles at one point of time, Microsoft HoloLens, Amazon Echo and Facebook's Oculus are all products that were or have been around for some time, make little money for the companies so far, yet are powerful image-bearers for their brands.

In fact, a failed product or a half-satisfying experience today doesn't have the same stigma as it had in the pre-digital era. Even though a Google Glass could never be practical and popular, it served a great purpose for many years in helping position Google as a company that gets the future and is well-positioned to tap it. The world's most valuable brand, Google, between 1998 and 2011, churned out 251 independent new products, but 36 per cent of Google's products have been failures.[2] Google has built its brand as much on its successes as through its failures. The world clearly loves betas and therein lies the opportunity for brands to use relevant 'beta' experiences— around the product, shopping or communication—to inspire, engage and win consumer commitment.

In every category that is high involvement with long purchase cycles and requires significant information, there is an opportunity to intervene at several points in the customer journey using micro-utilities that add value to the decision-making process by answering real questions or solving issues a customer may have (such as an app to calculate loan instalments by a bank, or a paint volume calculator by a paints company). Using the data customers share, the brand can offer a high level of personalization, building credible rapport. Successful branded utilities can help create a powerful impenetrable ecosystem around a brand, thus boosting its competitive position.

As Industrial Revolution (IR) 4.0 technologies transform our lives, more and more things are getting connected. In the eventual future, one's fridge and washing machine may socialize with the car, the shoes and the grocery app in a matrix of pervasive AI, making our lives easier, helping us pack in even more life per life. A lot of these IoT technologies are designed around people trading their data for a tangible utility solving some real customer problems.

As brands across commoditized categories seek to differentiate themselves from each other, they will try to solve larger customer problems in and around the needs the category currently satisfies by deploying consumer IoT devices. It could be embedded in their packaging, it could be an add-on device, a service device (say in-store), an innovation in media or communications or it could be something embedded in any of the other partner devices.

The future of living will reside in a matrix of sensors that work in tandem to simplify and enhance our lives. A new level of anticipatory intelligence to assist people in the more mundane tasks will be deployed in every aspect of our lives. In a world deeply impatient with sales pitches, an AI and IoT-based brand value, can establish a more meaningful value exchange between people and brands. IoT in the B2C (business to consumer) space can enhance brand power by using connected objects to better customer experience as well as to solve unmet customer problems.

From personalization to convenience to speed to image to cost-efficiency, it opens up a whole new world of customer-value propositions that have the power to transform many categories. A bevy of everyday branded objects whispering to each other discreetly via smart data streams—anticipating, curating, personalizing and serving our myriad needs, is a dream made in future for brand and marketing as a discipline.

Extended reality technologies such as augmented reality and virtual reality will, in addition, provide new form factors—much more immersive and intelligent ones—to create brand experiences. A parallel world is being cast inside metaverses, allowing people to be whatever they want to be on a given day in a given world (and many things at once), allowing unmatched real-time efficiency in how information is served, how self is expressed and how people can participate together in new living experiences. Let's look at this in more detail in chapter 11.

* * *

Designing the Perfect Brand Experience

With the fragmentation of prospects, channels and touchpoints, more and more categories are having to contend with highly fragmented customer fulfilment pathways. This requires brands to manage a consistent experience across the multiplicity of pathways for its gamut of stakeholders, while maximizing business—not easy since, for example, social media has its own cultural norms and expectations from a brand versus a call centre versus a physical customer-service counter versus a chatbot. As we discussed, this is ensured via consistent personality, navigation, rituals and communication.

It also requires the internal organization to mirror the same brand values, in a personified state (personified by internal leadership, high performers and champions; an objectified state (day-to-day objects and habitat, whether physical or digital that people encounter); and an institutionalized state (rituals, processes and organizational entities, for example) in order to truly live the brand. As mentioned before, this requires the right platforms, structure, processes and internal currency (for example, key performance indicators).

An integrated brand experience design in these times must stretch seamlessly from product design to service design to behaviour design to communication design. Apple is a great example of how the essence of its product design—simplicity, intuitiveness, cool factor, ingenuity and refinement—seamlessly extends across all its communication design: launch events, packaging, advertising, PR stories, social-media presence or even device notifications. But the way Apple customer executives behave online, or its Genius Bar interacts with the customers also extends the brand smoothly into the behavioural traits and aspects of personified culture. Underlying this behaviour and communication is a service design that ensures that the external manifestations can live up to the high standards that the brand holds itself up to. The Apple brand is also suitably personified by its leaders such as Steve Jobs, Jonathan Ive and Tim Cook. And their commitment to design is reflected in their office design, their work processes and zero-compromise quality control.

Over the last decades of the twentieth century, 'customer value added' rose as a central concept in management. The principle was that everything that a business does—activities, decisions, investments—must be evaluated against one simple question as to whether it adds value to the end customer. Today, that customer value is best captured as brand experience, in every way that the business touches the customer. More than ever, the notion of brand experience includes customer experience, but covers both the functional and emotional dimensions of experience. It also emphasizes how a brand is experienced within the company as key to how it's experienced by the customers. Lastly, it must also cover the gamut of key stakeholders.

SUMMARY:

A. We started the chapter with a quick discussion on the subjectivity and hence the difficulty of conceiving a brand experience that meets the strategic objectives yet is steeped deeply in human insights. Then we discussed a brand house as the soul of the brand-building process. We also discussed how a brand ecosystem can be carved around it, in order to ensure the brand is expressed in every aspect of an organization and its interactions with its customers and other stakeholders.

B. Thereafter, we delved into how brand experience has evolved across four generations. We started with brands built for millennia on the power of anecdotes. Then we spoke about brands built by the highly controllable advertising machinery. Then we discussed building brands with content, not just ads, delving deeper into the five pipe content architecture.

C. We spent some time discussing fourth generation brand building around data-driven experiences—user experience, barely: user experience, finished but edgy products (called betas), and the role of micro-utilities in solving tangible customer problems in the journey. We also discussed how IR 4.0 technologies are opening several new opportunities in the space.

D. We closed the chapter with a quick summation of how it must be all brought together in a seamless integrated brand experience that's lived internally within an organization and is reflected in every interaction that a business has with its various stakeholders.

Having dwelt on the brand experience in some detail, let's spend the next chapter focusing on the creative aspects of conceiving a great brand experience. Brand creativity as we knew it in the last century versus where it is today, the expectations, the mechanics, the benchmark, is vastly different. That would be the topic of our next chapter.

7

The New Creativity

'Imagination is the only weapon in the war against reality.'

—Lewis Carroll

In 1964, Arthur Koestler wrote his book, *The Act of Creation*. In it he tried to develop a general theory of creativity. One thought that stands out clearly is the 'Theory of Bisociation'. In a nutshell, it defines creativity as two disparate thoughts colliding together to create something new.

In the context of marketing, creativity may often be triggered by an insight—conscious or subconscious—and is expected to solve a marketing problem in an engaging way.

Creativity rooted in human insights actually sits right at the heart of marketing. This is the reason that marketing exists as a distinct discipline, as apart from sales or technology or finance or production. Insights lead to creativity. And without insightful creativity, marketing is probably just sales with good looks.

Steve Jobs spoke the famous line: 'Real artists ship.' A good creative idea in the context of a brand ought to be judged by how well it can serve its role for the business. To ensure that, a good idea must sit inside a triangle representing three important considerations: A good idea must be aligned with the brand equity, ensuring it deepens the brand rather than dilutes it. A good idea must also address a consumer-side bottleneck so it can unlock growth (see diagram). And finally, a good idea must be relevant to the target audience that is considered the lowest hanging fruit in the context of the bottleneck.

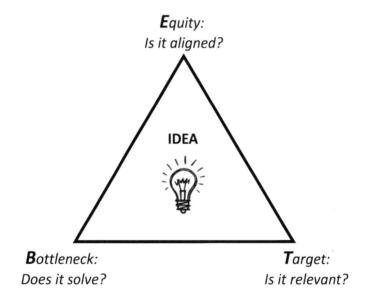

IDEA AND THE EBT TRIANGLE

In the last two decades, while the soul of marketing, that is, creativity has remained a constant, its expression, the craft, the form factor, have changed considerably with changing technology and people's relationship with media and businesses. It is important to ponder over the important ways in which this has affected the nature of creative ideas in our times.

The Enemy at the Gates

In the digital era, with Silicon Valley hype providing a powerful tailwind, there has been a serious effort by technology companies to take over and turn marketing into a set of algorithms. Martech evangelists have stood at podiums and proclaimed marketing dead, some among them subsuming marketing into technology by treating human creativity itself as an error margin in the marketing equation. The ship is pretending to be the cargo here.

This aberrant interpretation of marketing plays well to the culture of quarterly sales targets, where short-term certainty of average returns may sometimes be prized over longer-term bets on extraordinary returns. Activist investors, corporate raiders and private equity players are being groomed on the misleading notion that marketing-by-spreadsheet is synonymous with effective marketing. The skeleton is denying the soul, raising the spectre of what could be only seen as some sort of 'zombie marketing'. The truth actually, as always, is in the middle.

As organizations seek to transform themselves, trying to balance the old business model with the new, they are adopting a multitude of new weapons. This has led to a new level of complexity in marketing departments. In addition to all that existed before, a marketer is now expected to harness the areas of search, social, website, apps, CRM, content, e-commerce and so on. To mirror the emergence of these needs, the marketing services ecosystem has thrown up newer and newer departments and a plethora of new start-ups. This has quickly created silos that are often jostling to maximize their share of the pie, and few are willing to share accountability for the final outcome with the marketing decision-maker, making his or her task that much trickier.

As the marketing ecosystem gets more and more bogged down with managing the plumbing of marketing, there is a real fear that its complexity can kill the soul of marketing. In order to ensure creativity holds its own in the new milieu, it is important to understand the new vocabulary of creativity.

A broad glance at the nature of creativity in the new age lends us at least six new dimensions on which brand creativity is evolving. The new creativity is contagious, moment-aware, personalized, texperiential (related to new technology-led experiences), multicontent and performance-ready (see diagram). Let's have a look at these in more depth.

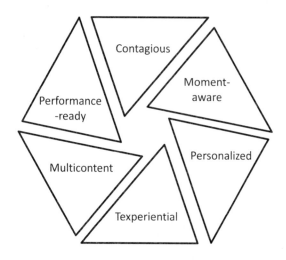

SIX DIMENSIONS ON WHICH
CREATIVITY IS EVOLVING

* * *

Contagious Creativity

Contagious creativity is based on the premise that people are the most important medium today. A share-worthy message will get passed along from people to people and people may add to the message or create their own take on the message in the process. As brands sit in networks that connect people to people, contagious creativity is the fuel that keeps these synapses alive. Clearly the implied notion is that what's creative must be share-worthy. A great creative message must invite people to participate in its propagation.

This aspect of creativity, of course, changes how creative teams and workflows were designed in the past. Professional creativity is getting increasingly challenged by the 'creativity of the crowd' in the battle for people's attention. In professional creative set-ups, origination, crafting and selection is controlled by a small bunch of professionals. Crowd creativity, however, involves origination by millions of freewheeling ideators (who may not even consider themselves ideators). And then, out of a plethora of useless stuff, a one-in-a-million piece of work that has extraordinary appeal and share-worthiness may emerge, self-selected by the Darwinian algorithms.

> Professional creativity is getting
> increasingly challenged by the 'creativity of the crowd'
> in the battle for people's attention.

So, the main advantages of a creative professional today against this crowd creativity are the skills of her or his craft (more likely to be the result of professional training, seasoning, process and infrastructure) and the ability to ensure the strategic relevance of the work so that it actually solves the brand's problem and drives business. Also, creative leaders can regularly take inspiration from trending crowd content or even tap the crowds directly in order to be able to 'curate' ideas rather than always originate.

Contagious creativity, while much celebrated in the social age, however, remains an aspiration for marketers for the most part. Most ideas, however great the creative team behind it may be, in reality fail to generate the virality that can attain the type of reach that a mass brand needs to maintain. The good news is, what one shares or reacts to has a better recall than what is merely seen, so the required frequency of exposure to a message gone viral is minimal.

Hence, a brand committed to contagious creativity but without push-based media investments can only hope either to get very lucky or to aggregate critical reach over several campaigns (even with the best catalysts deployed to help propagate it). That's why significant push-based media support (déjà vu) is still required to get the message out to a sufficient number of people in order to be able to exercise some degree of control over a brand's fortune. What goes viral gets extra organic views from social platforms, thus creating a multiplier effect on its reach. This also serves as a reward or discount for creativity that enhances user experience. This reward forms the difference between a post and a meme.

One of the most powerful examples of contagious creativity will be the purpose-driven Dove campaigns around real women. Dove chose to focus on the notion of beauty that goes beyond the shallow, photoshopped, notion of beauty. Given how such unattainable-for-most notions of beauty damage the self-esteem of women around the world, the campaign had an extraordinary resonance with people in general and got viralled around via social media, public and private to possibly hundreds of millions. The campaign put authenticity and empathy, in the front and centre of the brand, and got hugely rewarded for its courage and leadership.

Virality, in practice, is an elusive bonus everyone can strive for, but most will have to make do pretty much with media exposure they actually paid for. When it comes to making money from marketers, in this sense social media behaves just like the good old TV. There are no free lunches—unless the crowds really love you. (The edgiest Silicon Valley icons have a cult following that in turn creates a global viral machine which does allow them a lot of free lunches. A Musk can say a few words to himself on Twitter and the Tesla stocks, or Dogecoin, may move up and down a few billions of dollars. This pattern has given rise to the phenomenon of *meme stocks* as well.)

Moment-Aware Creativity

As discussed in the chapter on the new prospect, creativity today also has an opportunity to be moment-aware. As people live more and more in moments rather than in broad, diffused segments, and media access to moments gets much easier, brands can map and target specific moments in the category—functional, emotional, purchase or usage moments—and seek to convert the share of moments into share of market.

A functional moment for a skin-care brand could be, for example, a young woman named Lauren Kelly looking at her pimples in the bathroom mirror early in the morning while getting ready for work. An emotional moment could be the same pimple gnawing at her confidence when she is sitting in front of her date. A purchase moment could be when she is out on the weekend, shopping at the pharmacy with her mom. A usage moment could be when she is washing her face before going to bed.

Each moment, even though they relate to the same person, and is around the same product need, engenders different states of mind and mood with different levels of receptivity to a brand message. For example, a message on being her best may work better while driving for the date; a message of overnight efficacy may work better before bedtime; a message of staying in control of her day may work better in the morning; and a value-for-money message may work better in the pharmacy.

There could be several moments in her life for each of the four moment buckets. Each of those moments have their penetration (how many people it is relevant to) and frequency (how often the moment comes). Each moment may also have its sensitivity based on the degree of relevance to the product (so, for instance, skin-care sensitivity may be higher while going out with the date, than while going out with the mom). Together, the three determine the business value of each of the moments. Market shares of brands can be seen as a weighted total of the share of moments. This becomes especially relevant for categories where people use multiple brands in the same category. In such categories, frequently market-share battles are basically battles to own the moments.

The associative structures of human memory often tend to store brand imageries in the language of associative hooks. Moments tend to make excellent hooks, sort of the brain's favourite little timeless boxes of memories. A brand with dominant association to the moments with maximum business value earns the right to become the market leader.

> Moments tend to make excellent hooks,
> sort of the brain's favourite little
> timeless boxes of memories.

Moments can also be a powerful bridge between creative and media as, unlike a lot of other media considerations, creative professionals find it easier to visualize moments in the lives of people with all their contextual richness and be able to play with that. For instance, Johnson's baby bath wants to own the moment of connection when a mommy gives a bath to her baby. Similarly Coca-Cola wants to own the moments when people share an uplifting moment of togetherness. The Axe moment focused on that sexual tension as a young man tries to attract a young lady.

If stories are but a collection of moments stitched together with an engaging intent running all the way, then moments are the best mode for short-form storytelling, that brand messaging often is.

Personalized Creativity

As against the 'one brand, one segment, one creative message' principle that informed much of the mass-marketing era, brands today can deploy creativity at a granular level, where each person (or each microsegment) sees his or her own message. Each message builds on a specific insight into one's state of being with relation to the brand.

This personalization may be something as simple as addressing the consumer by their name in an emailer sent to them (not new, as direct marketing of yesteryears managed to do that too, albeit at a much higher cost per contact). Or it can entail making simple but useful customizations in a standard creative template—like changing the last frame to add the local dealer address in a location-targeted car campaign. Or it can be an airline campaign where the creative changes by route adding a different photo for each city along with the latest ticket price.

It can also be a deeper creative personalization, where the larger creative strategy and crafting is conceived in an insightful manner, so that any individual version, out of the thousands generated, feels almost as polished as a normal, single-version creative in a traditional mass campaign.

Generally speaking, creative personalization may involve five key steps—diagnose, define, architect, imagine and optimize (see diagram). In the 'diagnose' phase a strategist must look at all the various micro-barriers and drivers that may exist for a brand. He or she must also consider the saliency of these barriers and drivers to be able to filter and shortlist a set or a dimension along which personalization is expected to be most meaningful for a brand.

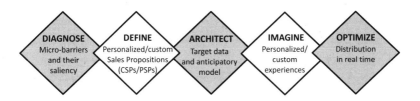

FIVE STEPS TO CREATIVE PERSONALIZATION

Each brand is a bundle of benefits and advantages—both functional and emotional. The 'define' phase needs to assign an aspect of this benefit bundle to each of the micro-barriers and drivers shortlisted above, in order to make the best of it. In the 1940s, Rosser Reeves coined the term USP—Unique Selling Proposition. The idea was that each brand must focus on a USP that's best placed to differentiate it among others and help drive its growth. However, in the world of personalized creativity, it is important to reframe this. Within the larger territory that the brand operates in, a brand can have a multitude of CSPs—Custom Selling Propositions— each for one microsegment (or PSPs, Personalized Selling Propositions for the segments of one). So, arriving at the CSPs for each micro-audience with their unique wants and fears is the natural next step.

At this stage it may also be realized that certain resolutions by the brand are not convincing enough, given its real comparative advantages, and hence may be dropped.

The next step is to 'architect' and relates to media targeting. The salient bottlenecks identified in the diagnose stage are of limited use if they can't be micro-targeted through media. So, we segue into identifying data on the relevant micro-audiences and architecting it so it is possible to deliver different messages to different micro-audiences with high fidelity. This step may also necessitate an iterative relook at the 'diagnose' step to ensure that the media targeting has sufficient specificity and scale.

In the 'imagine' stage, the brand needs to apply creativity to how the resolution identified can be brought alive in a sharp yet engaging manner. A creative framework needs to be conceived with both copy and design with a strategy of how they will be mixed and matched in order to look complete, yet do the required job. The raw ingredients of copy and art are then fed into the versioning technology, that will allow personalized versions to be brought together in order to take it to the people. This is, of course, the stage where the heart of personalized creativity sits. (A similar process can be applied to other formats such as video, for instance.)

As soon as this is done, the campaign can move into the 'optimize' phase, where it can be distributed in real time, with low-impact versions dropping off and the high-impact versions taking a bigger and bigger share of allocations. Of course, fresh versions must be introduced every once in a while, as a sort of mutant agent in a process closely mimicking the evolutionary process.

It is important to remind that personalization is not just an opportunity for campaign creativity. As discussed in earlier chapters, it is possible to indeed activate each of the five content pipes with the power of personalized creativity. Also, personalization can be applied to UX and can be delivered via branded IoT devices as well. In each case, it works best when the right creative strategy is backing it.

Last but not least, since, by definition, personalized creativity is built around a person, it offers a particularly powerful opportunity for brands that can track an individual's journey across different touchpoints. So, for example, if Lauren Kelly, in the skin-care example above, clicked on a brand campaign that spoke about boosting confidence, read an article on oily skin on the brand website and our customer database shows her thirtieth birthday is coming, we have an opportunity to upgrade her by sending a personalized email wishing her a happy birthday and appealing to her desire to feel her radiant best on her thirtieth by using the oily-skin variant of our brand.

Creative personalization as it exists today is often shorn of real creativity. Cookie-cutter automated versioning overseen by left-brained analysts often oversimplifies creative messaging with generic photos and banal text. A famous quote by Bob Hoffman from *Ad Contrarian* puts it quite well: 'The aesthetic lineage of online advertising is not "Madison Avenue". It is the maddening tackiness of junk mail direct response.' Online ads often have the heritage of classified ads and what they lack in creative power, they seek to make up by having a powerful and efficient machine. The reality, however, is that the plumbing can complement and supplement but can't substitute the magic of poetry.

As discussed in earlier chapters, creative personalization can be transformational in many ways for marketing. Some believe that the marketing wars will increasingly be won by masters of personalization. There are also those who believe that at some point in time in the future, mass marketing may be dead (or mass marketing may become a 'niche' inside the larger marketing mass).

Creative *Texperiences*

Texperience is a word we will use in this book for technology-led experiences, and denotes all the myriad, new, exciting experiences that the emerging technology has made possible. The texperiential dimension refers to how creativity can leverage these new experiences to step-change its power, and this theme has been discussed in some detail already in the chapter on brand experience.

A good example will be Hyundai's 'Mobility adventure', a metaverse space on Roblox, targeted at its young customers. 'Gucci Garden' on Roblex as mentioned before is another example. As visitors enter the Gucci Garden, avatars became neutral mannequins. Wandering through the different rooms, each visitor's mannequin absorbs different elements of the experience. With every person experiencing the rooms in a different order and retaining other elements of the spaces, they emerge at the end of their journey as unique creations. Balenciaga partnered with Epic games to integrate high-fashion skins on Fortnite as well as accessories such as a designer pickaxe or a bling backpack. The experience was amplified in the real world via billboards. Similarly Coca-Cola auctioned an NFT lootbox on OpenSea containing digital apparel that can be worn in the virtual world of Decentraland.

The texperiences can also be integrated into the physical world to create novel experiences. Among a few examples of works by Entropia, Pepsi Black pasted tiny screens on the newspaper page to announce the drink from the future. The screens switched on and much like the *Daily Prophet* in Harry Potter movies, presented the news in video. In another texperiential innovation Pepsi labels activated an augmented reality concert using the bottle as the backdrop. Faced with the pandemic, BMW in order to launch its X5, used an augmented reality showroom to have people experience the car. We also got Alcon to use augmented reality application to monitor the blinking patterns of people to gauge dryness and recommend the right contact lenses. And KFC released limited edition NFT tokens of its most savoured moments for the keepsakes by its loyalists.

To be able to brainstorm along this dimension, it's important that the possibilities and constraints of each of these technologies—social, programmatic, mobile, AR, VR, AI, etc.—are ingrained in the creative mind. Creative origination is a subconscious process and for it to spring up a new idea based on a new technological possibility, what all it can do and what it can't need to be assimilated into the cast of the mind where ideas are forged.

Multicontent Creativity

Also, the multicontent dimension refers to how creativity doesn't need to constrain itself by the traditional content pipes of advertising and editorial but needs to be able to imagine how the five different content pipes—advertising, editorial, peer-to-peer, influencer and utility—can be leveraged in different roles in the campaign designed to multiply impact. (This has been discussed in some detail in the chapter on brand experience.)

Performance-Ready Creativity

The sixth and the final dimension is the need for creativity to be performance-ready. Traditionally, the onus of creative effectiveness was usually left to the brand strategists, media planners and marketing leaders. Now, as digital operators have shifted the norms on performance expectations and crowd creativity has shifted the standards of core creativity, creative leaders are being held more and more accountable for the effectiveness of their work. It's a tricky subject as performance measurement is a highly numerate task and there is clearly a dire need to simplify performance metrics to an essential minimum so it is not too difficult for creative leaders to be able to check what worked and what didn't, and be able to introspect in order to hone their creative power campaign after campaign.

Numbers are power. And for a new generation of creative leaders, who can understand basic data and are not in denial of their importance (and are not afraid to engage with them), this puts a unique power in their hands. Also, now they can be less dependent on others to interpret for them what worked and why. Performance-ready creativity is the gateway to power for creative leaders in particular and marketing leaders in general. Let's spend some time on these creative leaders in the next section.

* * *

The New Creative Talent

The new generation creative talent is less of an originator and more of a curator and co-inventor. He or she is a fluid collaborator, who can work with different specialists (an IoT product designer, a UX expert, a performance buyer, a data scientist, and so on) in the knowledge that the creative cue and magic will come from the sparks at the interface of these disciplines. A creative leader of tomorrow is able to evoke a creative vision born of and hence relevant across the consumer journey and is able to work across the full spectrum of segments—from the mass segment to the segment of one.

So, just as the creative talent of today must know how to create, they must also know a bit of how to count its impact and learn from it. Given the new vocabulary of creative thinking—the digital formats and experiences—needs to be coded in, a creative must have a broad understanding of the possibilities that related technologies offer. Also given the rise of experiential content pipes and the advent of IoT in the IR 4.0 era, they need to possess a tinkerer's attitude and have the mindset of a maker. In summary, the new-age creative leader ought to sit at the cusp of create, count, code and make. And empowered with all four, they can once again regain the respect as the central force of marketing.

> The new age creative leader ought to sit at the cusp of create, count, code and make.

Some of the greatest creative geniuses in the history of mankind have possessed similar lineage. Da Vinci's scribbles on flying machines were pictures of beauty conceived at the cusp of engineering and imagination. His drawings of the metastructures of shapes and forms in his paintings could be both anatomy and art. So could be said about Renaissance masters like Albrecht Durer.

Ancient Indian philosophy believed that music was the language in which the gods created the universe, as they saw recurrent rhythms, vibrations and cycles everywhere they looked. They believed that all linearity was myopic and defined the conception of time itself as cyclical. It today finds its resonance at the peak of science in 'string theory', a theory that seeks to unify and explain the four fundamental forces in the universe around the premise that matter can be broken down beyond the tiniest particles into tiny loops of vibrating strings.

Truth at its imaginative best has always emerged at the intersection of art and science. Imagination at its true best also lives there now.

SUMMARY:

A. We started with a discussion about the centrality of creativity in marketing and how it is different from creative arts in general. We also discussed how marketing creativity is being threatened by the current focus on marketing infrastructure.

B. Then we considered the six dimensions on which creativity in our times is evolving (contagious, moment-aware, personalized, texperiential, multicontent and performance-ready) offering a new vocabulary of ideation, in line with changing expectations.

C. We also delved deeper into the five-step creative personalization process from diagnose to define to architect to imagine and optimize.

D. Finally, we closed the chapter with a discussion about what the new creative talent looks like at the cusp of create, code, count and make.

Having considered the role creativity can play for marketing and how it's evolving, let's delve deeper into the media touchpoints that eventually carry the creative message to the audience. Magic happens when you can't make out whether an idea is a creative idea or a media idea, so let's look at how creative and media can work together to create magic.

8

The New Media

'Media are means of extending and enlarging our organic sense lives into our environment.'

—Marshall McLuhan

The great prophet of media, Marshall McLuhan, is known most widely for the famous statement: 'The medium is the message'. He emphasized the primacy of the medium and how it changes people's lives over the content of the message itself. He believed, rightly, that the way the content of the message affects people depends on how, when and where the medium is consumed. The effect also depends on the role the medium plays in people's lives and how consuming the medium as a whole changes the essential dynamic of their perceptions and beliefs. For example, if a new brand appears on the front cover of a national newspaper, people see it as a big and important brand that they should learn about, because that is what the front cover of a newspaper stands for in their lives. However, if they saw the same new brand in a display banner on a clickbait but fun website, it would evoke more casual and passive imagery, because that is the relationship people have with that medium.

Just as the electronic age extended our eyes and ears (and the mechanical age extended our hands and legs before that), the age of consciousness has extended our brains via digital media and all the machine intelligence it puts at our disposal.

People are living through media today. Out of about sixteen waking hours each day on an average, the world's Internet users in 2021 spent about seven hours each day online. The real business of living is today being conducted on media—learning, socializing, shopping, working, banking, entertaining, falling in love, having one's heart broken and deriving sexual gratification. The Internet is a medium of living in so many ways just like the physical world is. It won't be long when most people spend a majority of their waking hours in the digital world and a small minority in the physical one.

That would change the definition of 'reality'—hitherto pegged closely to physical living experiences. Digital living could be delusional in certain ways, yet could be deeply liberating in others, as people are freed from the myriad limitations of the physical world in terms of speed, access, choice and replicability. It would drive superiority of perception (or let's call it 'digital reality') over physical reality, of mind over body and of energy over matter. At some stage of its evolution, digital reality, instead of aping physical reality in a skeuomorphic inspiration, would conjure up its own independent norms of human relationship, organization and societal living. Life and the very state of being may eventually have a new meaning, as virtual relationships and experiences—learning, working, shopping, copulating—may suffer less of the legacy sentiments of being inferior to the 'real' experience. The absence of certain sensorial dimensions may be more than made up for by the data-driven efficiency, choice and pervasiveness of the virtual.

Centuries ago, René Descartes proclaimed: 'I think, therefore I am'. It was a declaration of the dominance of mind over body. Today, social media operates as an 'ubermind', emergent from the billions of minds sparking a global consciousness in real time. Through this planetary social graph, we may just be building the next great instrument to supercharge the survival of the human species—one that is spectacular in its scale, diversity and synchronized Darwinist power.

Television with a Vision

For more than five decades, television has defined and dominated our cultural zeitgeist. Before TV came, there was the magical medium of cinema. Now with TV, everyone had their own little cinema in their living room. Its power to hold an entire family's unbroken attention for hours on end, day after day, was unparalleled. Characters in popular dramas felt like extended family, visiting regularly and mirroring our everyday joys, woes, dreams and drudgery.

For marketers it was a dream medium. For those thirty seconds, they had the viewers' unbroken, unskippable and unscrollable attention—there was no editorial lying next to it to take attention away and less than 15 per cent of people on average took a break in the ad break. And even if people sometimes complained about too many ads interrupting their favourite dramas, to the extent it paid and subsidized the price of TV programming, it seemed like a fair exchange.

Television tried to bring the linearity of radio, the editorial quality of newspapers and the audio-visual impact of cinema in a perfect concoction. Television brought marketing to its peak respectability at the turn of the century. And eventually it ended up building some of the greatest brands that came to define the power of marketing.

Television tried to bring the linearity of radio, the editorial quality
of newspapers and the audio-visual impact of cinema
in a perfect concoction.

As TV's delivery technology evolved, IPTV (Internet Protocol
TV) came via private dedicated digital networks (it was
primarily a pipeline innovation against terrestrial, cable
and satellite). TV also tried to adopt some of the qualities
of digital. Recording boxes allowed people to do time-shift
viewing, adding more viewers who wanted to watch their
favourite dramas at a later time (thus making it non-linear).
Set-top boxes also offered video on demand. However, it was
the OTT streaming (over the top streaming, also simply called
OTT) technology that truly blurred the line between television
and digital, by allowing people to watch any time, anywhere
via any device using the Internet—be it the on-demand video
or the live streamed one.

Today, the very definition of television is a tricky one. It
could be defined by the screen size (home-based, larger than
PC but smaller than outdoor screens usually) or linearity
(scheduled content watched mostly as it gets broadcast) or
editing (professionally produced and aggregated content)
or by the lean-back mode (typically long-form content
consumed passively). At the end of the day, the soul of what
can be called television lies in professional mediation, lean-
back mode, linear viewing, living-room friendly screen and
at-home consumption. Of course, all these criteria are typical
and not an absolute.

The soul of what can be called television lies in
professional mediation, lean-back mode, linear viewing,
living-room friendly screen and at-home consumption.

Television, unlike OTT, was also defined by 'channels'—the professionally aggregated and linearly scheduled plans of content. Of course, behind every channel there was a creative vision of a target focus, content quality and schedule that would presumably have sufficient and dependable worth to make you sit back, relax and keep watching again and again.

A successful TV programme has a much larger life today beyond TV. A popular programme triggers conversations and memes; mash-ups and fan fiction; communities and followers; reviews and ratings; likes, loves and shares, across all the digital platforms. *Game of Thrones* managed to garner huge merchandise sales as well as a tourism boost to the locations of its shoots. In fact, an episode on TV is merely the seed, the total story gets played out across media, which in turn reinforces viewership on television. A blockbuster TV series may end up creating its own mini-culture, fans and followers, rituals and role models, believers and symbolisms.

For marketers, historically, television has been used for roles across the purchase funnel—to build rapid awareness, to create interest and to elicit desire and drive action. Those roles in the digital age have shrunk significantly as the place that television occupied in people's lives has undergone a shift. The Internet has repositioned television's status as a passive, linear, lean-back medium to be highly limiting. It is often watched in split-attention mode—in conjunction with other activities, such as checking your Instagram feed, sharing a photo on WhatsApp and talking to your daughter. If one wants to explain cognitive information, there are better ways than TV to do it. If one wants people to interact with the brand, seek more information, check out other's opinions or register for test drives, there are much better alternatives that new media offers. Those legendary, thirty-second slice-of-life commercials have lost part of their magic as digital media offers much more flexibility, body, participation and after-story to the message.

For marketers globally, television in the new age has come to serve more as a gateway—building rapid brand awareness due to its vast reach, interruptive format and cost-efficiency, but leaving the deeper tasks of driving consideration and preference to digital media. Of course, it still represents a great way to convey controlled focused messaging at a large scale, which can intrigue people enough for them to search further, start an online conversation or visit the relevant website. It can initiate a powerful journey that other mediums can subsequently build upon to bring it to its logical conclusion.

> For marketers, television in the new age has come to serve more as a gateway—building rapid brand awareness but leaving the deeper tasks of driving consideration and preference to digital media.

Of course, to try and match the power of digital media, ad tech on TV has been evolving too. TV players are seeking to replicate the micro-targeting that digital provides. Set-top boxes in many countries allow targeting different ads to different segments of households, thus making television addressable. It also reduces wastage a good bit as only selected households are shown the ad, thus challenging the Wanamaker assertion of half of advertising being wasted, with which TV is often flogged. Further on, programmatic TV allowed buying of specific programmes on the basis of myriad audience attributes coming from different data sources as well as set-top boxes.

The Omniscient OTT

OTTs emerged to liberate TV content from the shackles of TV screens and traditional television pipes. It also brought a vast choice of content that people could watch at will any time, anywhere. Netflix as the pioneer in the OTT industry has today become a global platform with real-time access to about 200 million households around the world, paying monthly subscriptions. While traditional channel content has to move through a vast and complex matrix of local players to gain access to this global audience, Netflix has no such bottleneck. No wonder every major Silicon Valley platform—YouTube, Apple, Facebook, Instagram, Snapchat and, of course, Amazon are fighting for a share of the lucrative OTT pie.

In the world of Netflix, if content is the king, data is the queen. Netflix has data on each and every one of its subscribers around the world, which allows it to anticipate the viewing interests of its audience and be able to curate and create content that would attract their viewership. It deploys powerful machine learning to be able to create an unbeatable competitive advantage versus traditional TV. Its major weakness historically had been the lack of original-content IPs (Intellectual Property), which it has been aggressively investing in to reduce its dependency on IPs owned by other content networks. Major content networks, such as Disney, fearing eventual disruption by Netflix, have pulled out their content from Netflix and have launched their own OTT plays, seeing tremendous early success (especially for Disney which owns an unparalleled library of content IPs).

It's likely that due to the importance of original IPs, eventually Hollywood will end up building their own walled OTT gardens. In anticipation of this, large-scale consolidation has already begun in the media and entertainment industry. In such a scenario, typical households may have a multiplicity of OTT apps, which in turn may need cross-OTT search apps, which digital platforms and device makers would kill to own.

As the end game of the OTT industry is plausibly in sight, there is a new urgency for smaller native OTT players to get into profits, and hence a lot of them like Viu, ESPN+ etc. have started opening their platform to marketers. The data that OTT platforms have brings them powerful leverage in this process, and there are platforms that do not just allow custom-branded content, but have married data, content and commerce to create interesting cross-funnel plays. Having said that, the clear shape of what role OTT players will eventually have in building brands and businesses has not yet emerged, although, somewhat like Spotify, a free model for those willing to get ads and a premium model for others is likely to become the norm. Commerce will ultimately get weaved into most of the offerings too, on the lines of Chinese players.

> The data that OTT platforms have brings them powerful leverage . . . and there are platforms that do not just allow custom-branded content, but have married data, content and commerce to create interesting cross-funnel plays.

Although OTT is a digital platform due to its proximity to TV, it is in certain ways different from the usual digital platforms, in the way it garners lean-back consumption of professionally generated content. It has caused a wholesale switch from episodic viewing to binge viewing as a mass phenomenon—paradoxical in an era when attention is touted to be increasingly scarce.

If snacking platforms like TikTok hold one end of the entertainment spectrum with its six-second looping UGC (User Generated Content) videos to help fill the fun breaks between our everyday schedules, OTT platforms hold the other end, where high-quality PGC (Professionally Generated Content) can compel people to watch even six straight hours of a drama series in one continuous binge, putting aside all our daily routines. Between the snacking end and the bingeing end, of course, regular TV channels and cinema continue to stick to content durations of thirty minutes to 150 minutes typically. Somewhere between the one-minute and twenty-minute zone there seems to be the red ocean of entertainment, where everyone from Snapchat (closer to the TikTok end) to Instagram and Twitter to YouTube (longest form among these typically) battle on. The fact that PGC has the potential to get both subscription revenues as well as advertising revenues means that there is also a gold rush in this zone to develop PGC channels, that people eventually may be willing to pay for. YouTube especially would seem to be in a bit of a no-man's land right now as far as the trends go.

The choice of platforms also has created multiple options of video messaging for advertisers, depending upon the objective. Unlike TV, brands don't have to always pay by seconds. This means that video content can be used in very short durations, say six to fifteen seconds (*hook* video) or for durations that stretch from thirty seconds to several minutes (*dwell* video); or they can be full-length stories, infomercials and documentaries that are ten to twenty minutes or even longer (*dive* video). Each of the three formats can be used to address different types of bottlenecks for a brand.

Magazines and the Business of Relationships

The medium that got almost killed by digital media is magazines. Magazines had evolved in interesting ways. People had (and still have) a more private relationship with magazines than they had with newspapers or radio or even television. Most magazines were highly super-specialized, intimately curated by passionate editorial teams, who tended to have a firm finger on the pulse of their readers, and column after column, cover after cover, built a close relationship with them.

>People had a more private relationship with magazines
>than they had with newspapers or radio or even television.

While newspapers focused on news and currency—the urgent would always get precedence over the important—magazines tended to go one level deeper offering considered perspectives and in-depth research; relatively less about what was current, but more about what was truly important enough for a deeper dive. Also, the quality of production could be customized to the taste and context of the audience and their lifestyles. However, their most important differentiation came from the super-specialization itself. That also became their Achilles' heel.

In the digital age, given the nature of the medium and the low cost of entry, millions of content websites appeared, offering a whole new level of specializations, micro-aggregating their audience from a vast global catchment area. Readers could discover a website themselves, get referred by friends and family, or Google could be their editor-aggregator. The marginal cost of additional readership was nil. Reader-surfing data allowed for powerful customizations and one didn't have to wait for a whole week or month to get their magazine. The production richness could be highly attractive too.

There really was no reason for most magazines to exist any more (except maybe for some people's love of paper). In any case, the advertising spigot closed rapidly, with marketing investments rushing to online premium-content portals with rich media content. Many of the global magazines that have continued to survive today have aggressively diversified into award shows, networking events and sampling—leveraging their sharp brand image and relationships with their readers. Print versions of magazines have become a glamorous packaging layer over what is now essentially an event business for a majority of magazine titles around the world.

A few magazine titles, highly respected for their quality of content, managed to expand into digital platforms and build a business model based on subscriptions to quality research and credible opinions, and have managed to survive the onslaught. This validates that, in their own small way, magazines, like radio and cinema before it, will continue in a smaller way in their own moment and lifestyle niche.

Newspapers and the Power of the Written Word

If there is one medium that is second only to magazines in how it has been eviscerated by digital media, it's the newspapers. Thousands of newspapers around the world have shut shop since the advent of digital and many of those surviving are struggling to find their place under the sun.

Newspapers were invented some 400 years ago in Belgium and can be credited with giving birth to the mass-media era. Newspaper editors also played a major role in sanctifying a certain respect for the written word, which continues to be mirrored in how ordinary people instinctively believe a half-decent WhatsApp article that is forwarded to them by a fake-news purveyor.

For centuries, educated people around the world (at its peak almost 2.5 billion adults), opened their morning regime with a newspaper in their hands. For many of those, the fresh smell of a newly minted newspaper complemented with a cup of tea or coffee became the essential morning addiction. One rejuvenated the body, the other woke up the mind. People sat with a newspaper and reacquainted themselves with the fresh new world of the day, baked hot from the ovens of the most exposed, most resourcefully aware and most learned curators of information and perspectives in the world. A new context was gained, a new beginning was made, a piece of information here, an insight there; over time, people became the newspapers they read.

The indomitable power of the printed word moved societies, bred revolutions, won wars, jettisoned the past and augured the future. Headline by headline, picture by picture, column by column, editors carefully crafted the dominant narratives, shaping billions of minds each day towards a shared future. This shape of the future could vary a lot editor by editor, yet an unspoken circle of propriety often enveloped them by virtue of their shared experiences, intellect and wisdom.

> The indomitable power of the printed word moved societies, bred revolutions, won wars, jettisoned the past and augured the future.

And then with the dawn of the twenty-first century, the search engines came along. The search engines could be generic all-purpose ones or the more specialized ones—for jobs, property and cars, for example. Now if you needed to find any buyer or seller, you could just search specifically for what you needed. No more the necessity to go through page after page of classified ads in newspapers. Classified ads which had been the bread-and-butter of the newspaper industry (even if the least glamorous part) got disgorged first of all, taking away a very dependable source of income.

Also, with the advent of social media, as people started receiving breaking news via this medium, a new news post could spread across the world instantly. A daily newspaper in comparison was too many hours too slow. Newspapers soon followed with their online editions; however, initially it was literally the soft copy of the newspaper but accessible online, which didn't help at all. Later, they broke away from the format to come up with a native version, but the nature of news and how it was curated had already changed by then.

News in social media came through one's networks most of the time, so one's network curated the pieces of news that fitted one's individual context, thus making news a lot more relevant to individuals. Now one didn't have to flip through 200 pages to read the six stories that were interesting; one could just read the eight stories that the network of friends, family and colleagues considered interesting. Network was the editor now. One could also add to a news story's reach by merely reacting to it, contribute to the story by adding a comment or debating it out on the platform itself or share it with one's network.

As people reacted to certain types of stories more than the other, in due course the algorithm made sure they saw more and more of the type of stories that they expected to read and react to. Network was everyone's private editor, and everyone got their own front page. It was an editor with no institutional position or moral voice of its own. Algorithms don't have intellect, wisdom or souls. Some new-age players in the space, such as Toutiao in China, have tried to discover the model of the future by marrying data-driven curation with professionally generated news, with great success.

People, especially the younger ones who were native to the digital age, not yet steeped in the romance of newspapers, just loved the efficiency, the opportunity to participate and the unprecedented relevance. This generation would never truly understand newspapers. However, the problem was not limited to the young, as even those who liked their newspapers now woke up in the morning to first check, for example, their Facebook, Instagram, WhatsApp or Twitter feeds. Newspapers had forever lost their irreplaceable stranglehold on the raw morning moment, right when the mind was at its freshest and most receptive to know about new products, new promotions and new perspectives to reconsider the current choices. The medium just lost its clout of those golden twenty-two minutes,[1] when the world changed a wee bit each morning.

In fact, the nature of this change had another qualitative dimension now. The change had changed the change. Newspapers were a window to the world. This window was conceived with the interests of a large public in mind; there was nothing personal about it. So, each morning people saw a world view that became an important reference point for their own individual views. The broad, mediated world conjured by the editors collided with the narrow and situated world of readers to enable diffusion of perspectives, to negotiate balance and establish harmony. A mass newspaper typically covered a wide spectrum of news and views and prepared an individual in a subtle and powerful way to understand and accept the other. Among the readers, those radically minded could gradually inch towards the centre, while those in the centre could better appreciate the fringes. People who were unsure of where they stood on a certain issue pegged themselves to reference points they found in the stories and the columns, subtly infused with editorial wisdom.

In certain ways social media, by putting a megaphone in each person's hands, has brought a democracy of influence, yet its core logic leeches off the metastructure of democracy. It threatens to reduce the human collective to a set of binaries that their simplistic and arrogant codes can barely comprehend. It seeks to replace the enlightened harmony of the middle with the semi-literate brutality of the extremes. Freedom of speech and individualism has often been cited as a defence by the social-media oligarchy to protect its unaccountable algorithms; however, all freedoms must be contextualized with judicious responsibility. At the height of individualism is the undoing of individualism, as algorithms sap away the real underlying power individuals have over their opinions and judgement, while they pay lip service to the letter of this freedom.

In fact, large newspapers in a way ran a daily school of democracy—the spirit of mutual accommodation, diversity of views, acceptance of the 'different' and the middle path. Now, in the new world, each has its own headline and reads and knows things that algorithms, which reduce individuals to a simplistic logical construct, choose for them. You either love what you see or hate it, both eliciting reactions that are eagerly noted by the servers. The 'republic of me'—shorn of the collective moderation of earlier times—may finally end up destroying the republic.

> Large newspapers in a way ran a daily school of democracy—
> the spirit of mutual accommodation, diversity of views,
> acceptance of the 'different' and the middle path.

With the multilateral onslaught from search, specialist-content portals, online native-news portals and network-mediated propagation of news, marketers and brands have been switching out their investments en masse along with the associated flows of attention and engagement out of newspapers.

Today, some of the best among these newspapers have managed to stay around by focusing on quality, all manners of diversification and by finding ways to generate online subscription revenues. Their cost structures are now a lot sharper and more agile. In the fog of the hugely fragmented online news space, the preponderance of fake news and partisan perspectives, there is a rebound among the more considered to go back to the anchorship that curated news by respected editors provided. Also, the huge number of parallel narratives for people to discern the truth from has created a paradox where too much choice is actually less choice, more confusion. High quality, trustworthy, professional news brands in such a context have an opportunity to be a beacon of clarity.

The magic today is clearly no more the same, but there is a new respect for professionally mediated, well-researched and fact-checked news and perspectives among some quarters. That's the light at the end of the tunnel for newspapers. The world clearly still needs them, maybe a lot less in their print incarnations.

Newspapers that once held the anchor role in brand building can still be an important trust-builder for many target segments. They can rub off their still considerable credibility on the brand message and provide it with a measure of stature and validation. From being the all-purpose vehicle for brands, newspapers have taken on more specialized roles in the marketing plan for specific audiences. People approach newspapers with a cognitive mindset. Unlike TV and radio, newspaper ads also continue to offer reference value (you can keep the ad and refer to it later), and newspaper ads in conjunction with editorial coverage can help cement trust better than most other mediums.

> Newspapers that once held the anchor role in brand building can still be an important trust-builder for many target segments.

Although online news continues to thrive, it remains deeply underappreciated as a marketing vehicle. Impression to impression, it finds it difficult to compete with social media or the long-tail media inventory in terms of cost efficiency. And a clear currency to capture its contextual power and content rub-off has been missing as newspaper sales departments frequently seem to lack the will to create and popularize their own play in the new ecosystem.

Within online news, there are two distinct segments: online incarnations of printed newspapers and 'native' news portals or ones that do not have print versions (in most cases, never had). Some examples in India would be The Print, Scroll.in, The Quint, OpIndia, Firstpost, Wire, The Ken, etc. Even though the native news portals in general seem to better understand the art of online engagement and share-worthiness, their ability to monetize it has still been fairly limited. Few have been able to attain a measure of mainstream commercial credibility that allows them to command a sufficiently premium pricing in terms of advertising revenues. The higher quality ones have, of course, been trying to move to a largely subscription-based model.

If newspapers as a concept have to remain around in twenty years, they must learn to manage the ecosystem of all three—readership, currency (among the young adults especially) and revenues—to their favour.

The Radio Drive

Radio was a precursor to television, yet as a medium it works very differently. Much like newspaper, radio is a hot medium. You listen to radio and your brain has to work to conceive the image that it only provides clues to. That brings a certain richness to the medium if you put people and their imagination at the centre. However, television being a cold medium, fills one's senses with fast moving audio-visual stimuli that leaves very little brain space or need for people to imagine. The story on the TV screen keeps our senses overwhelmed, even if in a shallow way. It also expands our field of experiences, unlike in the radio world, where the image people would ascribe to a voice or a sound would be limited by their own narrow field of experiences. Television breaks those bounds and expands people's experiential horizon.

As the preference for low-brain-effort TV news and drama grew, radio took on a more and more niche role in people's lives. Due to the low cost of setting up radio stations, radio could be hyperlocal. Radio could become the background of our lives at home or at work, or radio could safely share our mindspace while driving, making it fun and sometimes informative. Once in a blue moon, radio could let us wander into the depths of our mind, making us happy or sad, in the later hours of nights or afternoons, just as our grandfathers would have enjoyed it in the days of yore.

Drive time became the crown jewel of radio inventory for marketers, especially in countries where cars were a primary mode of office transport. Radio DJs often became bigger brands than stations, and brands sought to benefit from their rub-off. Reading into the shifting sands of time, radio has diversified today into a hyperlocal, on-ground, on-the-move consumer activation machine.

> Radio has diversified today into a hyperlocal, on-the-ground, on-the-move consumer activation machine.

However, traditional radio is now increasingly threatened by pure-play digital-radio channels and has expanded, even if apprehensively, into online versions of themselves. The switch from analogue to digital radio is by and large constrained only by habit and car-audio technology. A higher degree of fragmentation is expected in digital radio eventually due to its low cost of entry. The success of Spotify has rapidly built a new market for streaming audio, thus setting the backdrop for digital radio to scale up. Existing brand equities of stations will be increasingly competing with the hyper relevance and sharper personality that online radio can bring.

For marketers, radio remains an option with very low entry costs, and hence allows for a much larger gamut of companies to advertise here than, say, television. It allows for a certain moment-based targeting that is a lot trickier to schedule in newspapers. While it may lack the slice-of-life messaging of television, its low cost also allows for higher frequencies to be delivered, and hence works as a useful reminder medium.

Radio, as mentioned before, tends to have a unique clout during drive times, only competing with outdoor media in these moments. Working people, the typical everyday drivers, are often the chief wage earners in households holding important roles in brand choices. In morning-drive moments, most radio listeners are alone in their cars, and they are in an optimistic yet control mode looking to process decisions that will help them organize and enhance their lives. The morning mind is also fresh and receptive to cognitive messages. In the evening, when people are driving back, they are tired, but many are thinking about their families and friends, happy and relaxed, allowing certain messages to graft themselves pretty well to this mood and moment. Radio, due to its strong share of driving moments so far, is less affected by digital media in many countries, although a disruption may not be too far away.

The Cinema Spectacle

Cinema is generally a medium for the young and the young at heart, though the omnipresent multiplexes theoretically allow a multiplicity of segments. Cinema faces a threat from video-on-demand and OTT players (a threat that exacerbated due to pandemic lockdowns); however, its larger-than-life format and highly immersive, spectacular ambience gives it, exposure to exposure, a relative power that few mediums can replicate. In order for it to compete, there has been an emphasis on deepening its differentiated experience, both in terms of technology as well as content. Large-scale blockbusters with big stars, tons of CGI (Computer Generated Imagery) to be best enjoyed on the big screen, and larger-than-life stories are uniquely placed to be enjoyed in all its spectacle on a big screen. It's also become an important part of going-out regimes culturally, offering a somewhat intense shared experience to gather around. Also, highly innovative new formats such as 4D, 6D, IMAX, etc., have turned cinema viewing into highly enhanced experiences, for which people are willing to pay a premium. In many countries, such formats have become a big portion of the cinema inventory.

> (Cinema's) larger-than-life format, and highly immersive, spectacular ambience gives it a relative power that few mediums can replicate.

However, marketers have so far been extremely slow in adapting to new formats, as they typically tend to be expensive to customize content for. The new cinema industry, however, is expected to hold its own in the digital world as it once again has managed to occupy a unique moment and niche in people's lives in the digital age.

The Omnipotent Outdoors

The last important medium that is set to thrive despite small-screen digital platforms is out-of-home. Out-of-home is not a medium in the traditional sense as it is an aggregation of highly varied contexts and formats in the out-of-home setting. It's the third space in our lives after home and work space (or education space depending upon one's life stage).

The medium has undergone a dramatic transformation in the last two decades by incorporating digital screens, turning what used to be a 'space' buy into a 'time and space' buy for marketers. Time-buy and the digitization of screens allows out-of-home screen networks to be treated in a manner akin to television networks (and within a large out-of-home network, different channels can be created to cater to different types of audiences and moments).

Given that outdoor formats typically work in the background of people's day-to-day lives, a lot of its effect is soft and subconscious, creating over time a sense of familiarity with the brand. Visible and trendy outdoor messages have a good probability to trigger conversations and give brands a sense of currency and buzz. Intriguing brand messages have the power to generate massive curiosity through search queries. The breadth of outdoor allows it a range of roles in the customer journey and communication. The bigger formats due to their larger-than-life status in the cityscape or on highways help evoke stature for the brands. Its moment-aware nature also allows for micro-content to be hyper-targeted via out-of-home, thus raising the effectiveness of investments. Last-mile outdoor formats can help people navigate to stores, bringing powerful proximity and ability to convert.

> The bigger (outdoor) formats due to their larger-than-life status
> in the cityscape or on highways
> help evoke stature for the brands.

Out-of-home is also the most local of all mediums, and this allows for a very high level of geographical localization in the messaging. Every outdoor site sits in the midst of a mini-culture that can often be quite specific in terms of audience profile, occasion and mood. In that sense, outdoor is the perfect medium to tap moments allowing customization by all three—time, place and activity.

The true magic of outdoor, however, lies in its potential to marry the physical and the digital world with exciting new-age participatory experiences. With a mobile phone in every pocket, it's possible to design real-time interactive experiences between the mobile screen and the outdoor screens. (Some have even gone to the extent of calling mobile an out-of-home medium—apps like Waze and Google Maps simulate that bridge even more closely.) Out-of-home screens can be further augmented with new-age technology such as augmented reality, virtual reality, facial recognition, etc. These could, in turn, be married to instore tracking to complete the loop in the purchase funnel. This is one of the most exciting areas in the out-of-home industry and the medium is uniquely placed to build on this opportunity.

Looking at the spectrum of roles that out-of-home can play, it can fulfil versatile communication tasks across the purchase funnel. To that extent, outdoor is a medium that pervades both the digital and the physical experiences; it can claim a certain superiority over digital media.

Having said that, outdoor also happens to be probably the most fragmented medium around the world in terms of ownership. Also, traditional sales pitches and buying conversations in outdoor have always been around locations, sizes and formats, and less around their strategic role in building businesses. It's important that this role be rediscovered. The outdoor story needs to be retold in the language of journey and roles; networks and experiences; moments and micro-cultures; curiosities, conversations and conversions. The case for outdoor needs to focus on what it does to people's minds rather than what it looks like next to a gas station.

The Dynamic Digital

Among the digital platforms, the role-plays are getting increasingly clear. For mass marketers, Google Search is the first port of call once people are intrigued by or get interested in a brand (which is typically triggered elsewhere). But while

Google has an important role in the upper part of the funnel where it's sought for research and information, Facebook and YouTube (along with several much smaller premium publishers) continue to have a unique relevance mid-funnel. At the bottom of the funnel, e-commerce players such as Amazon battle it out with Google Search, millions of faceless long-tail websites and a whole host of other e-commerce sites. Amazon, with vast amounts of data on people's purchase behaviours, is placed in a unique position to offer a data architecture that works backwards from the actual purchase. While Google owns the intent graph and Facebook owns the social graph, Amazon owns the purchase graph (along with other e-commerce marketplaces), although its full potential for mainstream marketers is yet to be realized.

* * *

Media, Roles and the Funnel

Among the traditional media, television and newspapers dominate the upper part of the funnel, working as rapid reach and awareness builders. Mid-funnel, newspapers can build strong credibility, while television and cinema continue to have a strong role in building desire by bringing impactful brand-communication experiences. Radio, with its familiarity and reminder functions, can play a strong role in both the upper funnel and lower parts of the funnel. Out-of-home, much like digital media, has the potential to work across the bottlenecks depending upon the format.

Not all exposure is the same. A display banner exposure on a mobile screen while having your dinner can't be said to have the same impact as a 1960s ad on a spectacular cinema screen in a dark hall. Nor can a scrollable mid-feed ad have the same impact as a linear TV ad during your favourite programme on a 56-inch screen.

Exposure to exposure, different mediums can be compared on the two key dimensions of attention and immersion as surrogates for their relative impact when taken as a whole (of course, this may vary moment to moment and individual to individual). In the high-immersion, high-attention zone lies cinema. Spectacular billboards and large digital screens sit in the high-immersion but low- or medium-attention zone, due to the backdrop nature of the medium. In the low-attention, low-immersion zone lie the small outdoor formats as well as radio. Social media and e-commerce sites sit in the mid-attention, low-immersion zone, YouTube scores slightly higher on attention and immersion due to its typical horizontal-screen consumption (in certain markets, already about half of the YouTube views come from the TV screen coming back full circle). Search marketing would belong to the high-attention, low-immersion zone. The bulk of television advertising and lifestyle magazines occupy the mid-attention, mid-immersion zone, while newspapers due to the typically active mental state of reading occupies the high attention, mid-immersion zone.

HIGH ATTENTION		
Search marketing YouTube & other horizontal screen platforms etc.	Newspapers	Cinema VR content On-ground activations
Social media e-commerce sites	Television Magazines	Spectacular billboards Large digital screens
Small outdoor formats Radio Physical point-of-sales	Ambient screens & light boxes	HIGH IMMERSION

TYPICAL RELATIVE IMPACT BY MEDIA: A HYPOTHETICAL MODEL
(EXPOSURE-TO-EXPOSURE)

Of course, digital platforms have multiple formats, each of them with their own relative roles and relative power but, by and large, the above makes logical sense. (Many studies have been done to find an apples-to-apples comparison of exposures across different media; however, most of such studies either make assumptions that are either too narrow to be generalized, or are 'ad sales studies' with a plethora of not-too-subtle, systematic errors willingly made by passionate sales departments.)

The destiny of each of these mediums eventually depends upon how well they carve out their share of moments in people's evolving lifestyles. In light of their unique strengths, they must stake a claim to their due roles in the customer journey, aligning with it their product development, collaborations, sales strategy and the measurement ecosystem.

The success of marketers in leveraging the new media spectrum to its best potential depends on understanding their prospects and bottlenecks, choosing and deploying the right media in the right roles, and tracking a simple and actionable set of metrics that matter.

SUMMARY:

A. We started the chapter with a discussion on how we live our lives through media today, beyond using it merely for information and entertainment.

B. Then, we delved into different media that exist today one by one to consider how each has been evolving in terms of technology and hence its place in culture and lifestyle. We then looked into how its marketing role has also changed to mirror that.

C. We closed the chapter with how the different roles that different media play come together around the DIET loop. We also discussed the relative effectiveness of exposures in different media on a two-dimensional grid of attention and immersion.

Having discussed both the creative messaging and the nuances of the different media touchpoints, let's look into the metrics that keep marketing focused and honest. With the whole ecosystem under ferment, clearly there have been some fundamental changes in the measurement approach too, which will be the crux of the next chapter.

9

The New Measurement

'In god we trust. Everyone else bring data.'

—W. Edwards Deming

The Grand New Auction of Intent

The origin story of Google is that of a company that invented an ingenious search algorithm and offered it via a brutally simple interface; however, much less appreciated is the fact that the real secret behind Google's rapid financial success was the AdWords tool. AdWords transformed the way online advertising would be bought and sold forever. In the process, it augured a way to price, place and optimize marketing budgets that was truly transformational.

For one, it was a fully automated process. For generations, media sales had always been a very high-touch process conducted over long lunches and much-fussed-over relationships. Even the first wave of digital-media players had followed that model. Scale had been the name of the game as large media agencies negotiated massive annual deals with deep discounts, building huge entry barriers. Annual upfronts, where a big share of the annual deals was made, became the most important milestones in media trading, allowing traditional media owners to lock in a good part of their targets early on.

AdWords threw the entire model into a bin. Instead of glamorous sales people and sleek agency deal-makers, all it needed was a bunch of outsourced analysts sitting at their desks and optimizing their investments. Scale made little difference as the whole process was auction-based, as what mattered was how many were bidding for a keyword and what price they were willing to pay against each other. A housewife who had recently become an insurance agent could technically use her credit cards to bid a few dollars against the largest insurance giants with hundreds of millions in investments and be able to get the same price for a potential lead (a better price if her landing page was lighter and more relevant).

In the world of business, large players have always used their scale to be able to snuff out smaller competitors; however, in the world of Google, entry barriers had suddenly been dropped several notches and a level playing field had been created, at least in terms of media access to potential customers.

But this was not all. AdWords brought a series of new thinking to the industry. Google search marketing didn't charge money for mere exposure to the text ads. It only charged money if the customer actually clicked on the ad. Its pitch to marketers was not based on the traditional spray and pray. A proactive intent had been expressed by a real person, and he had shown a clear behavioural interest in the ad by clicking on it. It was something that was rarely heard of before in the world of traditional media.

One of the other important factors in pricing was Google quality scores. Google quality scores depended on factors such as how well the brand landing page fitted the needs of the user, once he or she clicked on the ad, and also how relevant the ad was to the search term targeted, etc. So, it helped improve user experience and also discouraged blind mass-targeting. You could track the performance of the media investment and brand messages in real time through a transparent dashboard accessible from anywhere. You could also upload your actual conversion from the leads generated to optimize the cost per conversion and not just cost per lead or cost per click. It had all been the stuff of marketing utopia for a hundred years.

The explosive popularity of AdWords forever changed the landscape of media and marketing measurement. In industry after industry, namely airlines, hospitality, technology and e-commerce to begin with, new-age players building on the power of AdWords, started taking on the big incumbents. A whole generation of intermediaries rose up to tap its power to suck margins from traditional incumbents while bringing a new level of choice and access to customers. AdWords was truly the first major milestone in the marketing revolution that was to come.

Digital Trail and Broken Research

In the early 2000s, marketing research had been an eighty-year-old discipline. Over the decades, an elaborate ecosystem of measurement had been built consisting of brand and advertising tracks, usage and attitude studies, market-opportunity mapping, copy and concept tests, segmentation and positioning studies, etc. This was further augmented by qualitative research such as focus groups and in-depth interviews. They all fitted snugly before the digital age began. But a lot of this traditional research methodology was too little and too late for the speed of the digital age. The research not only suffered often from the limited perspective of the researcher when it came to designing the instrument, but also when it came to being able to anticipate and infer the unknown unknowns. In qualitative research, in fact, the researcher himself or herself was the research instrument.

A lot of traditional research methodology was too little and too late for the speed of the digital age.

However, as people started living more and more of their lives online, they left elaborate digital footprints, and these behavioural footprints (for example, the percentage of people who clicked on an ad could reflect the relevance or creativity of the ad) offered mines of insight into people's lives as well as how they perceived the brands. These insights were in real time, were based on actual behaviours of often millions of people and could provide a lot of depth, even if the data was sometimes highly unstructured, especially in the social media space. On the flip side, this new data didn't allow itself to be weighted back to the universe in order to ensure statistical representation; it had its own set of systematic biases—for instance, skewed towards heavy Internet users. The data suffered from gaps in the technology deployed (for instance, native mobile apps couldn't be tracked via cookies, and the IP address approach to identification of individuals had its limitations). New-age marketers particularly loved the speed, however.

Marketing companies, as they began to invest in accessing and inferring digital data, started making trade-offs with traditional research. Today, given the high level of penetration digital has attained in many target segments, it is possible to substitute, within limitations, the traditional insights and tracking techniques with approaches native to digital. However, given that the digital world isn't exactly analogous to the offline world, it also has thrown up its own native behaviours that could be important surrogates to tracking brand-effectiveness (for example, percentage of positive sentiments on social conversations).

The New Chain of Impact

In the old world, when a brand invested in media, they expected that ad tracking would be able to tell them how much the awareness metrics or the image attributes had moved and hence, how the purchase intent was affected. Between receiving the brand message (captured by opportunity-to-see research from the likes of Nielsen and Kantar) and real sales data (that came from the brand's internal sales figures or from sample-based retail audits, there was often a large information gap. This gap could only be filled to some extent with sample-based recall tracking, which told whether the opportunity to see converted into better recall of the brand and its competitive advantage, which may have impacted sales and shares one way or another.

Now, in the new world, when people see something in traditional or digital media, and are affected by it, some of them would go to Google and search to seek more information on it. Many may also go to social media and have conversations about it with their network. If brand messaging involved something new or intriguing or engaging, it would drive up the search volume for the related brand and its keywords (see diagram). It would also drive up the conversation volume and, hopefully, positive sentiments about the brand. These offered two very important leading indicators of purchase intent. Share of spends drove the share of curiosity (in search) and the share of conversations (as gleaned from blogs, discussion groups and public social profiles), and these two in turn drove up share of market.

CHAIN OF IMPACT

In high-involvement categories, where it was important to hand-hold people through information and influence in order for them to convert, SOQ (share of curiosity represented by share of branded search volumes in the category that a brand has) and SOC (share of conversations in social media, associated with a brand) have become important new markers. It was now possible to plan inventories or geographical focus in some categories using the volume and footprint of search as a surrogate. Looking at what people searched for, it was also possible to understand the zeitgeist in the category, consumer priorities, top associations with each brand and the day and time when the purchase decision was being processed most intensely.

Today, Google insights with millions of data points has become a powerful leading indicator. This also means that campaigns now need to be planned to intrigue people enough for them to want to search for them, thus engaging them with the brand choices. Campaigns also need to incite conversations, be the talk of the town as, not surprisingly, in most cases, that leads to people moving further down the funnel. Just as Google search trends indicate curiosity to know more, search queries on YouTube related to category or target relevant topics can offer useful indications of people's lifestyle and entertainment interests (sometimes people even search on YouTube for information, demonstrations or hacks), which can be useful for creative leaders looking to understand trends and preferences. Search patterns on e-commerce sites, such as Amazon, become a surrogate for purchase intent and can hide important cues to shifting consumer preferences.

Digital platforms also introduced pre- and post-techniques to measure ad and brand tracking parameters (such as image attributes) that a click could not measure—which was mostly analogous to how the old world functioned. Most of these parameters lived in the upper- and mid-funnel areas and were important for traditional mass marketers. It was a clever move, as now one could buy awareness, for instance, on Facebook (and not just views or reach). This pricing agility clearly helped Facebook open the next lock on media-investment inflow.

The speed of digital also changed advertising testing to a large extent. Unlike the ad testing of yesteryears, when it took weeks to test multiple versions with an offline sample of consumers (to assess which one should be launched), online panels could react at a much shorter notice. A/B testing (where you ran two copies to see which one got better clicks, for example), allowed for the copy or the concepts to be tested with real people in real environments and with much larger samples. In fact, you no longer needed to choose the copy, you could just throw a pool of options out there, and change budget allocations based on which copy seemed to be working better, and the best creative would survive in a self-select process.

The Fly on the Social Wall

The data that truly opened a powerful, real-time window into people's lives was social media conversations data. Massive crawlers scanned the part of the social landscape that was public to analyse billions of texts, images and videos to map what was trending in a given moment and what was not. You could map different emotions to those texts knowing how often these emotions were being expressed in relation to the brand. Sophisticated NLP (Natural Language Processing) and machine learning could be deployed to glean patterns that gave a vivid glimpse into what, when and where society was thinking, talking and sharing, in turn cueing what mattered and why.

This was in many ways more powerful than traditional qualitative research techniques, even if statistically less rigorous (which it made up for by its speed and vast number of data points). What's more, the data had some quantitative validity and could serve as a powerful directional surrogate to the real world. Traditional research had always made a trade-off between the rigour of quantitative research and the depth of qualitative research. One told us about what and how many, the other told us why. In social data, the two domains came together as one. And all this could be done at a lower cost and higher speed than usual. Social data also mapped stories and influencers at a very granular level, an aspect that usual market research had rarely focused on. Brands had not been seen as networks then.

Social data was not free of limitations per se. For one, it was able to scan only a limited part of all the conversations going on there. Private chats couldn't be accessed, nor could private profiles, and hence, even though the number of data points was huge, it was no census. Also, social data couldn't answer every question one may have had. It was a free-flowing unstructured data set that told its own story and gave its own answers unbeholden to any analyst's chain of logical thinking. Quite often, it told us a lot, yet it left a lot else unanswered. Traditional researchers hated the lack of control over the instrument, even if they admired the speed, scale, behavioural patterns and cost efficiency it brought.

Eventually, the truth, as always, sat in the middle. Smart marketers today must pick and choose from both traditional market research and social data depending upon what they are trying to measure and what the decision-making context was. If one were looking for some early feedback on a brand launch, social data would be perfect for that. If one were looking to track broad sentiments with relation to the brand across geographies and did not need exact percentages pegged to each image attribute deemed crucial for the brand, social data would be great. If you were looking at which influences were operative in your category, or which trends were taking over, social data would be just right. However, if one were trying to map the percentage of people in the universe who believed that the 'brand is for people like me' then the best that social data could give was directional surrogates.

Given the centrality of digital metrics for marketers, let us spend some time discussing its many limitations.

* * *

More than Meets the Eye

While AdWords with all its strengths works beautifully for measuring lower funnel impact, it is a very poor substitute for ad tracking when it comes to upper- and mid-funnel marketing effectiveness. As far as Google is concerned, it doesn't know what is happening off the Google network so, if a person clicked on a text ad on Google (or YouTube or its ad network) and converted, Google would assume that the conversion happened because of Google. In fact, the Google attribution that sought to improve this somewhat also allocated the attribution of conversion to only the touchpoints that its walled garden had access to, which was a very small set among all the touchpoints that customers would typically interact with.

This was clearly an incomplete picture. The reality is that a lot of people land on Google search after they hear or see or read about things elsewhere. The only problem is that this elsewhere—often the traditional media—is not measured in as good a way as Google measures its own footprint. Sometimes they are measured but cannot be integrated into Google's attribution system. This became the single biggest problem with justifying traditional media investments for many advertisers, against the digital onslaught. All you needed was Google, because all you knew was what Google measured (and later, independently, Facebook).

A preference for smarter measurement systems spawned by digital players became a preference for digital players at a huge detriment to the traditional players. And few traditional players had the vision to offer their own counter-narrative that went even halfway on this new path. They could have done much better than they did. In many countries, before digital media had won the battle for audiences and revenues, old media players had already abandoned the battle of ideas—half in denial, half in defeatism. The siege was a spectacular success.

Another important mistake that people often made while assessing Google return on investment (ROI) numbers can be encapsulated in the 'brand search' issue. When people searched using broad category keywords, it was assumed that people didn't yet know what brand they wanted, but when people searched for a specific brand term, there was a high chance that people already had the brand in their mind and may, in fact, a lot of the time just be looking for the website URL, which would usually figure among the top search results. However, Google ads would appear even above the top organic links, leading people to click on the ad rather than the organic link, and brands would have to pay for a customer that in many cases was already theirs to start with.

These brand keywords had typically the maximum ROI on AdWords for a brand and Google, by controlling the gateway and with the right to try to swing the user towards a competitor ad, made huge monies on this. It can be debated whether the money invested in brand keywords was worth as much as it seemed because, in many cases, people looking for a brand specifically would still skip (even if there was a competitor ad in between) and click on the organic link. If, say, two in ten could be dissuaded by Google and its competing brand ad, in truth, the ROI of branded, keyword investments was one-fifth of what was mistakenly believed. This is an approach that later the big e-commerce platforms with their own search function would also use to make their most profitable advertising sales dollars. (To be fair, Google didn't invent these sales practices; and clearly was not the only one who practised this; point-of-sales ad sellers in supermarkets before that would sometimes show research attributing the entire sales to itself as well.)

The pedigree of digital media numbers has always been somewhat doubtful. The first metric touted in the dot-com bubble was 'hits'. Hits on a website referred to how many files got downloaded from all the webpages of a website (a webpage can be seen as a collection of image, video or text, etc., files organized in a particular way). A page could be made of twenty files or a page could be made of a hundred files depending upon how you organized the page and how you split the files. In fact, you could have a million invisible pixels, each of them with the status of a file that could be counted as a million hits (a method that later many used to try to game Google's organic-search algorithm by embedding these pixels in the invisible metadata).

Hits was the wonder currency of the dot-com era. Mind-boggling valuations got pegged to the number of hits that a website could get. However, the bursting of the dot-com bubble put paid to that metric, and was soon replaced by views, which was a more robust metric. Yet there was many a slip between the cup and the lip in defining what a view could actually mean. And while the standards still tend to vary, IAB (Interactive Advertising Bureau) has tried to define it in an effort to develop some minimum common standards. Views today remain one of the most powerful currencies of digital media trading. The largest platforms claim billions of views a day, and often use it to emphasize their superiority over television, for instance. However, too often it is not an apples-to-apples comparison and once again, Silicon Valley players with all the newest tailwinds behind them and a good dose of salesmanship have managed to successfully steal the perception game.

For instance, many of the percentages used in digital sales pitches have historically been shown on the base of online users, which, in the era when smartphone penetration was low, helped digital media look a lot better in front of mass marketers than their actual status. As before, digital cable and satellite salespeople used this trick often.

Imagine a sixty-minute television programme that gets a rating (also called TRPs—television rating points) of 10 in a population that is the size of 200 million. Put simply, what it means is that there were 20 million people on an average watching the programme in each minute. This also means that 1.2 billion viewer minutes were logged in. And that is at the level of a minute. An online video view is defined by IAB as at least 50 per cent of the ad must be in view for 2 seconds or more. The time is 1 second for a display ad.[1]

In 2019, YouTube claimed that every day, people watched one billion hours of videos on YouTube and it had 2 billion monthly active users worldwide. When it comes to television, at least 14 billion[2] households had television. At an average of, say, three to four viewers per household (often viewed as a family), television clearly had somewhere around 5 billion of what one could call monthly active users—almost 2.5 times that of YouTube even today. Television viewing hours have tended to be 2.5–3.5 hours[3] a day across countries despite the Internet. Hence, if we take even 80 per cent of people logging in every day (television viewing tends to be a habit-led ritual), then we are talking about 12 billion hours of video watched on television every day against one billion hours watched on YouTube.

Now consider the fact that unlike TV, more than 60 per cent of the people watch online videos with the sound muted.[4] And, in the context of advertising, also consider that television ad breaks ensure that your entire ad is played and seen (typically around 15 per cent of the audience stop watching in the ad breaks),[8] whereas for online videos 50–60 per cent of the people drop out by the mid-point of the video on YouTube[6] and yet are counted as views and charged for.

There is little doubt that YouTube revolutionized online videos, and that YouTube and other OTT players are the future in many ways. However, the good old TV continues to be strong, even if not at the peak of its power.

To be fair, the traditional media measurement techniques were by no means perfect. Radio has often been measured on recall of whether one listened in to each of the fifteen-minute segments of a day—not particularly nuanced. Newspaper planning often ignored the percentage of newspaper read and assumed that the figures of 'read or looked at the newspaper yesterday' could apply to every placement, where the truth was people rarely read every page and hence, had the opportunity to see ads on every page (newspaper pricing, of course, charged a premium for the higher impact of say, page 3, versus pages further inside, but readership numbers per se used in most countries remained the same whatever be the page.

Television, typically measured with higher robustness, could still have reliability issues for small programmes and channels due to sample insufficiency issues. Also, if one were busy talking to someone during an ad break and not paying attention to the ads, the measurement techniques would be hard-pressed to account for that—well, the research designers, to their credit, did have the peoplemeter boxes (along with a special remote, they measured viewership) in people's homes flash these surprise pings asking people to confirm if they were still in the room. Outdoor measurement, in most cases, forgot to factor in the viewability of the billboard assuming the total traffic as their audience.

The Gardens of Walled Currency

Things changed on the syndicated research side as well. Companies like Nielsen, with a monopoly in many markets, refused to adapt to the changing times. The money from TV was too good and as the powerful arbitrators of media currency and ruled by the grand old bureaucrats of market research—somewhat fossilized like regulators of a government that is in rapid decay and denial—their measurement system forever kept trying to play catch up. They kept expecting digital to play by the rules of rigour and the systems of comfort that the industry had got used to.

The mountain, as it were, never came to Mohammad. Giant digital platforms—each a somewhat unique ecosystem in itself—instead perpetuated their own metrics measured by their own opaque servers as per their own methods and algorithms according to what suited their own specific narratives. This was a big blow to the time-honoured convention of neutral, industry-approved, third-party measurement. The player was the referee now and the referee, the player.

Obviously, a lot of what was measured was not right, even though, as a broad principle, a lot of it made sense. Massive overclaims of views were found in one of these cases.[7] IAB and the WFA (World Federation of Advertisers) along with other industry bodies have sought to fix many of these issues, but with limited success. The digital platforms tend to have their own game and make their own rules in many ways.

In the world of TV, if you placed an ad on a programme on a given day, you could sit in front of the TV screen and see your ad being played. In the world of the Internet, where each had their own screen, it is hard to tell when and where the ad appeared and to how many, unless you took the platform's word for it. And a claimed exposure was often not as real as many marketers believed.

However, a popular trope and a nasty trap of our times was and is that we intuitively associate sophisticated technology with robustness, transparency and accountability. In truth, a claimed exposure could have been a banner below the scroll which no one scrolled down to or it could have been a bot pretending to be a human (30 per cent of all views are often believed to be from bots). It could have been a pixel that is invisible except to the server, or it could have been a 0.2-second flash of a banner on a page with seven other banners. The great viewability crisis took the world of digital advertising by storm—marketers realizing that a large number of their digital ads were never really 'exposed'; it wasn't just the long-tail programmatic players who were complicit in it, but even the giant platforms were found wanting, who, in turn, scrambled to address the issue—somewhat—only in the aftermath of the big hue and cry.

The Creepy Frequency

The other big issue with walled digital platforms is the crisis of reach. In the pre-digital era, even though cross-media reach measurement for a given plan was still a tricky subject only to be accessed by probabilistic models of overlap, within a media—especially within television, newspaper and radio—unique reach could be measured with decent statistical fidelity across different programmes and channels. In fact, sophisticated distribution models, such as BBD (Beta Binomial Distribution), were deployed to model reach by optimization technology to approximate the best possible reach obtainable for a given budget.

In digital media, however, although the basic currency was behavioural (an improvement) and 'almost' census-based (also an improvement), there was no similarly reliable way to know unique reach across YouTube and Facebook, for instance. Third-party players such as Nielsen and ComScore got into the act, approaching it from the sample-survey perspective. Audience measurement studies have often discovered that digital campaigns that do not track unique reach tend to deliver an extremely high average frequency, thus resulting in extremely high wastage. Basically, it meant that without any unique reach measurement, even if a cookie-based frequency cap was assigned within a specific platform, brands would be reaching many of the same people, many more times with the same message since it was difficult to know whether it was the same person.

Much of the digital buying was based on optimization algorithms that sought to minimize cost per thousand exposures or increase click-through rates and so on. In the vast lot of inventory pools, algorithms and their runners were programmed to look for pieces of inventory that provided the best propensity to view or click with the lowest cost. For brands that focused on exposures in order to drive awareness or desire, in the absence of reach as a constraint, the optimization just zeroed in on a small but highly efficient lot, and kept spending more and more money on that group. An analogous situation in TV would be that, if a specific programme has very low cost per exposure for a given audience, the brand starts investing the bulk of its money into the programme, even if the cumulative reach of that programme and hence, the unique people that the brand ever reached, is only, say, 24 per cent of the target audience.

P&G was one of the advertisers that acknowledged this issue publicly[8] but many mass marketers suffered tremendous wastage on this account apart from annoying customers so much more. It is unbelievable that the giant platforms weren't cognizant of this; however, the power to optimize had been passed on to an automated console and so the blame lay on the marketers and their agencies. Third-party reach validation, priced by cost per million views, are perceived to be rather expensive by many, usually to be deployed at scale.

The Crisis of Context

Yet another fundamental limitation of digital inventory, the bulk of which tends to be user-generated content, was contextual quality. While traditional media players put up edited content and hence took accountability for the quality and context of the content, digital media players saw themselves not as media companies but more as audience aggregation technologies (at least in situations like these), and hence to begin with, took little accountability for content control. In any case, with hundreds of millions of content pieces being uploaded each day, it was impossible to censure content in a traditional sense.

As a result, it was not uncommon for brands to end up with their ads being shown on sites run by deceptive players of all kinds, along with all sorts of undesirable content. Once again, third-party players kicked into action qualifying ad-ready inventory on a huge number of criteria, some for general control, and some that a specific category or brand may care specifically about.

Given the fragmented data sources involved in measuring marketing in the digital age, it has the ability to ironically create more confusion than clarity. So, let us spend some time discussing how a focused measurement model could be conceived with the marketing objectives at the centre.

* * *

The Single Source of Truth

When it comes to campaign-effectiveness measurement, given that there are so many more media choices today, and given that the largest digital-media platforms are all walled gardens with their own roles in people's lives and their own currency, campaign measurement has become that much more complicated. For a marketing leader who must balance the macro with the micro, the hard with the soft, and the strategy with the operations all the time, keeping track of so many metrics from so many players—each with their own version of truth—and yet being able to consistently connect it to his final, key performance indicators can be highly confusing. So, customized dashboards have emerged to collate together what could be used as the single source of truth.

Probably the best way to organize data in such a marketing-effectiveness dashboard so that it has a single-minded focus on what truly matters, is to build it around the customer journey and how people are being processed through this journey. So, a string of metrics must be shortlisted for each step of the DIET loop that one can optimize for, see where the bottlenecks are, and which bottleneck offers the most opportunity for value if focused on.

The right metrics for the discovery stage must consist of total exposures, cost per thousand exposures, unique reach and share of curiosity (see diagram). In TV, GRPs (Gross Rating Points) become a measure of gross exposures, different from 'exposure' being calculated as the total number of exposures divided by the total population and multiplied by 100. CPRP—Cost Per Rating Point—on the other hand is analogous to cost per thousand. Online exposures must be filtered by the IAB viewability criteria.

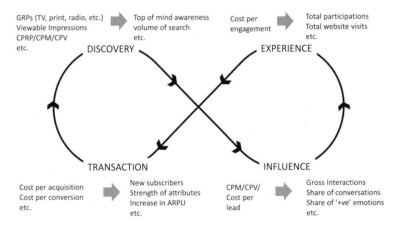

DIET LOOP AND THE MEASUREMENT: A TELCO EXAMPLE

Influence can be measured by the share of conversations in the category as well as the percentage of people with positive sentiments towards the brand and gross interactions. Experience can be measured by total participations and, where e-commerce is involved, one may want to look at total and unique website visits, and cost per engagement. This is also the step where one may want to measure changes to specific image attributes.

Last but not least, the transaction stage may be measured by the number of new customer acquisitions or incremental sales metrics. Of course, the ladder of metrics aligned to the journey needs to be customized to the specific category and brand context.

The Holy Grail of Attribution

One of the time-worn challenges of marketing has been attribution. Of all the different investments a brand makes in marketing inputs, knowledge about which one deserves how much credit for the final outcome, which could, in turn, tell what combination of inputs maximizes the return on investment, is very useful for marketers. In the beginning, ambitious marketing departments with a scientific bent of mind or researchers at universities and industry bodies tried to model experiments with control cells and experiment cells, so that the marginal impact of a marketing input could be calculated. However, while these experiments, at their granular level, were rigorous in their own right, the real world of marketing was often too subjective and high context to lend itself to any decent degree of scalability from these results.

The second wave of researchers applied multiple regression to model the market mix, where sales or brand or ad-tracking outcome would be the dependent variable, and there would be a whole host of independent variables across the 4 Ps (Product, Price, Place, Promotion) and other macro variables that may apply. While at a broad level, many of these models offered some useful directional learnings, a marketer's ability to apply it at a micro level when making specific decisions remained limited for reasons of practicality, relentless change in the competitive dynamics, the fact that creativity worked in ways mathematics could never truly quantify and several other subjective factors.

Also, a major issue was the black-box nature of such econometric modelling, using which practical marketers were not always willing to risk their careers and bonuses on decisions that they could not understand very well, or recommendations that sometimes seemed counter-intuitive. And so, despite the mathematics of econometric modelling having been around for decades, its practical application remained sparse. Marketing remained, at best, a discipline of informed intuition, complemented by robust execution.

Attribution was one of the many problems that digital media claimed to solve. New third-party attribution companies arose, and major platforms started offering attribution as an integral part of their optimization suite. However, in practice, attribution continued to raise as many new questions as it sought to solve, especially for categories where online sales were a small part of the total.

The first type of attribution was simple. You saw a text ad on Google, you clicked on it, you went to the website and you bought a product. Full attribution for the sale went to that Google click. However, as the Google ecosystem itself became smarter and more complex, new attribution approaches were introduced by them, where the credit for the sale could be attributed, for example, to the last click (among the clicks tracked by Google), first click or the distribution could follow a U-pattern of allocation or some such simplistic rules of thumb.

There was no real science behind this choice—although conceptually it could be modelled—and most media buyers chose last-click attribution, which hugely favoured Google. Imagine a travel ad, where people, after watching all the ads and checking out all the photos on social media, finally turn up at Google search and click on a text ad to go to the travel site and book the tickets—and that last click gets all the credit for the sale.

Subsequently, savvy marketers started upgrading to multi-touch data-driven attribution, which is based on logistic regression and looks at individual journeys across different touchpoints to attribute outcome in a statistically more rigorous way. However, this attribution still suffered several limitations. For instance, there was no way to incorporate the impact of offline investments in this model, even though everyone knew that it had a great role to play in bringing people to the Google search engine. Also, all those online investments whose data could not be integrated into the Google suite couldn't be counted in this model (there were other third-party attribution model providers but, due to the walled gardens that the digital world was made of, they all suffered huge limitations of similar kinds). The models were also sometimes limited by only factoring in the clicks rather than the exposures, thus pretty much ignoring any upper- and mid-funnel impact that marketing investments may have.

* * *

The Drunkard and the Lost Key

'Not everything that can be counted, counts.
And not everything that counts can be counted.'

—Albert Einstein

There was once a drunkard who was staggering back home from the pub late in the night, fully sozzled. The street was dark, and he could barely find his way. He stumbled several times on the way and closer home, fumbled for his door key. He couldn't find it and realized he had dropped it somewhere on the dark streets along the way. He looked back. It was all dark, but far away he saw a lit lamppost with light beneath it.

He walked over to the lamppost and, for the rest of the night, he kept looking for his keys under this lamppost.

Just because there was light under the lamppost didn't mean the key was there too. Data is great, but in the marketing ecosystem today, there's an interesting scenario of too much data available for a small fraction of the total area that marketing covers. In fact, it is the walled gardens that painstakingly control what data they want marketers to see, and what data they don't want them to see. However, in a world with a sometimes irrational obsession with data, there is a real danger that we may keep looking for the key where the light is and not where we may have actually dropped it.

> In a world with an irrational obsession with data,
> there is a real danger that we may keep looking for the key
> where the light is and not where we may have actually dropped it.

Just because the light is there, doesn't mean the key is there.

* * *

SUMMARY:

A. We started with a discussion on how Google Adwords revolutionized the world of media planning and buying—heralding a new democracy of buying, the centrality of user experience and charging for effectiveness.

B. We discussed how the digital ecosystem made a lot of the traditional research increasingly obsolete. We also had a balanced discussion about both the opportunities and limitations of digital and offline measurement.

C. Then we considered the DIET loop and what metrics would give us the best way to track what works what doesn't and fine-tune our investments depending on where the inefficiency and the bottleneck were. We also discussed the pros and cons of different attribution approaches.

D. We ended the chapter with a need to prioritize focus on where the knowledge gap may lie in the decision-making process rather than what metrics or data may be easily available, so that we do not put the cart before the horse.

After having pondered over the new measurements, let's look into how marketing technology aided by the vast data being generated by digital systems is trying to automate marketing and hence, bring back some sanity into an otherwise highly complex marketing ecosystem that exists now.

10

Data and Marketing Technology

'Maybe stories are just data with a soul.'

—Brené Brown

Navigating the Frankenstack

As marketing became more and more complex, and data sought to play a bigger and bigger role in marketing sophistication, technology moved in to make things easier. This gave rise to the whole field of marketing technology (martech). In the last decade, the field has become one of the most hotly contested arenas of marketing, even if the plethora of jargon it has spawned can be difficult to keep up with for most marketers.

The two largest players in the arena of marketing technology globally are, of course, the pioneering AdWords-led Google stack—and the Facebook Ad Manager (with Amazon Marketing Services slated to become increasingly important, along with Adobe and Salesforce dominating the wider end of the martech spectrum beyond adtech). Both have tried to create a complete ecosystem within their respective walled gardens by arraying different types of technology that marketing may need. Google also allows inventory to be bought on non-Google sites via its own demand side platform (more on this later). However, much as the duopoly has revolutionized media access by putting it into the hands of anyone with a credit card, their ad stacks are also limited in many ways by the walls around their gardens.

To start with, an important challenge that digital media presented for marketers was its extremely fragmented inventory. Google and Facebook today sit on one end of the spectrum owning the largest chunk of ad-ready inventory. This is followed by tons of new-age digital portals as well as the traditional publishers gone online sitting in the middle. This is further followed by a massive number of individually small, long-tail sites. Having said that, in a disproportionate skew towards the bigger players, the share of the duopoly in the digital-advertising spends amounts to more than 60 per cent globally.[1]

The dominant norms of buying online inventory had already been set in place by Google AdWords. But not everyone—especially those who see Google and Facebook as a threat—wanted to be confined to these walled gardens. So, a whole host of independent ad exchanges appeared as auction houses for the independent digital media, to allow for bidding and buying inventory pools.

But rare publishers had the technology and know-how to convert their inventory into exchange-ready assets. So, they needed partners who could look into all the inventory they had, classify them, price them and set other rules of engagement with the ad exchanges on the supply side. These players were called the supply side platforms (SSP). SSPs became a critical bridge between the publishers and the ad exchanges, helping publishers maximize their revenue yield (see diagram).

However, on the other side of the ad exchanges sat the media buyers representing the marketers. And the media buyers needed their own technology to specify what they wanted to buy, how much they wanted to invest in what kinds of buys, the messages they wanted to place in what they bought and various other rules and constraints of the buying engagement. This set of technology came to be called demand side platforms (DSP). The tech that allowed optimization across several of them came to be called Meta DSPs.

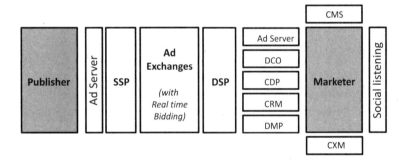

A BASIC MARTECH STACK

In due course, marketers and media buyers realized that the online inventories were vast and a certain exposure was worth a little or a lot based on what we knew about that exposure—who, when, where—the more the better. With more and more knowledge about an exposure, a piece of inventory can evolve from anybody to somebody to a target to a high-propensity prospect for a brand. As with any auction economics, the key to getting a great price here is asymmetry of information. If an exposure was getting bought and sold on the exchange as a generic commodity, but the marketer had the unique intelligence that here was a person in the market to buy a luxury car or take a home loan, he could realize disproportionate value on that buy.

With more and more knowledge about an exposure,
a piece of inventory can evolve from anybody to somebody
to a target to a high-propensity prospect for a brand.

However, most marketers had limited first-party data, data that they owned, that is, and so they needed external data for this information advantage. Even those who had decent first-party data would often need this third-party data, because first-party data by definition consisted mostly of current customers and hence it somewhat defeated the purpose of campaigns that sought new customers from competitors, or worse still, to attract non-customers entering the category for the first time. In categories like durables or services like travel or insurance especially, where at any point in time a small fraction of the population is in the market, this data becomes especially important in order to avoid wastage. Publisher data, of course, constituted second-party data, and publishers would deploy it to offer smarter targeting to marketers, where inventory was being directly bought.

So, a whole new technology emerged to collect and provide access to third-party data, and this was called the data management platform (DMP). DMPs sourced data from all publicly available databases, as well as from any for-purchase sources not protected by privacy regulations, to triangulate elaborate profiles of hundreds of millions of individuals (in some cases, information was consolidated on up to fifty different parameters across a billion profiles).

Platforms are transitory, but data and relationships are for keeps. Of course, marketers who had a large first-party data pool built their CRM programme around it. First-party data could also be integrated with global digital platforms via custom audience integration, so that those in the database could be targeted with the brand messages on these platforms, rather than only via owned media channels such as websites and apps, emails, text messages or notifications. Many corporations also invested in data lakes like snowflake and databricks that basically housed vast pools of raw structured (for example, number of items bought by each customer) or unstructured data (for example, social conversations data about a brand) with an open-ended purpose. This was different than a data warehouse, which contained structured data with pre-determined purpose.

Looking at the bigger landscape of data today, despite the powerful DMPs, some of the largest and most precious pools of data remain under private ownerships. Retailers, banks, telcos, airlines, major apps, broadcasters and governments possess a massive amount of individual data; however, most of it is not available to be tapped by external marketers.

Ad-serving technology emerged to allow the serving of creatives to DSPs and also to be able to track unique exposures. Tagging technology emerged to allow websites to track their users' online behaviours via cookies. These were little codes left in user computers to not only allow a website to identify if the user had visited the website earlier, so the experience could be made easier (this is also useful for re-targeting those who checked out the website but didn't register or purchase, just in case they changed their mind) but to also send back other surfing information of the user). Players like Nielsen and ComScore provided the ability to measure unique reach and frequency levels across sites based on people-centric sampling. Further on, players like Integral Ad Sciences and Moat (later acquired by Facebook) emerged to help qualify the inventory in terms of quality parameters such as viewability and context.

Of course, if the unique power of digital media lay in being able to micro-target with highly specific messages, then the world needed a technology that could automate the creation of these hundreds or thousands of ads, and this tech was called dynamic creative optimization (DCO). Google and Facebook also integrated basic DCO capabilities within their stack.

Clearly, with all the new opportunities came the measurement technologies. Website-measurement tech allowed one to track visitors on the website in the minutest detail. Customer data platforms (CDPs) went one step further, allowing a marketer to be able to see across a customer journey—when he clicked on the campaign, came to the site, got an emailer, booked a demo, purchased a product or had any other trackable interaction with the brand. Dashboards emerged as the single source of truth to simplify the plethora of metrics that the servers generated. CDPs also included tag management and typically had a digital asset management integrated within. Attribution players emerged to allow brands to use those metrics to triangulate which ad interaction contributed how much to the eventual goal.

Content management systems (CMS) allowed websites to change their content in the most user-friendly way possible, and hence, typically came with e-commerce functions built inside. Also, a lot of listening tools emerged to track publicly available conversations in social media for brands to benefit from. To handle customer service, research and elements of in-store marketing and supply side e-commerce functionalities, customer experience management (CXM) tools were developed by players like SAP and Oracle.

Of course, the multiplicity of tech tools involved in the marketing ecosystem created tremendous complexity and confusion—apart from an alphabet soup of jargon. In order to bring some sanity into this, some players organized the chain of technology required in a typical marketing ecosystem into a stack, put it in the cloud and called it the 'marketing cloud'. Adobe and Salesforce marketing clouds are among the key players in this space.

* * *

Trouble in Paradise

Much as the rush to collect and monetize data has accelerated, not all is hunky-dory with data-driven marketing. Here we will discuss three most contentious issues, which can put the future of data-driven marketing at peril.

Better Data for Better Marketing

Half-baked data that knows a person can buy a product but doesn't know that the person has already seen the ad several times and not shown any interest or doesn't know that the person has already bought it recently, means that people keep seeing the same ad again and again and again. This is in direct contrast to the original promise of digital media to be smarter and less annoying than, say, a TV ad, where, with much less data, the notion of effective levels of frequency had existed for long. Also, as mentioned before, a majority of the digital ads tend to be very clumsily put together like junk ads, further increasing the annoyance factor.

Part of the targeting process deployed due to the extreme specificity of targeting can also be very creepy when seen from the consumer point of view. By 2020, ad blocking had risen to more than one quarter of the users, and unless stricter protocols on privacy are applied, this number is set to rise.[2] Apple has taken a lead in this area, and its vision of a more private web is in line with its commitment to impeccable user experience. With Google planning to remove the third party cookies, the picture on data privacy is getting better. As a result, a marketer's own first-party data is becoming more important. Of course, the reliance on large digital platforms for quality targeting will increase.

Let's now zoom out a bit to consider the larger implications of lack of data privacy.

The Trusteeship of Data

In the history of the world, never before have private corporations (and some governments) had second-by-second access to the innermost secrets and the most intimate conversations of individuals. This has raised a fundamental issue about individual freedom and empowerment, where corporations and regulators have struggled to draw the line between collecting data to enable better convenience, choice, customization and delivery of governance; and collecting data with the potential to invade privacy and freedom. A beginning has been made with General Data Protection Regulation (GDPR) in Europe, but a lot more is needed to be done around the world.

A fundamental difference between a liberal democracy and a totalitarian government has been the bounds of government power. In a democracy that thrives on individual freedom and choice, under normal circumstances, the state only needs to know about individuals what its citizens, by way of constitution, allow it, as necessary for governance. This is the opposite of totalitarian governments where states choose the freedoms that individuals are allowed, because the default position is the omnipotence of the state. To that extent, in a democracy, the state must not bother with or interfere in the private behaviours of an individual unless the behaviour is detrimental to another individual's freedom.

However, the availability of such granular and comprehensive data on individuals poses a new conundrum.

On one hand, it presents great opportunities to step change the quality of governance (better security via pervasive surveillance, for example) and yet on the other, it creates new moral questions in relation to the state's interference with individual freedoms and rights, and indeed the role of the state in the societies of the future. A system of 'quantum governance', where the state is simultaneously everywhere and nowhere, is a vision that evokes both fear and inspiration.

The Bad, Bad Coder

> *'Algorithms are opinions embedded in code.'*
>
> —Cathy O'Neil

The big question of ethical coding, a war cry of Silicon Valley conscience-keepers, is what moral codes should coders play by. Just as doctors are expected to play by the Hippocratic Oath, lawyers are expected to play by the bar's code of conduct, should there be a moral code for coders, whenever coding-for-profit comes in conflict with what's right for the world? Because coders get paid to write algorithms to maximize engagement and profits, instead of simulating real-life social dynamics as closely as possible, virtual living has the potential to distort the fine equilibrium of how physical world lives. It actually would be fine if that was for the better, but the profit motive means there are gaps between what is the state of social media and what it should be.

Clearly these gaps create a big disconnect between the real world and the simulated society on social platforms. Also, ordinary people are unable to internalize this difference and accordingly adjust their response to social media stimuli. This has the potential in its extreme manifestations to contribute to extreme events, for example, depression—sometimes leading to suicides at an individual level; and social hatred—sometimes leading to riots at a public level.

Whether the culpability for aiding this can be attributed back to the human coders or their organizations is an area that the laws of the times have not been able to catch up with. Technology is moving at the speed of light, and while the adoption curves get ramped up to global scale within a span of months, the regulators often move at the speed of sound, opening vast legal grey areas that can lead to manipulation and mass disasters (the Cambridge Analytica episode provided a good example of what's possible).

Data can impede freedom and choice in many other ways. Loss of serendipity is the big casualty in the age of answers. An algorithm that's designed to show the content that fits the 'type' that one has clicked on in the past, even with the best of machine-learning algorithms, typecasts people into a very narrow straitjacket of consistency and predictability. And gradually, the person can be led into an obsessive data tunnel, where only one's own echoes can be heard. You know more and more about less and less. You keep becoming more of your own reactive self, suppressing the more reflective part. This dramatically narrows real choice, reduces serendipity and mutant perspectives—factors essential to one's intellectual well-being. Shorn of the natural-learning ecosystem, in due course, the person can lose his sense of perspective and proportion of things.

> And gradually, the person can be led into an obsessive data tunnel, where only one's own echoes can be heard. You keep becoming more of your own reactive self, suppressing the more reflective part.

One of the other disconnects between reality and the virtual modelling of reality is that the digital never forgets. Digital footprints persist year after year, decade after decade, and like 'Hotel California', you can log in any time, but you can never leave. High-school boys caught on camera, high on drugs, must fear a rediscovery of their private little scandal job after job, interview after interview, all their lives. Just as in the natural world, people and their images and their deeds have a right to be forgotten but digital algorithms today are not designed for that. Data policies and algorithms must do a lot better to protect human dignity and people's right to a second chance.

As more and more of living gets digitized, it leaves very little choice for those not on the train to hope onboard. As services after services, in the garb of being pure play digital, shut down their doors on those who can't access it through internet, right to disconnect is being denied gradually. It could give rise to a new digital apartheid.

The ruling algorithms of the era have often defended themselves by claiming to further the essence of the modern, Western society—individual will and freedom of speech. Freedom of speech and individual choice rose as the dominant ideal in an era where society imposed suffocating strictures in the forms of tradition, religion and elite interests to the detriment of individual dignity and possibilities. It was a deeply liberating idea, and still is.

However, these principles assumed that people are 'aware' or can be made 'aware' of the true choices they have in relation to interests, both personal and public. They also assumed that people will be able to exercise their speech within their limited sphere of communication access, and that anyone with access to mass communication would be sufficiently accountable for his or her ideas. All these assumptions are in tatters in the social-media era. For one, the mechanics of how reality and facts were established traditionally are broken and there is a preponderance of fake narratives that create dummy 'awareness', thus effectively restricting real choice ('deep fake' technology adds to this threat further). Also, real choice is narrowed by the echo-chamber syndrome that data-driven feed curation can create. Secondly, everyone has the instrument of mass communication at his or her disposal, yet the accountability that must come with public communication—both at the originator or the media-platform level—is missing.

Data and the Sacred Tryst with the Future

After 500 years of 'enlightened' individualism, freedom of speech today has become a textbook caricature to be fetishized by the prophets, profiteers and punters of Newism threatening the core of democracy.

All in all, there is little doubt that, facilitated by technology, data will eventually enhance the sum total of human happiness. However, there is still many a wrong that needs to be made right towards that. Giant walled gardens with unprecedented powers have little incentive to do this of their own volition. Only in a truly open architecture system, where there is ample competition along with relentless pressure from the civil society, can there be an incentive for accelerated correction of these irresponsible algorithms.

Monopoly breeds stagnation. The moral immunity that the Silicon Valley future-makers enjoy—on account of their being at the frontiers of human possibilities, a status that also allows them to cumulate extraordinary wealth and power within a short span of time—must also come with a curse of relentless insecurity. To allow them to stagnate is to compromise the better for the sake of the good enough.

Lest all this conversation around the omnipotence of data (and its indecent flaws) should give the impression that data-driven marketing is all about data, this picture needs to be set right.

* * *

The Plumber and the Poet

'Data data everywhere, so much data we will sink.
Data often without meaning, who will help us think.'

—Rishad Tobaccowala

The last ten years have seen a flurry of investments in marketing technology and data infrastructure by marketers. But after a few years of making these investments, they increasingly realize the age-old truth that technology is technology, merely a tool. The ability to make the best of the tool still requires strategic thinking, creativity and the analytical ability to convert data into insight, foresight and farsight. The most important marketing technology is still the human intelligence, imagination and ingenuity. Micro-targeting is rarely enough; it's the micro-delighting that really moves the needle. We decide with our hearts and then conjure numbers to justify what we did all the time in our lives. Plumbing can't replace the poetry when it comes to marketing (but, of course, it can create a more powerful platform for poetry).

> The most important marketing technology is still
> the human intelligence, imagination and ingenuity.

The truth today is, most marketing organizations—the skill sets, the workflow and the processes—may not be suited to deploy a full-scale marketing stack. In many companies, it is still not clearly defined as to whether the ownership of making the stack work lies with the chief technology officer or the chief marketing officer. Also, its strategic role in driving business needs to be carefully defined beforehand with a model of cost-value analysis in place. And a phased approach can be calibrated to keep pace with the ability to actually use the technology.

The irony of automated marketing—even for the savviest of marketers—is that it's a lot less automated than people think.

SUMMARY:

A. We started with a story of how the modern marketing technology stacks came about, discussing the various components and the roles they have in automating the marketing ecosystem.
B. We also discussed the flip side of how data-driven marketing can sometimes be blinkered and a good marketing plan needs to be mindful of these limitations.
C. We closed the chapter with a discussion of how the plumbing of marketing technology can enable and complement but can't substitute the poetry and power that powerful human insights and ideas can bring to a marketing plan.

Having discussed the data and marketing technology central to contemporary marketing, let's move towards the larger transformation that some of the key IR 4.0 (fourth industrial revolution) technology is expected to bring to marketing in the coming decade. Due to the complexity involved with each technology, for each we will first spend some time discussing what it is. Then we will move to the implications it has for people and society in general and thereafter, we will focus on its implications for consumers and the marketing value chain in particular.

11

Marketing and IR 4.0

'I am not crazy. My reality is just different than yours.'

—Cheshire Cat, *Alice in Wonderland*,
Lewis Carroll

The industrial revolution began in the United Kingdom about 250 years ago, where production was mechanized using steam power. The second industrial revolution came when electricity was used to scale up vast assembly lines and mass production. The third industrial revolution was brought about when computers and automation arrived. Now we are entering the era of the fourth industrial revolution where connected and autonomous systems fuelled by data and machine learning are once again slated to step change the industry—thus heralding the advent of IR 4.0.

As IR 4.0 takes over the business world in yet another wave of transformation, it is indeed worth pondering as to how the new wave of technologies may change marketing as we know it today. Some of the key technologies that are expected to have a big impact on marketing are extended reality (XR),

IoT, AI and blockchain—eventually auguring the arrival of Marketing 4.0. We will use this chapter to delve deeper into these. Given the novelty of these, we will also spend part of the time fleshing out each at a fundamental level, parts which more tech-savvy readers may be happy to skip.

Reality is Overrated

XR covers the entire spectrum of experiences on the reality–virtuality continuum—starting with forms of augmented reality to mixed reality to virtual reality. It's a field of spatial computing that can add a layer or create an alternative to actual physical reality. Google AR already allows for fun 3D layering of animals, objects or places in our natural space. Anyone can bring a Royal Bengal tiger in their living room, for instance. It may also often allow for smart participative experiences. Infused with haptic feedback, in a 5G future, it is set to revolutionize human living beyond one's imagination. The business of living is set to be further pixelized.

For millennia, knowledge sat in songs and ballads, papyrus and parchments, and books and treatises. A powerful Google search algorithm allowed much of the knowledge of the world to be freed up from locational and physical constraints, and access met intent in the epoch-defining text-based search bar. Knowledge in an augmented world of the future is likely to be accessed as an all-pervasive layer on physical objects and spaces, wherever they are and activated via AR—rather than people coming to a search engine as a destination. It could be a highly decentralized and contextualized vision of information working in sync with computer vision and sound recognition.

Technology such as Amazon's Flow provides cues to what search could be like in the future. Flow uses both bar code and image recognition to continuously recognize tens of millions of products in a live camera view. Users can just point to an item and flow can overlay availability, pricing, media content, reviews and various other information directly over the item in the view. It is easy to imagine a future where every surface or object (or faces, privacy laws allowing) around us has an AR information or experience tagged to it.

Industries and functions starting from education to customer service to information departments of governments to signages on roads, in hospitals and in stadiums to tourism information may get transformed by this technology.

Knowledge, however, is just one dimension of what AR has the potential to bring to us. The opportunity that this layering of content over physical reality brings can go beyond normal experiences—Pokémon Go which became a global rage was the earliest example of this. Awareness of locations, situations, surfaces, objects and faces could create participative experiences leading to a new genre of games and entertainment.

AR's ability to influence marketing will depend upon how it changes ordinary people's day-to-day lives. As the most accessible technology within the XR portfolio, AR is already scaling up fast via smartphones. Web AR has further removed the need to download the app, thus eliminating an annoying bottleneck. The launch of Facebook's AR format and loads of assorted AR filters gave it a truly global scale (even though almost every major social media platform now has AR elements, the real pioneer among them was probably Snapchat, which has consistently innovated in this area). AR-based photo filters are already morphing the 'photo me' into the 'dream me'—and it could be a different 'me' depending on the place, time and mood on a given day. Car heads-up displays are coming in rapidly, too. As mentioned before, Ray-Ban Stories, a collaboration between Facebook and Ray-Ban, represents yet another step towards bringing an AR layer to people's everyday lives.

E-commerce is being slowly augmented with the help of AR too. AR-enabled sites allow for people to use their mobile, tablet or PC cameras to try out the look and feel of a watch, a pair of glasses, a piece of jewellery or an item of apparel or accessory on their own body. Retailers can add a parallel augmented e-commerce layer tagged to their real-world stores, shelves and SKUs. Department stores can provide information and advice on the items they are selling through AI-based virtual advisers activated through AR. Museums can recreate times bygone and galleries can offer yet another dimension of imagination for artists and their audience to play with.

For marketers, AR allows a new canvas that can be layered to provide customized information, advice, demonstration, participation or other types of engagement across packaging, point of sale, in-store or in-screen. A paint marketer can allow painters and customers see what their houses will look like in different shades and textures; an interior decorator or a proud house-owner can check what the new sofas will look like in their drawing room—and a food marketer can layer the calorie count for each item on the tray.

Unlike VR, mobile and tablet interfaces allow a ready-to-scale interface for AR. However, many battlefronts remain—from device sophistication to GPS accuracy to AI software—before it becomes an inseparable part of the day-to-day lives of more than 4 billion netizens.

AR introduces a new level of interoperability between the digital and the physical world, in a mutually reinforcing loop to enhance the total joy of living. It augments our real lives, making it more informative, engaging and enriching. In fact, in humankind's quest to live more life per life, AR adds a new layer.

Everyone Has Their Own Reality

Virtual Reality or VR is different from AR in the sense that it first isolates the viewer with the help of a pair of VR goggles and then creates an alternative reality in front of him or her, which can be a highly immersive, full-sphere experience. It also allows people to interact with the new surrounding space, creating highly engaging space-and-motion-aware experiences. New dimensions can be added with the help of haptic and psychosomatic feedback among others (Oculus headsets already integrate basic haptic feedback). If AR has the potential to revolutionize how our reality can be enhanced, VR is patently suited to formalist fantasies due to its ability to focus human attention and its exponentially higher levels of immersion. Marshall McLuhan would have been intrigued finally to meet the ultimate 'hot' medium, several notches more overwhelming for the senses than plain old television.

VR has the potential to eventually take over the world of media and entertainment, education and tourism among others—industries expected to benefit a lot by evoking immersive, mediated realities for people. VR also has the ability to revolutionize human sexual behaviour, as VR can allow people to watch porn in first person and offers a whole new level of first-person intimacy and immersive simulation. Last but not least, today, much of the social-media interaction is mediated through flatter formats such as text, photos and two-dimensional videos. The story still has to be told. If you attended a party, you have to capture it via text, photos and videos in order to share it with friends but, in the world of VR, a group of friends experience the party in a 360-degree world, almost as if they were themselves present there too.

Mixed reality (MR) fuses the immersion of VR with the augmentation of AR, by creating virtual objects in the real world that one could interact with (this interaction marks a key difference between AR and MR, though sometimes MR is seen as a subset of AR). It still requires headsets, but it retains the real world as either a backdrop or a series of depth-aware layers, between which virtual objects can be integrated. MR gaming in indoor theme parks is becoming increasingly popular. The possibilities of MR carry AR and VR experiences to yet another level. In the home furnishing industry, choosing the right furniture size has been a task for several consumers—measuring the vacant space, finding the right match in stores, the possible back and forth with carpenters. Many such problems were solved with the app, IKEA Place. Users were able to browse and search IKEA furnishings and place furniture in their actual room and where it would sit and fit, capture it as a still or video, make a favourite list and buy via the IKEA website or the IKEA Store app. With mixed reality, it's possible to now layer alternative realities in the same space and time—and even achieve interactions between them. Finally, people can truly live more life per life.

It's possible to now layer alternative realities in the same space and time—and even achieve interactions between them. Finally, people can truly live more life per life.

Despite the potential, large-scale adoption of VR and MR is less common. The single largest barrier happens to be the inconvenience of wearing VR headsets for extended periods of time. Participative VR can be highly disorienting and one's sense of balance is often ill-prepared for it. For any long-form content, the battery charge is not enough either. High-quality VR also requires quality broadband speed, which 5G is expected to provide. Whether VR continues to be a niche technology for highly specialized roles or whether it becomes an everyday mass technology depends upon crossing this bridge between these physical limitations and our never-to-be-underestimated capacity for ingenious design.

A very central application of extended reality technology is the metaverse. The metaverse comprises the simulated 3D virtual worlds where people create their avatars and do various live activities (gaming, chatting, watching content). They have evolved from the massive multiplayer online role playing games (MMORPGs), which go at least two decades back. The first metaverse with global prominence was probably 'Second Life' which came about as early as 2003, promising to offer alternative realities inside a 3D gaming environment, selling lands and buildings inside the game. Roblox, Fortnite and Minecraft—all three focused on socially-infused gaming—are cited as the most popular metaverses currently. More than 3000 guests turned up for India's first wedding reception in the metaverse, hosted by newlyweds who wanted to avoid COVID-19 restrictions on their big day. The bride's late father, simulated as an avatar, also attended and blessed the couple.

The Creator said:
'I want to hide something from the humans until they are ready for it . . . it is the realization that they create their own reality.'

The eagle said: 'Give it to me. I will take it to the moon.'
The Creator said, 'No, one day they will go there and find it.'

The salmon said: 'I will bury it on the bottom of the ocean.'
The Creator said, 'No, they will go there too.'

The buffalo said: 'I will bury it on the great plains.'

The Creator said, 'They will cut into the skin of the earth and find it even there.'

Grandmother, who lives in the breast of Mother Earth, and who has no physical eyes, but sees with spiritual eyes, said:
'Put it inside of them.'
And the Creator said, 'It is done.'

—Creation story from the Hopi Nation, Arizona

The truth is, for as long as humankind has existed, each of us carried our own individual reality, deep in our hearts and minds. The way we saw the world in all our perspectives and prejudices; the way we saw ourselves in all our prides and pains; the way we made it our own in all our pursuits and purpose; the way we wanted it to be in all our dreams and desires. Our personal and private reality gave us the freedom to be the best of us, much as a shared notion of public reality gave us freedom to connect beyond ourselves, even though built by the norms of physical reality, it could be highly restrictive. Virtual reality and its prodigal progeny—the metaverse—has the possibility to help us live both the freedoms to the hilt, in other words, maximum life per life.

At the end of 2021, Facebook changed the name of its listed company to 'Meta' to signify its commitment to the metaverse, with an intent to popularize its usage beyond gaming. Facebook now offers meeting rooms as well as event spaces (and events) inside the VR world and eventually hopes that a whole lot of social interactions would happen live in the metaverse-like environment with voice, gestures and even expressions (things that are already possible to convey to some extent inside Facebook Horizon accessed via, say, an Oculus Quest VR goggle). As mentioned before, Microsoft is also looking to scale up business to business applications of the metaverse via its Microsoft Teams platform (imagine a group of colleagues having a presentation inside a VR space), Microsoft Mesh and HoloLens. Nvidia is another major corporation that has committed itself to the metaverse with its 'Omniverse' ambition. Apple is expected to be working on its own VR headsets. These developments together are accelerating a future where we may live a lot of our lives inside a metaverse—playing, socializing, working and learning.

In order to appreciate what industries could virtual reality disrupt first, we could take a value-based approach. At the moment, most VR apps tend to be in the areas of gaming, entertainment content and fitness based (reminding one of Nintendo Wii applications fifteen years ago). Here, the main value that VR brings is 'deeper immersion' than normal video or screen-based gaming participation. For events and work apps, the value is simulating 'superior presence' than video calls allow, without the traffic jams, red eye flights and dressing-up chores associated with physical presence. VR commerce has the potential to elevate the immersion that live-streaming commerce offers. It can also bring superior presence (you could window shop with your friend, for example) along with the easy searchability of normal e-commerce. Education is one area, where immersion can have a direct impact on learning, and is another sector that should lend itself to disruption early on.

* * *

The Mind Playing God

Another important technology that underpins IR 4.0 is artificial intelligence (AI).

Much has been talked about how AI will transform our world. Elon Musk, in his famous panel debate with Jack Ma in

2018, spoke about how humanity as we know it may merely be a biological boot-loader for digital super-intelligence (somewhat analogous to the role of a battery in kick-starting a petrol car engine).

Within the ambit of AI, a rapidly growing field is evolutionary algorithms which can allow codes to combinate, regenerate and mutate to evolve strands of code that best fit into a given problem–resolution environment. Science fiction has often spoken about the concept of singularity, a theoretical point of time in future, at which AI will surpass human intelligence to unleash rapid cycles of self-improvement, eventually creating a super-intelligent algorithm that will be far beyond human control (also called Seed AI—due to its ability to self-generate and evolve). Polls of researchers suggested a median probability of 50 per cent that artificial general intelligence (AGI—able to solve any problem, not just a specific one) would be developed by 2040–50. So, it's important to better understand what AI at its core is today and what it can and can't do.

It is important to clarify that AI is not equivalent to analytics, although it can be seen as a subset of the larger analytics discipline. AI is not equivalent to big data, but AI requires big data to be trained. Machine learning is a type of AI, and probably the one that is most often confused with the term AI (see diagram). Deep learning, in turn, is a type of machine learning.

AI in a general sense includes all those ways an algorithm can mimic human intelligence to solve a specific set of problems. So, for instance, expert systems based on a sophisticated decision tree designed to closely simulate expert decision-making can be a part of AI (however, they are not a part of machine learning). A lot of clinical decision support systems are based on such decision trees and bring a certain process rigour and easy scalability while still being transparent and easy to understand.

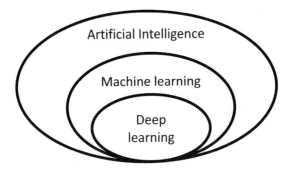

In machine learning, an algorithm is able to identify patterns on its own. For instance, with tons of photos labelled either 'car' or 'shoe, it may be able to train itself to recognize a photo as that of a car or a shoe and apply it to identify a new set of photos with a high level of accuracy. Machine learning mostly works with structured data with proper labels, so it can learn based on existing labels. However, machine learning may require human intervention, in case the accuracy levels are not satisfactory, as the accuracy depends a lot on the quality of data and the labelling that gets fed in.

However, the most sophisticated form of AI, deep learning, employs a mathematical process called artificial neural networks (ANN). ANNs are conceptually inspired by the way networks of neurons in the human brain learn since childhood. Deep learning can work with highly unstructured data but requires vast amounts of data (say over a million data points at least). Given millions of photos of cars and shoes without any labels, it may be able to classify the photos in two categories (one each for cars and shoes, though the two labels must come from humans after) by running the photos through layers and layers of algorithms each providing its own interpretation of the data.

Each network in the ANN defines specific features of the images through a hierarchy of different concepts. As soon as the photos are analysed through these nested layers within deep neural networks, each layer produces different outputs. These outputs are amalgamated to find the appropriate identifiers for classifying the two objects—if given a fresh set of images. Although deep-learning algorithms can improve accuracy dramatically in most cases, it still needs the quality of data to be good enough. The other problem that deep learning has is, while it may improve the accuracy over a decision tree or a machine-learning algorithm in solving really complex problems—for instance, diagnosing a tumour by studying the radiological output—the logic it takes to arrive at the decision is opaque. This means that when errors happen, it's difficult to understand why they happened. And it begets the problem of attributing accountability for decisions made—an ethical and legal dilemma that is set to trouble the world as we leverage deep learning more and more. Having said that, deep-learning algorithms can reveal patterns in unorganized data that simple machine learning may not be able to discover.

AI and the Unknown Unknowns

Theoretically, it's possible to know the unknown unknowns of cultural, social, economic and political behaviours of people and that can be incredibly powerful compared to known unknowns where humans know what the unknown is, for which they seek answers. When humans define what to look out for, it will always be limited by their knowledge or imagination. ANN allows the data to do the talking for the most part. Giant digital platforms sit on a treasure trove of data that can be harnessed by traders to make billions on stock markets; it can be used to discern political undercurrents and influence them to create revolutions and change governments; and they can be deployed as powerful weapons of mass manipulation (confusion, divisiveness, demoralization, etc.) in psychological warfare.

It is no wonder that China has built its own great-walled garden of digital platforms, with restricted access to US-based platforms. And there should be little surprise as to why the Trump government was so uncomfortable with TikTok—which is owned by a Chinese company—becoming so popular in America as well as the rest of the world. AI is also finding numerous applications in autonomous warfare, as drones and satellites develop smarter abilities to discern a terrorist from a civilian, or a cruise missile becomes AI-smart in detecting decoys from a target, and in avoiding a barrage of anti-missile hits from the enemy state. AI is a key technology in closing the loop in a sensor-to-shooter future of highly see-through and autonomous battlefields, where electronic warfare, cyberdefence and psy-warfare will come together to form the golden triad of advantage.

AI in Our Everyday Lives

We may not consciously realize this, but we already live in an AI-mediated world. Global digital platforms—Google, Facebook, Amazon, Netflix, Spotify and our iPhones etc.—deploy AI to curate higher quality user experiences and recommendations for us each day, all the time. Another common example of AI in our day-to-day lives that millions already use are Siri, Alexa and Google Home (in the area of natural language processing). Stock-market traders have applied AI algorithms to trading for more than a decade and, in fact, flash traders using AI caused a minor crash in American stock markets in 2010.

At the 2015 I/O conference, Sundar Pichai, the CEO of Google, gave a call to move from a mobile-first to an AI-first world. In the last decade, a host of companies, such as Amazon, Google, Alibaba, IBM and Microsoft, have ramped up their AI offerings that bring off-the-shelf algorithms along with their clouds (on-demand data storage and computing power that sit online), that can be further trained in specific contexts. These algorithms can conduct several tasks: they can understand natural language and translate; discern a colour; read the gender, age and mood; detect objects and backdrops in a photo or video; and recognize faces, voices or emotions. One can also deploy ready-to-use AI to train a keyboard to compose music or a camera to detect things; or to train autonomous vehicles; convert text into natural sounding voices, and so on. These suites are offered as a part of their cloud capabilities, and they open a whole new world of smart, yet fun, possibilities for any brand or business to apply.

One of the most powerful applications of AI might be in all sorts of advisory and consultancy services. For instance, wealth-management advice has historically been available only to high-net-worth customers given that the cost of service delivered by human financial advisers tends to be high. However, AI has created a new opportunity to bring relevant advice to many more people simply because the marginal cost of the service can be quite low. Similar innovations are being toyed with in the area of healthcare—with the notion of AI health adviser, and in the area of education—with AI-based personalized learning assistants. Towards that, some noteworthy developments have taken place recently with both Microsoft and Oracle having made massive acquisitions to develop their health cloud offering. Google is another platform developing a health play where they seek to bring the power of AI to healthcare.

AI and the Marketing Value

Just as the future of living is anticipatory and personalized, so it is true for commerce and marketing (see diagram).

Personalized propositions built around AI will be conveyed via personalized media and messaging.

AI could intervene at different stages of the value chain to enhance effectiveness (see diagram). AI can also be used to create personalized product and pricing propositions, thus helping businesses drive up their premiums. Facial recognition has already revolutionized surveillance, security and the payments industry in markets like China (although the first one does pose issues of privacy protection in many countries). With due permissions though, it can help personalize our day-to-day experiences further by integrating our visual signature with our intent and preferences—for instance, facial recognition may allow a shopping assistant or a waiter in a restaurant to be able to anticipate our preferences based on previous visits.

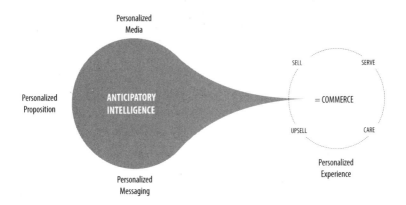

FUTURE OF MARKETING IS ANTICIPATORY AND PERSONAL

It can be deployed to curate a personalized and adaptive website or app user experience, thus enhancing the efficiency of information access. For e-commerce players, such as Amazon and Alibaba, AI-based search, curation and recommendation is fundamental to revenue maximization and user experience—in turn helping them sustain their dominance. Similarly, for a lot of online media and entertainment services, such as Spotify, Instagram shopping and Netflix, AI-based recommendation engines form the very core of their differentiation.

Social-media conversations tend to be highly unstructured data and more sophisticated social-tracking tools deploy AI-based natural language processing algorithms to make sense of the conversations. These social-media tools can use AI to glean deeper patterns in their categories—trends they could ride on, hot buttons they could own, hooks they could deploy, barriers they could overcome, moments they could own, emotions they could harness and locations they could focus on. It's already revolutionizing website and app experiences, as mentioned above.

Another opportunity for AI in marketing is media buying, which for many marketers is the single largest investment. Programmatic media buying is an ecosystem that must optimize in real time at many levels to maximize return on investment. A business may have a portfolio of brands; within a brand there may be different variants which, in turn, may have different micro-audiences. Creative messaging may have thousands of versions (including elastic pricing sometimes), and there may be a hundred different journeys to reach the end action. It can create a level of complexity that optical analysis by humans can frequently only fathom a fraction of. A well-designed and trained AI, however, can be able to bring a whole new level of effectiveness and automation to the end-to-end process, with minimal human intervention.

There have also been numerous applications of AI in the area of campaign creativity, where the idea is based on the application of AI, either to inform copywriting or art processes, or for personalization across media and creative.

However, the outcomes have frequently lacked in systematic and campaignable ideas that could be replicated as a model. Also, the applications have been sparse, given that most creative people see AI as akin to some nerdy witchcraft; and those who live and breathe AI can rarely fathom the nuances of the creative process or its junky purveyors. This should not be surprising, however, given creativity will remain for long the last frontier of AI.

Companies that incur huge costs in managing customer service have increasingly tried to automate at least a part of their customer-service system. For many such businesses, customer-service management is also an important instrument of upsell and cross-sell. One of the common alternatives for at least simpler or less important queries or contexts is the deployment of chatbots. While the first generation of chatbots were basically FAQ lists married with a simple decision tree and baptized with a cool name, they frequently left people unsatisfied once the novelty wore off. However, AI-enabled chatbots have been able to significantly improve the experience at better speeds and lower costs, even though they are still a poor substitute for the quality of human assistance.

As more and more brands seek newer ways to create differentiated value, AI can also be deployed to solve various other problems customers face in their journey. A paint brand may deploy AI to help people select the right colour for their home, an apparel brand may deploy AI to assess the virtual fit of a dress to a customer, a restaurant brand may use AI-based facial recognition to address loyal customers by their names. An e-commerce brand, of course, may use AI to recommend products on its site that may be most relevant to a customer. AI-based utility built to solve a customer's unmet needs has opened an important cluster of competitive differentiation and new customer value in many categories.

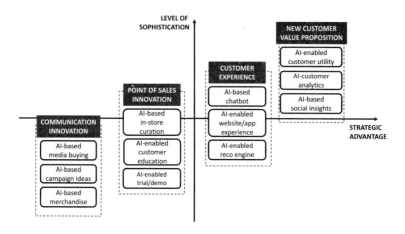

AI AND TYPICAL MARKETING VALUE OPPORTUNITIES

Thus, the applications of AI have the potential to transform each step of the customer journey as well as how the five content pipes are deployed by brands to convert people.

Last but not least, an important area of AI for marketers is their metrics. Every touchpoint that the marketers deploy—campaigns, content, website, CRM, customer service, sales interactions, in-store experience and actual transactions, among other things—often generate massive amounts of data. These hide precious patterns, opportunity cues, behavioural surrogates and leading indicators that are not always visible to the naked eye but can be discovered by AI algorithms. As the number of metrics in the marketing ecosystem has multiplied manifold, only a limited set can be realistically analysed by humans. But AI can be of great assistance in curating patterns in the overlooked or more granular data. And every pattern may hide a new opportunity for growth or cost efficiency.

Just as for marketing, so for people at large, it is quite clear that AI is set to revolutionize our lives like never before, providing us freedom from the banal and the repetitive, allowing us to focus on the more creative, more spontaneous and more high-touch parts of living. If happiness be the much-celebrated pursuit of life, against which all grand innovations ought to be measured, AI must allow us all to eventually fill a lot more happiness into one life.

* * *

The Society of Things

In the timeless stories of the *Arabian Nights*, one of the most loved fables is probably the story of Aladdin. Aladdin, an ordinary boy, finds a magical lamp in the cave of wonders. The lamp is extraordinary as, with a little touch, it can connect Aladdin to magical possibilities, where he can get done whatever he wants done.

If Aladdin lived today, he wouldn't have to risk his life to get the lamp. All he would need to do would be to learn to code the Internet of Things. IoT can allow him to convert random ordinary objects into connected things which, in turn, allow these things to serve tasks that are much beyond their usual jobs. You could code the genie into the lamp. Or better still, you could just code the rubbing routine into the lamp, and the genie would emerge from the cloud.

IoT at its most basic is about connecting everyday objects—objects embedded with sensors, software and electronics—to the Internet, enabling them to collect and exchange data in real time, in order to help them do things better or do new things.

To the extent it allows extracting and analysing digital data from the physical world, it offers a whole new interface between the physical and digital without much human mediation. It can also network one thing with another, thus potentially creating an interoperable society of things—a network of ambient intelligence sourced from smart sensors that work as a team to make our lives better.

In fact, we live in a world with millions of different types of sensors sensing and measuring everyday things like temperature, humidity, pressure, sound, light, proximity, acceleration, orientation, touch, colour, level, flow, image, motion, velocity, smoke, alcohol, and so on and so forth. The possibilities that their synchronized power can bring to make our lives more efficient and meaningful are myriad.

One of the earliest IoT devices to get global attention was Nike Fuel band launched in 2012+ FuelBand, a precursor to today's immensely popular fitness bands and Apple watches (given Apple is the market leader in the watches industry today, it could be called the first industry disrupted by IoT). Another pioneering effort was the Amazon Dash button launched in 2015. Dash Button—a simple and small IoT-enabled button that could be stuck to, say, a washing machine, and with one push, it could convey a signal to an app ordering replenishment for the detergent. (The innovation was dropped later as mobile phone screens offered a more scalable option to do the same.) However, the idea has led to the field of IoT commerce, also called iCommerce—IoT devices that are purchase-enabled. Google Glass sought to embed IoT and AR capabilities in its design. Even though it was a commercial failure, it became a precursor of things to come in the lifestyle industries.

The IoT device that we are all probably most familiar with are the AI-based voice-assisting speakers like Google Home or Amazon Echo; and climate-control devices such as Google Nest (let's leave aside mobile phones or PCs, as being connected is their avowed purpose to begin with). The largest IoT device is probably the Tesla car today, as the software can be booted, controlled and performance enhancement patches added via the cloud by the company, just like an Apple or Samsung would do with their mobile phones. Its connected features can also allow users to open garage doors, control the climate, better use in-car media and connect via Bluetooth.

In 2017, Tesla drivers were notified by the National Highway Traffic Safety Administration about a faulty charger plug that could catch fire. No recalls were needed, or rescheduling of appointments, or taking time off from work, or frustratingly long times in the waiting rooms. Tesla just updated the software from the cloud. We are moving rapidly towards a future where all cars will be connected one way or another, along with being autonomous, electric and a lot more fun.

The pervasiveness of IoT devices is also triggering larger cultural shifts. A wise man once said: 'You can't manage what you can't measure.' And, with IoT devices allowing us to measure different aspects of our everyday living, a whole new movement of 'quantified self' has been unleashed, where people measure their everyday behaviours in order to allow algorithms to track, train and optimize their lives. Wellness bands are becoming a cultural phenomenon. Smart sports equipment are becoming coaches by collecting and processing data. For example, a tennis racket with the ability to track its movement and its contact with the ball generates data that can be used to coach us better or may even be useful for self-coaching.

Marketing and the IoT

Within the ambit of marketing, IoT can play different roles across the value chain. However, its most powerful use could lie in being able to redefine entire categories by broadening the way the customer need gap is defined, or by tapping a higher order need state, in order to create a next level of differentiation.

For example, the premium milk category is usually a highly cluttered space with a flurry of brands offering similar products. It's plausible that, for a working mom today, when she thinks of milk for her toddler, the bigger unmet need is how to ensure that the milk, prepared to the right temperature in a germ-free environment, is fed to the child with consistent timing, and gets replenished at the right time. She may also want the right amount of milk powder to be mixed with the right amount of water to suit the child's age, weight and the height-weight ratio. Further, she may want that while the milk is being fed, it reminds the child of her. And she wants to be able to do all this with minimum demands on her time and attention.

It is possible to conceive of an IoT device that can do all these and more. One may hazard that such a device designed with great user experience and safety assurances may just have the power to disrupt the premium-milk category, by bringing peace of mind to affluent mommies around the world (if it doesn't get stuck in a 'Google-Glass trap' that is).

In the process, a more meaningful value exchange can be established between people and brands, where people allow brands to capture data on them via IoT devices and be able to give back hard, tangible value by solving unmet existing problems, thus enhancing the brand experience (see diagram).

IoT-based customer value could lie, depending on the category, in higher convenience, simplicity and speed. The sharing of customer data could also help companies personalize the product or service and even be able to personalize pricing.

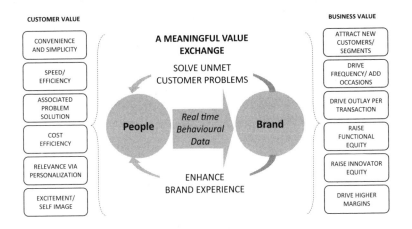

IoT CONVERTS DATA INTO HIGH ORDER CUSTOMER VALUE

For example, it could be UV patches that can tell on the basis of UV-exposure measurement as to what sun protection factor (SPF) will be needed to protect the skin of a person in a given moment. Or it could be thermal and humidity sensors embedded in the packaging of an isotonic drink that can tell you how many glasses to drink depending on the day's weather in a place.

IoT devices embedded into our everyday lifestyle products may also improve the wearer's self-image—both fitness bands and Apple Watch make a statement about the wearer—and sometimes may mean much more to them than their functional utility.

IoT devices can also expand a category definition by solving a completely new problem contiguous to the original category need state (see diagram). Refrigerators as a category have been built on keeping things cool and fresh. But a fridge that can, via visual recognition, tell the calorie count of all the things it stores, becomes an integral part of one's fitness regime. If it can order depleting stocks at the right time automatically, it can become a part of the shopping regime. And if it can tell automatically whether it contains all the required ingredients for a particular recipe, it can become a part of the cooking regime. Such category redefinitions can, in turn, help businesses attract new customer segments; drive frequency or add new occasions; drive basket value per transaction or generally improve brand equity and margins.

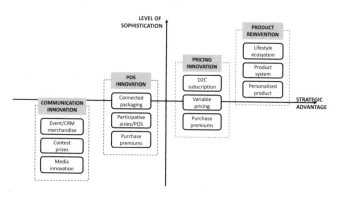

IoT AND THE MARKETING VALUE CHAIN

A new opportunity triggered by IoT technology is iCommerce. Between when a consumer is running out of stock for a certain product, and when he buys the replenishment from the supermarket is a highly vulnerable interval in most categories. An IoT device attached to the packaging that can time a reorder with minimum hassle for consumers has the potential to avoid churn significantly. It can also allow direct-to-customer commerce which may create not only new business models with inbuilt loyalty but also real-time data, inventory management, customer responsiveness and personalized customer-value propositions.

IoT can be applied to communication innovation, allowing for media or sampling or on-ground activation to be infused into connected devices. It can also create last-mile differentiation at points of access via smart packaging, IoT-enabled point of sales, or via IoT-based premiums.

A successful product reinvention with IoT can be highly disruptive, helping to potentially create a whole new ecosystem around the product, loyalty-walled and risk-proofed by margin-additive proprietary data, UX and brand value.

So, a pH sensor can accompany a face-care regime; a temperature and humidity sensor can come with smart water packaging; a connected comb can tell the hair health and a sunscreen can be calibrated with a tiny UV patch. Large consumer goods corporations like P&G, L'Oréal and Unilever—some of the biggest marketing companies—are moving rapidly to explore and capitalize on the IoT opportunity. For centuries, FMCG products were sold by adding a dash of storytelling around the otherwise mundane utility. In future, that magic could come more and more from 'storydoing'.

Also, as the number of IoT devices explodes into tens of billions, the size and cost of the components keeps going down, enabling even wider usage. Today, an educational IoT device—Pi Zero (a tiny version of Raspberry Pi), packs a 1GHz single core CPU, a 512MB RAM and a mini HDMI port. It could very well be the genie that would have excited a tinker-happy Aladdin.

Looking at the sea of sameness that most mass-marketing categories are today, it could be argued that more and more categories may eventually get disrupted by 'connected' physical products that are able to reconceive categories from a white sheet perspective. Uber pivoted the key value lever of the taxi industry by making data-driven access the epicentre rather than physical taxis themselves (and Airbnb did the same to the hotel industry). IoT is another powerful technology to unlock the unmet needs of customers on dimensions hitherto not imagined.

IoT is yet another powerful technology
to unlock the unmet needs of customers
on dimensions hitherto not imagined.

The physical would finally blend the magic of both the physical and the digital, and it can be argued that the business of living would finally be a blended, phygital one. In a 5G future, the reaction time of humans will become the limiting factor for remote apps that leverage 5G and IoT. So, a society of things based on machine-to-machine communications will become key to more life per life.

* * *

The Blockchain of Transactions

Transactional activity is one of the very underrated aspects of human civilization. Starting from the first barter between humans which established the notion of a win-win exchange based on a complementarity of one person's wants with another person's surplus, transactions have underpinned the development of human society. The more sophisticated society becomes, the more complex and higher order the nature of transactions gets.

In the beginning there was the barter system. Then precious metals—first money—became the surrogate for value. Then paper promises became the surrogate for money. Credit scores later became a surrogate for the dependability of these promises both at an institutional as well as at an individual level. In the world we live in today, there is a cornucopia of various higher order derivative instruments that get transacted in order to capture the full range and depth of risk and value (options and futures in the stock markets being some examples). In order to protect the sanctity and value of money, transactions and the underlying contracts, an elaborate chain of policies, laws and its enforcement apparatus have been erected. In fact, today, the governments, financial organizations, accounting, legal and security firms, and indeed all nature of businesses, spend a whole lot of time ensuring the sanctity and integrity of transactions. That's a whole lot of civilizational resources and energy invested.

Yet there are some obvious flaws in this model of managing transactions. Ledgers are owned, verified and controlled by a central authority—governments, banks and financial institutions of all sorts, corporations, etc., with a penchant for complex regulations and with layers of policies. Manipulation and fraud are not uncommon. The cost of governance is high in this centralized model with too many toll collectors on the way (say, if you had to transfer money from one country to another). Intermediaries and interlopers may have all manner of incentives to manipulate the system. At the least, they end up slowing down the system significantly. Given the fact that money is ultimately nothing but information—either as an entry in a ledger somewhere in one's name, or as currency note and coin, a miniature contract with the central bank.

The irony is, despite money being information, it's movement is often painfully slow, expensive and inefficient. This is the irony that has in the last few years captured the radical imagination of nerds around the world. Money is arguably the most important medium of universal trust ever devised and the coding evangelists believe that it needs to be freed from the shackles of centralization, opacity, vested manipulation, rampant toll-taking and technological lethargy. Legacy money systems have too much latency and error. Central authorities tend to edit at will the money database as if they are in some archaic mainframe.

The greatest barrier to erecting, say, a 1000-storey office tower is no more the structural engineering or the strength of materials, but the maximum speed at which humans will not get disoriented in the elevator. As a result, in tall buildings, elevator banks themselves take a huge fraction of the total space. Beyond a point, elevators which are to serve the tenantable spaces can occupy more area than the tenants themselves. In the digital era, as our lives get more and more complex, the average number of transactions a person engages in on a given day or in a lifetime is getting exponentially higher. Beyond a point, this can become too cumbersome to be handled by a complex, centralized operating system with too many choke points and vulnerabilities. The volume of transactions is rising exponentially in a world getting more digitized and global; and as wealth, investment and shopping break out of locational constraints. The exponential rise of fintech giants such as Paypal, Stripe, Adyen, Square, Robinhood, Wise, and a series of mobile wallets, etc., is a testimony to the latent need for change in this space. It's clear that a unified global architecture of money is a clear and present need. The world needs a new operating system of money.

The world needs a new operating system of money.

Blockchain is an IR 4.0 technology that holds a lot of promise towards changing the basic structures of transactions and contractual relationships (in any field indeed) underpinning our day-to-day lives. Although a lot of critical bottlenecks remain towards its larger adoption (for example, it can be rather slow, expensive and consumes a whole lot more energy and processing-power than current ways of doing things), it offers promising prospects due to its unique structure. Hence, it's important to understand this technology and what role it may have for society in general and marketing in particular.

First and foremost, a blockchain is a database. It's a very unique database in terms of its structure. Its basic unit is a transaction. A set of transactions—not unlike a ledger—make a block, and a chain of blocks makes a blockchain ecosystem. Each blockchain ecosystem has a set of protocols, which are the rules by which it is governed.

These protocols are defined by the blockchain creator. He invites other people to join in building the ecosystem. The extra capacity on their computers becomes a part of the ecosystem and they are called nodes. Together these components help run what's called a decentralized autonomous organization (DAO).

A block can be seen as analogous to an Excel file, where each row is a transaction. However, there are two important differences when compared to a normal Excel file.

First, as soon as the file is created, a huge number of copies get made, which are stored on the independent computers called nodes. This means that if a file is destroyed, stolen or modified, it doesn't matter, because there are so many copies to authenticate the true copy. If someone hacks several copies and modifies them, then the authenticity is verified by a vote by each node storing the copies. So, to be able to modify a transaction, one needs to modify 51 per cent of total computers carrying the copy, which is almost impossible due to the vast number of computers involved and the fact that they are each independent.

The second difference is that each transaction is recorded in a way that's connected to the last transaction, so that the sequence of entries is sacrosanct. So, if John gave US$100 to Vijay and Vijay in turn gave US$70 to Xue Xin and US$30 to Faiz, then one can't modify Xue Xin's takings to US$80, since Vijay gave her only US$70 and he had only US$100 to give between Xue Xin and Faiz. To change one entry, you must change every other entry that came before it. In effect, a record once created practically can't be destroyed or modified.

The important part to note is that, although the core protocol is set centrally, there is no other central filing or intermediary role. Also, anyone inspecting the blockchain is capable of seeing every transaction between blockchain addresses creating a high level of transparency. All communication is peer to peer. No one can turn off the network, as it's not dependent on a single computer or server. This 'lightness of being' allows many DAOs to have a non-profit core (e.g. Bitcoin, Ethereum), though for-profit companies can use the kernel to build profitable businesses (not unlike an open source software ecosystem).

A large part of what governance constitutes today will either become redundant or will get substituted by peer-to-peer blockchain networks—much like how peer-to-peer loans, insurance and investments are disintermediating financial businesses; or how peer-to-peer exchange of information and perspectives has substituted a large part of mass media's centralized news-and-views machinery.

In terms of technology and business, billions of connected IoT devices can exchange data on the basis of smart contracts enabled by blockchain, and one rogue device can't take the system down due to its distributed nature. Online identity data can be stored and accessed in a decentralized way making it difficult to hack. Certain types of insurance pay-outs as well as derivative trading and warranty claims can be automated via smart contracts, making it much more efficient and secure.

People in general tend to be open to sharing their data as long as there is a fair value exchange, but the current state of data ownership makes users sign platform-created contracts that allow the platforms wide and deep rights. People's personal data—content, interactions, health data, wealth data, credit scores, educational data, professional records and even their social graph and preferences and propensity data—can eventually be owned by them and be protected and allowed qualified access using smart contracts with digital platforms, contracts that will sit on independent blockchains. People can also securely store their own files via a system of decentralized and distributed storage managed via smart contracts. DAOs, for example, can be a great alternative to totalitarian data access by governments, allowing for qualified usage of data based on blockchain-based smart privacy contracts, while individuals still control access.

The Chain of Money

One of the most popular applications of blockchain has been in the area of cryptocurrency—digital currencies that operate on blockchains. Cryptocurrencies have risen to a scale where it's already being treated as an asset class comparable to gold in terms of its scale and independent risk profile compared to the stock markets.

Bitcoin was the first cryptocurrency created by a mysterious persona called Satoshi Nakamoto (there is still debate about whether he actually existed). Bitcoin remains the largest cryptocurrency today followed by Ether. Bitcoin is a pure cryptocurrency whose maximum number allowable (21 million) is already decided by Satoshi in order to control supply. Bitcoins are released by the code to reward the miners—parties who own the nodes in lieu of the verification jobs. In line with its limited maximum number, fewer and fewer bitcoins are being released by the code; however, the coins' high price makes up for it. An uncertain point, however, may arise if the price inflation of the coin is unable to keep up with the effort required in mining it (in other words, the required volume of verification work). Still, bitcoin is being seen increasingly by investors as digital gold due to its limited supply (even if it tends to be highly volatile).

Ether is the currency needed to operate on the Ethereum blockchain. Ethereum is more of a blockchain-based 'operating system', as it allows for smart contracts to be hosted on the blockchain too. Thus, one can build decentralized apps on this blockchain that are based on those contracts. A whole world of decentralized finance (DeFi), mainly exchanging currencies, buying virtual assets, peer-to-peer lending and borrowing against the holdings, and various derivative products, has arisen as a result, on Ethereum.

Also, a new class of assets called non-fungible tokens (NFTs) has taken birth. Basically these are blockchain-based smart contracts for unique digital property, such as a piece of virtual art, digital content, a piece of virtual property, etc. Sometimes an NFT may come with real-world assets; however, in most countries these must be accompanied by real-world contracts in order to be enforceable in the court of law. Apart from the NFTs and DeFi, cryptocurrencies can also be used at several online and some offline retailers, and items ranging from cars to electronics to luxury goods, can now be purchased with cryptocurrencies. One can also convert it into real-world currencies. In fact, a class of cryptocurrencies called stablecoins is pegged to real currencies.

The Chain that Unchains

A whole new vision of Web 3.0 has been imagined with the ideal of freeing the Internet from centralized profiteering platforms (this is reminiscent of the early days of the Internet and the open source movement in software). This means individuals will have a high level of control over their data and a lot of centralized functions—that of trust, security and rule-making—will get distributed via blockchain and designed around leaderless consensus. The Internet then would be truly bottoms-up and democratic. It is a revolutionary vision, that in its full manifestation has the potential to blur the boundaries between nation states, diluting a lot of legal, fiscal and monetary silos that exist today. However, revolutionary ideals usually tend to lead to a new pragmatic compromise, albeit of a higher moral order. The open source software revolution eventually made some core platforms open source; however, it also gave way to the rise of a new generation of platforms with an even greater concentration of power.

> A lot of centralized functions—that of trust, security and rule-making—will get distributed via blockchain and designed around leaderless consensus.

It is sure to lead to a whole new generation of human organizations—more efficient, more agile, more adult (rather than patriarchal), more open and transparent, and hopefully with a lot more freedom and real choice. As Peter Thiel summed it up: 'If AI is communist, crypto is libertarian.' AI assumes centralized control (and enablement); crypto's origin story is steeped into the liberal end of the spectrum.

It is not clear, however, as to who will write and evolve the protocol (is there something like too much democracy?); how can the distributed verification mechanism be more efficient, cost-effective and eco-friendly (which it is not at the moment); and how to monitor tax evasion, money laundering, terrorism financing in such a world (governments are still playing catch up). It is also arguable whether a cryptography-based trust will not be easier to build the future of money around than infrastructure-based trust (distributed servers as verifying nodes), which tends to consume a lot of processing power and energy and, as normal people don't like to own servers, may eventually lead to a new generation of massive global platforms who act as the centralized gateways to the blockchain servers. Already most users interact with the consumer-facing apps such as OpenSea, Coinbase, Metamask, Binance, Solarna, etc., which in turn may access the blockchain via Etherscan, Infura, Alchemy and so on, creating multiple layers between people and the blockchain. A peerage of people is becoming a peerage of servers and those who run them.

Blockchain and Marketing

The application of blockchain technology to marketing is still in its infancy. One important area is procurement, where blockchain can bring a high level of transparency to all transactions from the farm to the shelves allowing end customers to verify the quality and ethicality (including sustainability) of suppliers in the chain. The other area of opportunity is digital media-buying, where marketers can have a clear view of the inventory and its vital characteristics all the way through to the individual publishers. Blockchain technology can also allow the plethora of gift cards, loyalty programmes and customer service commitments to be connected and redeemed via smart contracts.

Blockchain will, on the whole, make marketing a lot more transparent both in its internal processes as well as towards its end customers. It could help protect personal data and unleash the full power of connected devices. It could also allow higher interoperability between a set of businesses looking to collaborate at a micro level. NFTs offer yet another opportunity for strong brands to build and sponsor unique assets that help drive relevant imagery.

* * *

Marketing 4.0 and the Kingdom of the Mind

Marketing 4.0 envisions a world where corporations and brands would deploy layers of enhanced experiences—anticipatory, personalized, connected and immersive—in everyday consumer lives to provide information, win trust and build imagery. Smart connected products would similarly simplify and improve people's lives by communicating with and learning from them, as well as exchanging data with an ecosystem of other connected objects. Enabling transactions of all sorts could be managed by autonomous, immutable ledgers improving transparency and replacing centralized governance with distributed trust and leaderless consensus. All this could be further underpinned by highly intelligent algorithms and cyber-physical systems run from the cloud.

Mankind can finally transcend the physical to embrace an uber-life with multiple realities. It will also become possible to infuse elements of its sentience into inanimate objects which, in turn, will serve to liberate the human living experience from the mundane and repetitive so that man can focus on the unbroken pursuit of stimulation, origination and self-propagation.

It would be the kingdom of the mind, as billions of curious, connected brains would synchronize as a supermind to dedicate themselves to the task of maximizing happiness and meaning and originating the next level of civilization. It will be an interesting time.

Having discussed the exciting possibilities for redefining marketing with IR 4.0 technology, in the last chapter of this book, let's zoom out and take a helicopter view of marketing as a discipline, how it came about, what role it plays in human society, and how marketing can be deployed for higher meaning and towards a better world.

SUMMARY:

We started with extended reality, discussing how augmented reality can layer information and content in our natural everyday living, thus taking information productivity and access to another level. We also discussed how virtual reality with its highly immersive experience can create a new alternative reality disrupting the world of media, entertainment, virtual work and potentially, even education. As people's lifestyles change, it opens excellent opportunities for marketing too.

A. Thereafter, we discussed how AI works, and how it has already pervaded different aspects of our lives in general and is increasingly influencing marketing.
B. Then, we discussed how the Internet of Things (IoT) is infusing everyday objects helping us lead smarter lives. We also delved into how it could transform different steps in the marketing value chain.
C. Last but not least, we discussed how blockchains work, what are cryptocurrencies and NFTs, and what opportunities for society in general and for marketing in particular, it may hold. We ended with capturing the key challenges blockchains must surmount in order to be all-pervasive.

12

Marketing, Meaning and Mankind

'Why do we let the one thing we don't have,
affect how we feel about all the things we do have?'

—Carrie Bradshaw, *Sex and the City*

The Merchant of Happiness

The spiritual origin of modern marketing can in many ways be attributed to the Renaissance. An important socio-cultural transformation that the Renaissance brought was the change of focus from the afterlife to the given life. It was the acknowledgement that there was a lot more to the here and now of the human condition that needed to be inquired about, improved upon and celebrated, than accepting the fait accompli and resigning oneself to pursuing salvation. It was a shift from 'god will help' to 'god helps those who help themselves.'

This renewed emphasis on the rational enterprise to rethink the world around an ordinary individual and the capacity of various social configurations to add, multiply or mobilize its power on its own or as a collective was transformational. The ordinary temptations of ordinary people, their very human desires for material and emotional betterment, were now the focus. And this was in striking defiance of dominant religions that had hitherto played the role of a very useful servant to material elites in confining the dreams and ambitions of the masses to an abstract eternal heaven for their souls—only after they die. It was a controlling trick that had worked for millennia.

An incisive understanding of these ordinary human needs and desires for material and emotional salvation eventually became the god particle of marketing.

An incisive understanding of these ordinary human needs
and desires for material and emotional salvation
eventually became the god particle of marketing.

The first lot of mass production organizations was centred on factories and workers. The broad idea was that if you can make a quality product, customers will come (aptly captured in Henry Ford's quip about the Model T). You could build economies of scale, be able to offer the product at a lower cost and wipe out your competitors. Just as product design followed the technology, pricing, by and large, followed the cost-centric approach. Geographical expansion was slow as the world was not as globalized. Engineers, accountants, salesmen and operations managers ran the show, and did what they were good at. There was little reason to think beyond the product, the pricing and the distribution.

However, as the marketplace evolved, and categories or product life cycles matured, the differentiation between one brand and another was difficult to discern for ordinary consumers. The number of years it took to discover the next significant innovation was much more than the time it took for competitors to catch up, and this had the potential to lead to increasing commoditization. This necessitated faster innovation—innovation in product design, pricing strategy, distribution channels and the way the brand was promoted. The success of innovations lay in businesses being able to listen in closely to the market, at the macro level as well as at the micro level. It required listening to the early adopters; keeping track of the trends and innovations in similar or contiguous categories; and, where relevant, anticipate the latent needs of people, before anyone else did. This is how marketing came to be.

Marketing had to, with the finesse of a sommelier, mix just the right concoction of product, price, place and promotion to create the most salient customer-value proposition. And while engineers would know the product, finance would know the pricing, and sales and distribution would know the channels, marketing had to know how each of these, along with the promotion, jived together to create maximum business value. In order to have a sharp customer-value proposition, a brand couldn't be all things to all people. So, segmentation became a common method to help gain audience focus. The concept of the Unique Sales Proposition (USP) was developed further in the 1940s and 1950s to help brands focus their marketing.

Marketing became the bridge between the hard of business and the soft of people. It was a whole-brain discipline, bringing together the left brain and the right brain, the magic and the logic, the plumbing and the poetry. While the mathematics of a business could be optimized in a given time and place, marketing offered open-ended opportunities. The power of a great insight into what people really wanted had no limits as the insight itself was often subjective—at best a sociometric construct.

The power of a great insight into what people wanted had no limits as the insight itself was often subjective—at best a sociometric construct.

As categories became more and more cluttered, the supply side became subservient to demand. Marketing owned demand generation, and thus gained importance within the organization. However, with subjectivity also came risk. A seemingly great insight could be a blockbuster or it could be a dud. No amount of marketing research was a fool-proof buffer against this risk. Marketing, at its most spectacular, became a high-risk high-gain discipline, something that other parts of the organization struggled to comprehend. And this struggle continues till today in many companies.

As a discipline, marketing was pretty much bred in the fast-moving consumer goods (FMCG) industry. It was an industry of lotions, potions and solutions—where entry barriers had historically been quite low. It didn't require much upfront capital investment nor complex technology, the operations were relatively simple and the products frequently needed very little real technical explanation. Often, the consumer decision-making didn't involve large outlays per transaction, purchase cycles were shorter and people were often willing to try new things, without laborious consideration. It had been an industry where sufficient differentiation was tough to create and sustain, whether in capital, manufacturing, technology or operations. (Repeated tests have shown that only a small percentage of people can really tell the difference in the taste between a sip of Coca-Cola and Pepsi, and that includes many diehard loyalists of each brand.[1] The FMCG industry was a perfect incubator for marketing. People no more bought sweet, aerated water—they bought instead a feeling, an image, a story and were happily willing to pay much more for it.

In due course, FMCG companies with a vision realized that the most sustainable differentiation they could have was in terms of the imagery. This imagery could be conveyed not only through packaging, in-store displays, high-context sampling, but could also be conveyed via advertising, PR and associations that came with being in the right place at the right time and espousing the right things. And, much as the image was cued from various disparate sources over a long time, the image itself sat inside people's minds. This image told people something about the brand which, in turn, made people derive their own self-image when they used the brand. It also told people functional and emotional attributes of the brand that made people prefer the brand over others. So, the concept of positioning was discovered to be able to map a brand's place in the customer's mind vis-à-vis its other competitors.

The power of marketing helped businesses liberate pricing from the cost. Price was no more about how much it cost to produce and distribute the product, but more about what the brand's target prospects would be willing to pay for a brand. Product innovation didn't always have to originate in major technological shifts, it could originate in size, shape, packaging format or just about any other aspect of the product, that need not require engineering magic (Ivory soap's ability to float broke the market for soaps—no one had imagined such things could constitute customer value before that in the category). Distribution became about closely following a customer and being available for purchase in the right format, size and price in the place, time and moment they were in. And promotion got elevated from mundane price-offs and extras to alluring emotional storytelling built around brands.

> Price was no more about how much it cost to produce, but more about what the brand's target prospects would be willing to pay for a brand.

This branding allowed businesses to own a share of real estate in consumers' minds which was much more lasting. It allowed them to command better margins and created a buffer against the competitive risk, thus enhancing its net present value. Brand became the new business; the rest getting easy to commodify. And marketing was the custodian of the brand.

> This branding allowed businesses to own a share of real estate in consumers' minds which was more lasting. It allowed them to command better margins and created a buffer against the competitive risk, thus enhancing its net present value.

Global brands such as Nike, Coca-Cola, Disney, Ikea, Pepsi, Apple and McDonald's, many with hundreds of millions of users took on the stature of cultural icons which competed regularly with human leaders in their ability to inspire and energize people. Mass-media editors, in large part funded by advertising, were a lot harsher on human leaders than they were on iconic brands, which allowed them to develop imageries that were carefully carved to perfection. Entire generations of individuals defined themselves by the brands they wore, drank, used and showed off (and continue to do). Brands also became the most benign instruments of cultural imperialism in the hands of dominant economies as bearers of global soft power. Everybody loved brands—and people became the brands they loved, in due course.

Marketer of the Future

As digital media and the advent of data and tech disrupted the marketing ecosystem, the early adopters of the new way were those who could sell their products or services online, e.g., airlines, hotels, books, toys, consumer electronics, online delivery services, etc. For these categories, the entire funnel from discovery to influence to experience to transaction could be online now. The ability to track real conversions against their marketing investments was magic for these categories, as it was now possible to calculate marginal profits per dollar of investment. And conceptually, if you knew the lowest profitability a business was willing to accept, media investments could keep scaling up. In fact, one could play with the pricing in real time to maximize profits.

Savvy marketers in these categories typically tended to focus on the lower part of the funnel in the digital sphere, as this allowed them a certain direct measure of accountability. As this model started scaling up, elaborate technology stacks were put together and skills were assembled to give the model a reliable industrial scale. A slew of data and tech-led innovations were tried out. The categories were disrupted and these marketers typically became the alpha marketers of the digital era, developing cumulative knowledge and scalable best practices in order to stay ahead of their analogue competitors (a whole host of aggregating intermediaries arose to further threaten the margins of those who couldn't evolve rapidly).

The priorities, however, at the top and middle of the funnel remained somewhat different. Marketers who couldn't sell online or for whom a very tiny percentage of their sales came from online sources (most FMCG categories fell into this set, as did a lot of high-touch, high-consideration and high-overlay per transaction categories), were primarily focused on driving their awareness and desire online, and there was no clear proof that online did that better than analogue media. Most of these marketers continued to hope that digital media platforms would play by the same rules whether in terms of technology or currency as the one they had perfected in the analogue days of yore with the likes of newspapers and television. That didn't happen really. Many of these marketers struggled to develop capabilities and experience in the new territory. The world of marketing had become highly polarized with very different norms and principles at the two ends.

However, with the growth of e-commerce, decline of analogue media, greater understanding of the new opportunities, as well as creeping threats from pure-play digital competitors, the two poles are now gradually coming together.

Notwithstanding this, some major challenges remain for marketers fighting to carve their own place in the corporate boardrooms. For one, the new tech-aware marketing ecosystem requires a deeper understanding of technology and data than what most marketing departments have ever been equipped with. This also means that the marketing and technology departments must be able to collaborate seamlessly in order to be able to integrate the marketing technology in the larger tech infrastructure of the company as well as to actualize maximum business value.

Added to that, the centrality of data in marketing necessitates that marketers need to be truly whole-brain— to be able to read the story behind the numbers and stitch together mental models of how customer minds work and how it relates to their business in one coherent qualitative-cum-quantitative picture.

As UX, XR and IoT, etc., become essential tools in the marketing toolbox, marketers need to be able to understand these at a strategic and conceptual level. As marketing and sales increasingly blur into each other in the world of e-commerce, there is also a need for marketing to develop deeper commercial acumen. With all the multiple demands on a marketer's skill sets, a truly holistic marketer is clearly a rare creature today. (Having said that, the good news is that many of the digitally native marketers are naturally attuned to develop into one.)

The new marketing organization requires talent, structure, work processes and appraisal systems that are naturally comfortable with the perilous job of building a margin advantage in the midst of tremendous uncertainties. They need to be able to peer into the blue horizons and the cornucopia of new toys it offers for play, and be able to discern what matters and what doesn't to the specific business objectives at hand. They also need the ability to learn from new entrants—tiny or big—from their own category or the adjacent ones, and rapidly assimilate what the new customer-value opportunities could be.

The new marketer should be able to move fast to time the market well in order to tap the most lucrative windows of margin; yet not be afraid to unmake and remake the customer-value proposition—and realign the organization behind it—just when the gravy is flowing out to move on to the next S curve, within the typical category cycles today of three to seven years. The new marketer is able to wear both hats—that of a pirate and a navy officer—at the same time. He has a judicious understanding of the difference between a martyr and a game changer when it comes to dealing with change. In that sense, every marketer wears a venture marketing hat every once in a while, comfortable with the uncertainties, yet smart and thorough in making his bets.

The new marketer is able to wear both hats—that of a pirate and a navy officer—at the same time. He has a judicious understanding of the difference between a martyr and a game changer when it comes to dealing with change.

Most importantly she or he watches the competitors, but always follows (or leads) the customer. She or he is the ultimate custodian of customer interests in the organization. In any decision room, he or she wears the customer hat, debating with the central premise that true business value must always derive from superior customer value (or experience).

She or he is a hipster, hacker and a hustler, all at the same time. A marketer of the future is an artist able to conjure up a 'reality-distortion field' around the product, yet knows that real artists ship (as Steve Jobs himself would put it), and that's the only true validation of a great marketing plan.

Marketing and Human Society

In the world which we live in today, rapid climate change is forcing human society to reconsider if rampant consumerism is sustainable. Every once in a while, the arrow of responsibility points towards marketing due to its ability to tap latent human desires to create a want for new products, as well as its influence in putting relentless consumption at the centre of living experience. We are moving from a 'market economy' to a 'market society' where the market and marketing mindset are getting infused into the farthest reaches of human relationships—their collective interactions, values and organizing principles.

We are moving from a market economy to a market society, where the market and marketing mindset are getting infused into the farthest reaches of human relationships.

Marketing has been accused of converting ordinary lives into a never-ending ladder of fleeting material gratification, leading people to buy stuff they do not really need or to buy stuff for instant gratification only to throw them away. The cascade of seductive imageries attached to countless products, etched into people's brains from childhood, end up grooming people arguably into short-sighted, carbon-crunching, consumerist bozos. An industrial culture of rapid obsolescence designed into products to ensure shorter purchase cycles, has also seeped into human relationships with other humans.

However, while marketing must accept its share of the blame towards this, there are a few important things to consider in favour of the role of marketing in our society.

Marketing has been a potent contributor towards human progress by virtue of driving awareness and removing the deep seated psychological and cultural barriers progress often faces. Some good examples would be the use of sanitary napkins, purchase of insurance products, use of birth control pills and condoms, education on good hygiene, healthy food choices, good social etiquette, respect and dignity for individuals, oneness of humanity, inspiring one to be one's best self, etc.

Marketing is the engine of innovation by keeping businesses pincer-focused on what people really need and want. In an engineer's lab, a hundred products can be invented based on what is technologically possible; but out of the hundred, very few may actually serve a need gap that exists. Marketing creates that bridge between all that can be made and what is truly needed and under what circumstances (place, time, price, message, etc.).

> Marketing is the engine of innovation
> that keeps businesses pincer-focused on what people
> really need and want.

We live in an era of human society where a majority of the people (not all, unfortunately) have their very basic needs taken care of. The dramatic rise in productivity due to education, technology and efficient design means that a small fraction of the total human population is truly needed to ensure ample supply of our basic needs. Ordinary people need an everyday purpose in life, a reason to wake up in the morning, something to strive for, something to work towards, something to desire and dream of. The role of marketing in fuelling people's higher order needs and giving expressions to people's latent wants and desires should not be underestimated.

Someone may go to office each day and work hard in order to upgrade to a dream house. Someone may be toiling two shifts a day in order to be able to afford a diamond ring for his beloved. There is dignity in that hard work and there is stasis and lack of purpose without ordinary everyday dreams like these. Marketing keeps relentlessly churning these desires and dreams—a whole ladder full of it—that keep billions motivated each day to give their best to whatever they do. Money is not equal to happiness, but money can be a fairly dependable bridge to happiness if it's used in the right way to enrich human relationships.

> Marketing keeps relentlessly churning these desires and dreams
> that keep billions motivated each day
> to give their best to whatever they do.

Imagine a poor, suppressed manual rickshaw-puller at the very bottom of a steep pyramid still living in a semi-feudal country like India. He sees the popular Bollywood icon—Shah Rukh Khan—using a bar of Lux in a dreamlike advertising imagery. He buys one for a few cents. At the end of a thankless, back-breaking day of work in 45°C of heat, honk and bullying on the roads, when he comes back home and uses the bar while taking a bath, for a fleeting moment, he feels like Shah Rukh Khan himself. Let's not underestimate the meaning it has in his practical day-to-day drudgery of life, however small and transient it may actually be. To be able to climb those little steps in the ladder of consumption towards a better quality of life is an important part of his everyday sense of significance.

In many ways, the question of consumption is closely linked to the sense of significance and human dignity.

Brands like Unilever's Dove have brought a new level of social responsibility that is somewhat contrarian to what many in the category have been focused on. By emphasizing that beauty is not about being perfect, they have stood for the notion that there can be beauty in every woman. The new generation of marketing lives where authenticity meets social responsibility. As the true derivative of the Renaissance, marketing could at its best be seen as the purveyor of significance, meaning and everyday purpose for ordinary people.

For thousands of years, religion served as the opium of the masses. Now, consumption is the new religion. And it's not too bad—at least people don't kill each other in the process. Marketing has, through its messages, mostly preached love, idolized goodness and spread positive values and behaviours. It has been a civilizing force, creating a win-win between business and society so far. Marketing keeps human society focused on the marketplace and trading happiness is a lot preferable to battlefields and trading blows.

Marketing, Planet and Purpose

Brand purpose is one consideration that's increasingly gaining currency in a discussion on marketing, planet and society. Brand purpose espouses the concept that every business and brand needs to have a sense of higher societal purpose, and must commit itself to that beyond its profit focus. In a way it's meant to provide focus and expression to the corporate social responsibility of an organization.

But it is important to resist brand purpose becoming yet another hypocritical fad of those who are too rich and too guilty. First and foremost, it's important to recognize that conceptually, all bona fide businesses are meant to serve a purpose in society by their very reason to be (or they may not survive). If Walmart has kept the American cost of living low for four decades (and now along with Amazon), that is an incredible societal purpose being served. It's a purpose that may lack the heart-rending appeal of breast cancer prevention; nevertheless, it's a very important purpose. A Walmart need not build a school in Nepal to deliver its purpose.

It would be better if it used its funds and its core expertise in the supermarkets' value chain to instead lower the cost of living in other parts of the world—for example, Central Africa, by enabling more efficient warehouse and delivery systems for the thousands of small grocery shops there—or by offering better benefits to its own shop-floor employees, or driving a larger and larger share of sustainable products in their portfolio. Many large global corporations who talk the big talk, but have created elaborate schemes to avoid paying taxes where they belong, may want to start paying taxes honourably as a great starting point for more nobler conversations. Taxes build schools for poor children, lower cost of healthcare or help fund reskilling of the jobless, all very purposeful and responsible activities. Many global financial corporations which have been regularly accused of helping launder wealth—stolen from the poor—of developing country kleptocrats, must start their CSR policies by denying access to such monies.

In order to help corporations discover their brand purpose, the true north, it's useful to borrow from the Japanese philosophy of 'Ikigai' (literally, the reason to exist) and apply that to the business and the brand. The Brand Ikigai framework allows a business to leverage its core strengths, things it does really well to serve a larger purpose that goes beyond pure financials. Let's take Coca-Cola as an example to demonstrate the process.

> *'Humankind has not woven the web of life. We are but one thread within it. Whatever we do to the web, we do to ourselves. All things are bound together. All things connect.'*
>
> —Chief Seattle, 1854

First and foremost, a company needs to look deep within and ask itself what are the core values that it holds close to its heart—positive values that it follows internally in its beliefs, policies, internal processes and culture, and also what it represents in the outside world. For example, the Coca-Cola Company holds the values of passion, integrity, quality, collaboration, diversity, leadership and accountability[2] close to its heart in how it operates internally as well as how it engages with the wider world (see diagram).

The next step would be to analyse what the business is really good at doing. Every organization is a bundle of assets, competencies and advantages. A successful organization always does certain things better than most others, which plays a critical role in its success in the marketplace. The Coca-Cola Company runs one of the best marketing machines in the world, overseeing one of the most iconic brands of the last 100 years. It also has a best-in-class beverages R&D, the widest bottling network as well as the widest and most efficient access to the points of thirst—places and moments—across the world. Together, these competencies make it one of the most successful corporations in history.

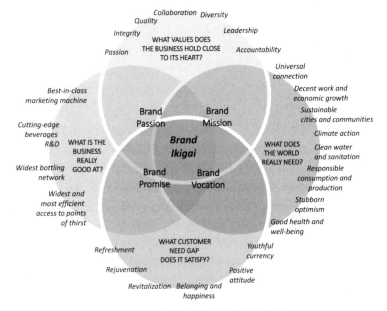

Collaboration Diversity
Quality
Integrity   Leadership
Passion   WHAT VALUES DOES   Accountability
           THE BUSINESS HOLD CLOSE
           TO ITS HEART?
                                     Universal
                                     connection
Best-in-class   Decent work and
marketing machine   economic growth
                    Brand   Brand   Sustainable
Cutting-edge   Passion   Mission   cities and communities
beverages   Climate action
R&D   WHAT IS THE   *Brand*   WHAT DOES   Clean water
      BUSINESS   *Ikigai* THE WORLD   and sanitation
      REALLY   REALLY NEED?
Widest bottling GOOD AT? Brand   Brand   Responsible
network   Promise Vocation consumption and
                                              production
Widest and   Stubborn
most efficient   optimism
access to points   Good health and
of thirst   well-being
                WHAT CUSTOMER
Refreshment   NEED GAP   Youthful
                DOES IT SATISFY?   currency
Rejuvenation   Positive
                                attitude
Revitalization Belonging and
                happiness

BRAND IKIGAI FRAMEWORK AND COCA-COLA

The next step would be to look at what customer need gaps it satisfies. Every category is positioned against a need gap that people have, and a brand is deeply planted in that need gap, evolving as the need itself evolves. For the Coca-Cola Company, on the functional side it means bringing refreshment, rejuvenation and revitalization to its consumers better than any other. However, clearly the brand brings a lot more to its consumers on the emotional side. It can lift people's moods, making them feel more positive and happier. It's a drink often shared with friends, family or sometimes strangers, helping people feel more connected. And the brand brings a certain youthful currency, making people feel young and hip.

The last step would be to define what the world we live in really needs. In the proximity of the category and the communities it operates in, the world needs, for example—borrowing from the UN's sustainable development goals:

good health and well-being, reasonable consumption and production, clean water and sanitation, climate action, sustainable cities and communities, decent work and economic growth. Beyond the functional needs, the world also needs the shared spirits that Coke has often tried to champion, such as stubborn optimism in the face of difficulties and crises, and the 'one world' message of universal connection.

At the cusp of what values a brand holds close and what the business is really good at doing lives the 'brand passion'. The Coca-Cola Company's passion is to conceive and bring to people the most widely loved drinks in the world.

BRAND IKIGAI FOR COCA-COLA

At the intersection of the customer need gap and what the business is really good at sits the 'brand promise'. And the company's promise is to deliver the most refreshing and uplifting drinks within an arm's reach of desire for as many as possible.

Where the customer needs meet what the world needs is the 'brand vocation'. The brand vocation for the Coca-Cola Company could be to bring everyday positivity in harmony with the long-term health and well-being of their customers.

Similarly, one can define the 'brand mission' at the intersection of what values a brand holds close to its heart, and what the world really needs. For the company, it could be to aid and inspire shared optimism via sustainable and genuine relationships with individuals, community and the planet (sustainable water tables, recyclable packaging and fair labour and procurement practices, for example).

Last but not least, the overlap of mission, vocation, passion and promise helps a brand identify its Brand Ikigai— the true north of the brand. It forces a brand to consider why the world really needs it. And what would be amiss, if anything, if the brand and the company behind it suddenly vanished from the world. It also compels a consideration as to how a business can balance its more material needs with the higher moral imperatives.

Coca-Cola's Brand Ikigai can be 'to be a Catalyst for a Can-do humanity'—to be an agent of the indomitable shared human spirit. It has done a good job of purveying the spirit in its communication, but that is surely nowhere near sufficient. It must also seek to expand beyond the transient gratification it brings to the people of the world to take reasonable and genuine cognizance of their long-term health and well-being. It could also be more decisive in addressing the genuine sustainability concerns that its operations beget. It's difficult to be a champion of stubborn optimism to a generation increasingly pessimistic about the future of the planet and its dispossessed. Also, humanity is much broader than its loyal drinkers.

As for a person, so for a brand; as in social media, so in the larger world. Finally, brands must learn to be truly whole. Not merely a manifestation of a capitalistic drive to maximize margins by packaging glib and glamorous dreams—but a true expression of an other-aware society's authentic aspiration to better itself by acting as a responsible, organic whole.

The business of goodness is here—as an opportunity, as an accountability or as meaning and fulfilment.

A New System of Credit and Deficit towards Sustainability

Looking closely at the interface of society and businesses, on the credit side, a new company can add economic value (profits, taxes, salaries, vendor sales, etc.) and social value (job creation, skills building, business and tech ecosystem creation, community building, etc.) to society (see diagram). On the deficit side, there are sustainability costs—companies can end up raising pollution levels, lowering water tables, automating jobs, sometimes corrupting governments, skewing the distribution of incomes, and so on. These costs are effectively borrowings not just from today but also from the future.

SOCIAL VALUE
(CREDIT)

Expensive greentech	Job creation	Profits and dividends
High cost of labour	Skills cultivation	Taxes
Investments into local community	Vendor development	Salaries, etc. paid
Sustainable sourcing	Technology and innovation	Interests paid
	Ecosystem development	Vendor revenues
	Business culture and	Capital and human
	reputation	productivity

ECONOMIC VALUE   ECONOMIC VALUE
(NEGATIVE)   (POSITIVE)

Resource pilferage and corruption	Environmental damage	Automation and outsourcing
Tax theft and manipulation	Aesthetic damage	Resource extraction
Cartels and price manipulation	Extreme wealth	Consumerist values
	inequality	Hyper competitive stress
	Monopoly and supplier	Extreme individualism
	squeeze	Social alienation

SOCIAL VALUE
(DEFICIT)

SUSTAINABLE VALUE BALANCE

A new socio-economic classification (SEC) system needs to be instituted for companies in order to assess their holistic impact on society. Such a classification should be based on social value added in addition to economic value added. A brand has a purpose if it creates maximum economic and social value with minimum damage on the deficit side. That ought to be a priority for all sensible CSR programmes. In fact, tax policies could evolve to incorporate such an SEC classification. It would encourage companies to deliver their individual purposes by focusing on their core competitive advantages within the bounds of the most sustainable processes possible.

It would encourage companies to deliver their individual purposes by focusing on their core competitive advantage within the bounds of the most sustainable processes possible.

Sustainable Living Needs New Ladders of Pursuits

Striking a better balance between the planet's limited resources and people's propensity to consume requires a major cultural shift. Most ordinary people in the consumerist world tend to map their life's journey around two key ladders. The first is the ladder of relationships, which defines the various life-stages we go through, the relationships we build and love we give and get. The second is the ladder of possessions—from durables to semi-durables to FMCGs. Our natural instinct is to climb as many steps on this second ladder as possible. Our sense of accomplishment, happiness and meaning are closely tied to these two ladders.

It can be argued that a richer and more fulfilling ladder of relationships could obviate the dominance of the second ladder. But in a practical world, humans need more than that to stay occupied and focus their energies. So there is also a need to create alternative ladders of meaningful pursuits that humans can keep themselves busy with. These need to be able to serve as bona fide substitutes to the ladder of possessions in terms of a sense of accomplishment, happiness and meaning. These new alternative ladders of meaning could be built around accumulating planet-positive experiences or around intellectual, creative, altruistic and spiritual fulfilment.

> These new alternative ladders of meaning could be built around planet-positive experiences or around intellectual, creative, altruistic and spiritual fulfilment.

Many ancient cultures have a strand of heritage and living philosophy which sees humankind as a seamless extension of nature as one organic whole (somewhat like the planet of Pandora in the movie *Avatar*). A certain respect for both—the living and non-living—as part of the same fabric of being was intrinsic to many ancient cultures, thus minimizing wastage and frivolous, flippant consumption. Today, bringing back elements of this thinking requires human society to develop a new level of awareness against hurting nature in irreversible ways. Social currency, reputation and prestige should be tied to being sustainability positive.

Transparency on 'Total Cost' of Product

The obsession with economic growth cannot lose sight of the real total cost of this growth, when fuelled by rapid obsolescence and repeat purchases with high costs to the planet, for instance. Towards that, the current metrics of economic growth are inadequate and require a new perspective.

Manufacturers building rapid obsolescence into their products must be required to publish sustainability costs incurred per year of the product's expected life on the packaging itself. Regulations on obsolescence can seek to strike a balance between the length of innovation cycles and the consumer's replacement cycles. Regulations must also necessitate cost-effective repair services to be available in order to discourage unnecessary replacements. The efficiency logic of the use-and-throw culture works because the non-economic costs are seldom accounted for. Packaging must come with the sustainability costs incurred per unit on the label, so that buyers can calculate the true price that they are paying for the consumption.

Gross Domestic Products (GDPs) of countries need to factor in not just the economic and social value of goods and services produced, but also sustainability costs incurred. Research and development into sustainable production technologies needs to be prioritized and a judicious patents regime built to encourage affordability. Tesla's marketplace success has begun a new era of sustainable energy. A new level of global awareness aided by activist funds such as Engine1 and giant asset managers such as Blackrock have raised the cost of capital for businesses not committing to ESG governance and the net zero vision.

Ideologies of an era are inextricably linked to the economy and the mode of production underpinning it. We need to change how we look at, organize and measure economy and production if we are to change the culture around sustainability. The subjectivity of the matter and regulatory interventions required towards this may appear tricky to begin with, but with the larger cultural impetus, they would be deemed negotiable and necessary.

And it should be great to market all this new thinking with the best of the latest marketing tools, until it pervades people's minds and the contemporary cultural fabric.

* * *

SUMMARY:

A. We started the chapter by establishing how marketing is a true manifestation of the spirit of renaissance with its focus on enhancing the here and now of the human condition.

B. We delved into how the industrial evolution led to the centrality of marketing and the rise of iconic brands that became bigger than human icons and provided critical reference frames of self-image.

C. We discussed what the new marketer and the new marketing organization in the changing business ecosystem needs to look like in order to live up to its mandate.

D. Thereafter, we appraised marketing's larger role for human society today.

E. Finally, we talked about companies and the need to have the right kind of purpose-centricity. We discussed the Brand Ikigai framework to find the larger purpose that's in harmony with the company's role in society. We also learnt about the need to balance economic value added with social value added, both on the credit side and the deficit side. Finally, we added some thought-starters for business and marketing to help build a better world.

Epilogue: Return on Empathy

Marketing is to business what empathy is to the human society. When a famous archaeologist was asked about the first evidence of civilization, she did not talk about the weapons or the pottery or the jewellery or the size of settlements. She spoke about a really old human skeleton which had a broken leg bone that had healed. When animals in the wild break their legs, they can't walk to the water hole, they can't move around for food, and they can't hunt or protect themselves from the predators. So they simply die. However, the fact that this leg bone had healed showed that someone had, for a long period of time, been a caregiver for the injured human. Bringing food, fetching water and protecting from beasts. That ought to be the true origin story that all religions must begin with. Empathy is the true god particle of society.

When it comes to businesses, marketing is where business meets people. And hence, consumer empathy becomes the god particle of businesses. Where there is empathy, there is magic. There is the magic of revelation, as deep human insights are discovered in the subconscious recesses of our minds. There is the magic of imagination, as an understanding of whys leads to a conception of why-nots. There is the magic of connection, as the more personal the insights we get, the more universal the ideas we beget. And there is the relatively unsung, but yet all pervasive magic of the win-win human spirit that informs all bona fide market transactions. Financial returns in any business are, in that sense, return on empathy.

In this book, we have tried to capture the type of marketing that remains relevant to how the digital natives in particular think, feel and act today. That should be a good starting point on your own journey of empathy as a student and practitioner of marketing, media or content industries.

There is the book on the paper. And then there is the book that happens in your mind, as you read the printed paper. I can only hope that in the process, you turned a few pages of your own thoughts, predicaments and decisions.

They say that in the classical Greece, when Cicero had finished speaking, the people said, 'How well he spoke', but when Demosthenes had finished speaking, they said, 'Let us march.'

I too hope that reading the book helps you act better and therefore, makes a real difference to your return on empathy.

Glossary of the Future

Consulgency: A portmanteau of consultancy and agency, consulgency is an organization, whose offering is a hybrid of what consultancies offer in the marketing space, and what agencies have historically offered.

Digital immigrants: The generation before digital natives (see below), who have known a world in their past where digital experiences were not pervasive. However, their lives are highly digitally-mediated now.

Digital natives: The generation that grew up in the post-dot-com era, which has not known a world where everyday life was not peppered with digital experiences.

Digital pilgrims: These are generations who continue to be resistant to digital pervasiveness and are adopting the digital lifestyle much slower than immigrants and natives.

Marselling: A portmanteau of marketing and selling, it alludes to a seamless interplay between marketing and sales. Marselling underlines the fact that in the digital world, pull generated via media is only a click away from the push generated via the shop and hence, the two need to be seen as one seamless discipline.

Momentness: The quality of being relevant in the right moment. A moment could be defined by time and place as well as the activity, the mood, the company, the device being used, etc.

Multicontent: A term used to define a combination of the five content pipes (advertising, editorial, peer-to-peer, influencer, experiential) that run between a brand and the people. The term has been used in the book to signify that different content pipes can serve different roles in the customer journey and hence, the right mix of these must be deployed.

Newism: The term has been used to define the cultural trend of obsession with whatever is new (mostly new products or experiences), irrespective of whether it is practical or ready to use or not.

Open house model: The model refers to a strategy of entry barriers, where competitors are free to use different elements of their assets and infrastructure, which in turn creates economy of scale and information asymmetry at different stages of the value chain. This heightens the competitive advantage at every stage, an advantage gained by co-opting the competitors rather than keeping them out.

Techsetters: A portmanteau of technology and trendsetters, it refers to the group of people who are usually among the first to try a new piece of technology and inspire others to follow them.

Texperiential: Made of two words—technology and experiential—texperiential relates to the specific experiences made possible by the new technologies.

Words of Gratitude

This book was in the making for almost two years, through months of late nights and exhausting revisions. Along the way, many came forward to help, so there is a little bit of all these people in this book.

I would like to thank friends and industry leaders who went through the very first draft and gave their precious feedback—Ranga Somanathan, Vishnu Mohan, Pratik Thakar, Ashish Joshi and Dr Atul Parvatiyar. Writing is easy; revising is the tough part. I would also like to thank Tuhina Anand, who reviewed the latter version and provided some invaluable advice.

A constellation of global leaders and marketing gurus came forward after seeing the manuscript to offer generous words of endorsement—Prof. Nirmalya Kumar, Matt Seiler, Pratik Thakar, Mauricio Sabogal, Jeffrey Seah and Vipul Chawla. Very grateful.

For someone new to the publishing world, the support and advice of friends—Niti Kumar, Dr Nidhi Agarwal and Dheeraj Sinha—were very useful. Gratitude is also due to my wife, Tulika Prakash, for her dispassionate opinions on the content.

It goes without saying that the Penguin Random House India team led by Radhika Marwah, and supported by Ralph, Rinjini, Vijesh and Alkesh (plus Nora Nazerene Abu Bakar and her team joining later from Penguin SE Asia) was just amazing. Without their belief in the book and commitment to see it out there in as many hands as possible, the book wouldn't be in its current form. Radhika, it's been an outstanding partnership, so thanks again!

Finally, deep gratitude to my English teacher, Ms Swati Das, who honed my love of books, and to my parents—Uma Jaiswal and Bikram Choudhary—for their unshakeable belief in me.

Notes

Chapter 1: The New Marketplace

1. https://appleinsider.com/articles/12/11/13/apple-doubles-tiffanys-in-retail-sales-per-square-foot
2. https://kr-asia.com/wechat-pay-surprise-attack-on-alipay

Chapter 3: The New Positioning

1. Aithareya Brahmana, 7.15, Rigveda

Chapter 6: The New Brand Experience

1. https://www.campaignlive.co.uk/article/advertising-facing-crisis-public-trust-heres/1524639
2. https://thenextweb.com/news/google-fails#:~:text=We%20discovered%20ther''s%20been%20a,of%20them%20have%20been%20cancelled

Chapter 8: The New Media

1. https://www.statista.com/statistics/1024296/apac-daily-minutes-of-newspaper-consumption/#:~:text=According%

20to%20data%20from%20Zenith,minutes%20per%20
day%20in%202021

Chapter 9: The New Measurement

1. https://www.iab.com/news/viewability-has-arrived-what-
you-need-to-know-to-see-through-this-sea-change/
2. https://www.sidmartinbio.org/what-percentage-of-the-
world-owns-a-tv/#What_percentage_of_the_world_
owns_a_TV
3. https://www.usnews.com/news/best-states/articles/
2021-07-22/americans-spent-more-time-watching-television
-during-covid-19-than-working
4. https://www.forbes.com/sites/tjmccue/2019/07/31/verizon-
media-says-69-percent-of-consumers-watching-video-with-
sound-off/?sh=3ed80bf735d8
5. https://www.nielsen.com/us/en/insights/article/2010/
research-study-shows-tv-viewers-really-do-watch-
commercials/
6. https://uhurunetwork.com/the-50-rule-for-youtube/
7. https://www.washingtonpost.com/news/the-switch/wp/
2016/09/23/facebooks-secret-way-of-counting-video-views-
was-wrong-all-along/
8. https://www.wsj.com/articles/p-g-slashed-digital-ad-
spending-by-another-100-million-1519915621

Chapter 10: Data and Marketing Technology

1. https://www.thedrum.com/opinion/2020/06/30/trust-
the-digital-duopoly-isn-t-what-it-was-advertisers-should-
take-note
2. https://blog.hubspot.com/marketing/ad-blocking-stats

Chapter 12: Marketing, Meaning and Mankind

1. https://www.washingtonpost.com/archive/lifestyle/
   food/1982/05/23/taking-the-test/ac0f3540-b670-468e-8afd-
   5b31c54d5514/
2. https://www.coca-cola.co.za/working-at-coke/our-values/
   mision-vision-values